FAMILIES, POLITICS AND THE LAW

Perspectives for East and West Europe

Edited by
MAVIS MACLEAN
and
JACEK KURCZEWSKI

CLARENDON PRESS · OXFORD
1994

Oxford University Press, Walton Street, Oxford OX2 6DP

Oxford New York Toronto
Delhi Bombay Calcutta Madras Karachi
Kuala Lumpur Singapore Hong Kong Tokyo
Nairobi Dar es Salaam Cape Town
Melbourne Auckland Madrid
and associated companies in
Berlin Ibadan

Oxford is a trade mark of Oxford University Press

Published in the United States
by Oxford University Press Inc., New York

British Library Cataloguing in Publication Data
Data available

Library of Congress Cataloging in Publication Data
Families, politics and the law : perspectives for East and West Europe
/ edited by Mavis Maclean and Jacek Kurczewski.
p.   cm. — (Oxford socio-legal studies)
Includes bibliographical references and index.
1. Domestic relations—Europe.   2. Privatization—Law and
legislation—Europe.   3. Family policy—Europe.   I. Maclean, Mavis.
II. Kurczewski, Jacek.   III. Series.
KJC1105.F36   1993
346.401'5—dc20
[344.0615]   93–38252
ISBN 0-19-825810-0

Set by Hope Services (Abingdon) Ltd.
Printed in Great Britain
on acid-free paper by
Biddles Ltd
Guildford & King's Lynn

Oxford Socio-Legal Studies
Families, Politics, and the Law

GENERAL EDITORS Donald R. Harris Keith Hawkins
Sally Lloyd-Bostock Doreen McBarnet Denis Galligan

Oxford Socio-Legal Studies is a series of books published for the Centre for Socio-Legal Studies, Wolfson College, Oxford. The series is concerned generally with the relationship between law and society, and is designed to reflect the increasing interest of lawyers, social scientists and historians in this field.

Recent titles in this series:

Preface

These essays were written by an interdisciplinary group of Polish and British lawyers, and social scientists who have a common interest in how the law both reflects and regulates the changing relationship between the individual, the family, and the state. The nature of these relationships is thrown into sharp relief at times of rapid change. Here we look closely at the underlying concepts, the developing vocabulary, and the behaviour of individuals in Poland immediately after the transition to democracy, and in the UK, during the long period of Conservative government, the transition to Thatcherism. In both countries 'Privatization' is used as a key political concept and we hear it applied to the family as well as other enterprises. We wish to examine what this means in different contexts, what benefits such a move might offer, and what may be a matter of concern.

The contributors have worked together over a long period, in some cases almost a decade. We do not offer a complete factual guide to the development of family law in Poland and the UK. We aim rather to do what artists do when they hold up their drawing to a mirror in order to see it more clearly, to check perspective and composition. By holding up our own observations of our own country to our European colleagues, we hope to see fresh aspects of the familiar, and to develop a new awareness of both countries from a broader perspective.

As Clifford Geertz declared, 'Like a nation's art, literature, science, production relations, religion or history, its law is part of a distinctive manner of imagining the real.' No branch of law is closer to the 'real' than that which regulates family life.

The editors would like to record their gratitude to the contributors, to Emma Bullard and Julia Barton for their editorial and secretarial assistance, and to the ESRC East West Initiative which supports our empirical work.

M.M. and J.K.

Wolfson College, Oxford
University of Warsaw
January 1993

Contents

List of Contributors

Anne Bottomley	Faculty of Law, University of Kent at Canterbury.
Artur Czynczyk	Institute for the Study of the Sociology of Custom and Law, WPRiPS, University of Warsaw.
Robert Dingwall Ph.D.	Professor of Social Science, University of Nottingham. Author of *Protection of Children* with John Eekelaar and T. Murray, Oxford, 1986.
Janet Finch Ph.D.	Professor of Social Relations and Pro Vice Chancellor, University of Lancaster. Author of *Family Obligations and Social Change* with Jennifer Mason, London, 1989.
Małgorzata Fuszara Ph.D.	Director of the Centre for the Study of the Position of Women, IASS, University of Warsaw.
Suzanne Gibson	Faculty of Law, Fellow of New College, University of Oxford.
Iwona Jakubowska Ph.D.	Institute for the Study of Sociology of Custom and Law, WPRiPS, University of Warsaw.
Heather Joshi	Department of Economics, City University. Editor of *The Changing Population of Britain*, Oxford, 1989.
Anna Kwak Ph.D.	WPRiPS, University of Warsaw.
Jacek Kurczewski Ph.D.	Professor of Sociology of Law, Director of the Institute for Applied Social Studies, University of Warsaw, Deputy Speaker of the Sejm. Author of *Resurrection of Rights in Poland*, Oxford, 1993.
Beata Łaciak	Institute for the Study of the Sociology of Custom and Law, WPRiPS, University of Warsaw.

Jennifer Mason   University of Lancaster. Author of *Family Obligations and Social Change* with Janet Finch, London, 1989.

Judith Masson   Professor of Law, University of Warwick.

Mavis Maclean   Fellow of Wolfson College, University of Oxford, Centre for Socio-Legal Studies. Author of *Surviving Divorce*, Basingstoke, 1991; with John Eekelaar of *Maintenance after Divorce*, Oxford, 1986; editor with L. Weitzman of *Economic Consequence of Divorce*, Oxford, 1992; and with D. Groves of *Women's Issues in Social Policy*, London, 1991.

Martin Richards Ph.D.   Director, Centre for Family Research, University of Cambridge.

Joanna Smigielska   Institute for the Study of the Sociology of Custom and Law, WPRiPS, University of Warsaw.

Robert Sobiech Ph.D.   IASS, University of Warsaw.

Andrzej Szlezak Ph.D.   Faculty of Law, Adam Mickiewicz University, Poznan.

PART ONE

Concepts: Words and Values

1. Introduction: The Issues in Context

Mavis Maclean and Jacek Kurczewski

In Western Europe family law has been described as 'rolling back' (Glendon, 1988; Van Houtte, 1990) increasingly leaving family matters for individuals to decide, focusing instead on protecting the individual rights of vulnerable family members—women, children, and the elderly. This development is sometimes described as the 'privatization' of the family, and is welcomed by those who see the family as a source of moral values and social control, but feared by those who, often from a feminist perspective, see the family as a battleground where stronger members can dominate the weak.

In Eastern Europe the family-law codes established after the Second World War look attractive to Western observers, at first glance, with their emphasis on equality of gender, civil status, and freedom for the individual to choose to end a marriage or a pregnancy through divorce or abortion. But these codes were imposed by an authoritarian regime, and are being reconsidered by the re-emerging democratic states of Central and Eastern Europe. Programmes of law reform are developing with the object of reducing state interference in the family, which always held a special place under Communist rule as the private place within which the open and meaningful communication took place between individuals which was impossible in any other milieu. In some Eastern European countries, notably Poland, state involvement in the family is being reduced, but the resulting 'privatization' could also be described as desecularization. The law reform policies which aim to move towards the rule of law in democracy are now subject to the influence of the Church, which sees marriage as a sacrament and abortion as a sin.

The family has suddenly become a political battleground in both East and West. In the East concern to retain welfare provision, to reject the past, and to reflect national values without reducing individual liberty now requires a balancing act of extreme delicacy. In the West, the family is held by the political right to combine independence from the state with interdependence within the self-sufficient family unit, and by the political left to pose the challenge of finding ways to safeguard the rights of individual family members while still supporting the institution. But at any point on the political spectrum there is a requirement, during the current economic climate of recession, to seek ways of regulating the relationship between the individual, the family, and the State in a cost-effective way. In the UK family law is withdrawing to some extent from court-based activity and seeking alternative methods of dispute resolution and regulation. Two examples of how this development is taking divergent directions can be drawn from the expansion of mediation at divorce or separation, and secondly the increased use of administrative agencies to regulate family matters, the most recent example being the Child Support Agency.

This volume addresses two sets of questions raised by the current move towards 'privatizing' or even 'reprivatizing' the family.

(1) The tendency to turn away from collective regulation of family obligations in the emerging democracies of the East involves rejection of state involvement and embraces the liberal values of respect for individual liberty, rather than equality. Unfortunately within the family any weakening of the ethic of equality may lead to problems for the weaker members within the family unit, in practice women, children, and the elderly. These are the groups on whom Western family law, functioning within a society which places less emphasis on equality and more on the liberty of the individual, has needed to concentrate its protective powers. In the East, state withdrawal from the family, leaving the family as a private sphere, seems to be accompanied by a new emphasis on fundamental religious values, which tend to stress the difference between gender roles and to limit individual access to divorce or abortion, in order to strengthen the traditional family. In this context there is a need to look more closely at the move towards privatizing the family and ask, however difficult this may be at this time, what can be found of value in the exaggerated collectivism of the former Communist regimes?

(2) The West has continued under a government which has stressed the need for individual freedom from the interference of the State (this resembles the liberty so attractive to the changing states of the East) combined with a belief in traditional Victorian values based on patriarchy without interest in equality of outcome between those of different gender, class, or race. In this context we record our concern for the rights of vulnerable individuals within the 'black box' of the family, and our questioning of the value of freedom of choice for the individual in situations where economic bargaining power is

unequal. But we also need to ask what we can find of value in the culture of opportunity, particularly at a time of recession and reduction in public-service provision, and why we are moving towards a residual role for the State in regulating family matters through the law.

This volume has four parts. In the first part 'Concepts: Words and Values' which follows this brief introduction, Kurczewski and Dingwall raise the political issues surrounding family regulation and discuss the conceptual frameworks which underlie policy developments: in Poland during the move towards democracy and the rule of law, and in the UK where both these concepts are stale and where market issues dominate public debate. Part Two 'Family Obligations' addresses the underlying social norms and values concerning the responsibilities of family members towards each other, presenting data from empirical studies in both countries; Jakubowska, Smigielska, and Czynczyk from Poland, Finch and Mason from the UK. These data provide a base from which to consider the legal intervention in private relationships dealt with in Part Three 'Families and the Role of Law'. We suggest that this can be divided into intervention at time of crisis when decisions must be made in matters, such as separation and divorce, where the parties have no previous experience and secondly the continuing responsibility to protect the interests of vulnerable family members particularly women and children. Part Four 'Family Law and Social Policy' is concerned with the relationship between legal regulation of family matters and the public interest, and thus brings us back full circle to the political issues presented in the first two chapters. These issues of cost effectiveness and resource allocation when private actions result in public expense are not currently part of the policy agenda in the East, perhaps because they are too close in flavour to the insistence of the old regime on socially acceptable behaviour, 'prevention and resocialization', but also because the concept of public expenditure is a difficult topic when moving towards the free market. This last section therefore contains British material which develops a critical response to the dominance of the free market, and Polish reappraisal of social policy in terms of the individual's expectations on emerging from reliance on a totalitarian state.

The second part of this introductory chapter presents the background to the issues discussed later in the book, and highlights the questions raised in subsequent chapters.

Part 1: Concepts: Words and Values

Every book has a starting point. For this volume the point of recognition was the realization of the paradox that, in Poland and the UK, the extensive and radical social change taking place in both was called by its protagonists by the same name, i.e. privatization. But the term came with very different associations and potential consequences. Privatization has little intrinsic meaning in isolation, it indicates no more than movement from one situation to another. When it acquires the prefix 're', as it has done in relation to the family, it implies the return to a former and probably preferred state of affairs. In the family context we have in Eastern Europe a clear preference for the remembered pre-Communist state of affairs, when families were thought to be free from State intervention, and privatization with or without the prefix 're' carries nothing but positive messages. In the UK we talk about a return to family values, meaning a particular view of the nineteenth century when heads of families took responsibility for and had control over their members (Mount, 1982). In this context privatization carries messages of a solution to the social confusion of libertarian Western society, which is interpreted as arising from over-reliance on the 'nanny state' and the failure of the family to accept responsibility for its members. In the UK we have some debate within fairly narrow parameters about the relationship between the individual, the family, and the State, concerned mainly with the need to protect vulnerable members of families from dominant members, or from excessive state intervention. In the recent episode of child sexual abuse reported in Cleveland, so many cases were diagnosed by the experts and so many children removed from their families that the predominant response at the time was concern that the State was interfering with family privacy, and to query the expert opinions (see Ch. 11). We also seek to protect the state from the consequences of individual freedom of action, for example, by instituting a form of tax on absent parents to protect the public purse from bearing the consequences of easy access to divorce. And there is a real difference between the views of the political left and right in their attitudes to family responsibilities. The right holds a view of the ideal family type with two parents, one of whom is the main source of social control, taking responsibility for its members and with authority vested in the male head of the household. The aim is to reduce government intervention in such 'good families' but, paradoxically, to achieve this withdrawal from the family, the Conservative Government has had to undertake a large legislative programme to place these responsibilities firmly back within the family (see Chs. 11 and 12 by Masson and Gibson). The left is more accepting of the new forms of family life, less insistent on the traditional structures, and more willing to offer state support to all vulnerable family members, i.e. to intervene inside the family Black Box; but at the same time it is concerned to support the family as an institution. We also have very different views on the privacy of the family, and the degree of autonomy to be exercised by heads of households among some ethnic minority groups, particularly the Muslim families from Bangladesh. But both major political parties are constrained in their policy by the need to control public expenditure in a period of recession. The choices to be made lie within a fairly narrow range of options. For example, we debate the maximum length of a pregnancy which may be terminated, but we do not seriously discuss abolishing abortion. There are new voices in the debate, with feminists talking about combating patriarchal values, and putting a new emphasis on children's rights, but we have no clearly defined and organized alternative value systems. We are basically a secular society, which has moved some way towards individualistic market-dominated rejection of communal responsibility for meeting the needs of vulnerable members. But our debates about reducing the commitments of the welfare state are couched in the language of economics, not in the language of increasing personal liberty. As Robert Dingwall goes on to describe in Chapter 3, recent prosperity has shielded us from the effects of market domination.

Poland, like most other European countries, and despite the atheism of the former regime, is not a secular country. As Jacek Kurczewski argues in Chapter 1, in Poland the Church constitutes an organized, popular, and long established value system offering a clear alternative to the ideas of the former discredited regime. The Polish Church has long been involved in political life. Since the sixteenth century when Poland elected its kings, the primate automatically became head of state during the sometimes lengthy interregnums following the death of a king while electioneering took place canvassing candidates from Austria, Prussia, or as far away as France. The Church, as Kurczewski describes, resisted the inroads of the Communists and, under the Polish Pope John Paul, played a key role in the Solidarity Revolution. The vast majority of the population describe themselves as believers (90 per cent). In seeking to return to the rule of law, that is a legal system based on the social norms of the society, what could be more natural than to move towards a system of family law based on the teaching of the Church? But here we have a far harsher division of values than in the UK. A return to the teachings of the church in family law has already resulted in the abolition of the right to choose abortion (see Fuszara, Ch. 13) and to restricted access to divorce by removing it to a higher court (see Szlezask, Ch. 7). Privatization of family regulation, in the sense of removing the influence of the state as typified by the Communist regime, may mean in practice the desecularization of family life. This is a matter of grave concern to those who are concerned about the liberty of the individual within the family setting, and in particular to those concerned with the position of women in a more traditional, Catholic, family setting.

In Poland the democratic tradition is strong and ancient. An elected monarchy, a democratic assembly with the famous *liberum veto* whereby any individual could bring proceedings to a halt, the liberal constitution of 1791, and more recently the emphasis placed on directly democratic procedures within the Solidarity movement indicate the strength and depth of the concern for democracy within Poland. The reality has recently been more difficult to manage in practice with the absence of organized political parties. And the monopoly of experience of administration among supporters of the former regime, whose expertise is not welcomed, has been accompanied by the development of interest groups with changing affiliations. Suspicion of representative rather than direct forms of democracy has been seen as naïve by Westerners. But in the light of the present state of 'damaged democracy' in the United States as described by J. K. Galbraith (Galbraith, 1992), a state of affairs which the UK seems to be approaching, such criticism seems in itself naïve. Less than 50 per cent of the American population vote in Presidential elections, and the UK was ruled for over a decade by a government free to put forward revolutionary policies with a large parliamentary majority elected by 40 per cent of the 80 per cent of the electorate who voted.

The drive towards democracy in Poland continues, with the emphasis on individual freedom of action, and the liberty of the individual to live under the rule of law. Equality of opportunity and public provision of welfare are associated with the former regime, as is administrative justice and interventionist court activity relying on expert prescription and judicial discretion. The rule of law requires a legal system in tune with the norms and values of the community. In this volume therefore, before discussing the role of law, we turn in Part Two to examine the evidence concerning the nature of existing private obligations as perceived and acted upon by individuals.

Part 2: Family Obligations

'The family' has always been a powerful rallying cry in politics, an entity which is almost universally valued but seldom defined. In Eastern Europe and particularly Poland the family had a unique role as the only institution supported by both Party and Church for different reasons but with a similar purpose in view: the family was seen universally as the institution through which moral values are best absorbed and reinforced, and as a powerful agency of social control. In times of intellectual and spiritual alienation the family became of primary importance as a place where trust predominated over suspicion, and where communication could be frank and open. When there were shortages the family also functioned as an effective searching, queuing, and allocating organization, providing specialists for the group in queuing for and bringing home goods in short supply (Jakubowska, Ch. 4) or helping with access to jobs or housing (see Czynczyk and Smigielska, Ch. 5). Both these aspects were familiar also in the UK during post-war shortages, though such team work is perhaps less familiar in the UK.

Following the period of intense interdependency, one of our contributors suggests that, if life becomes easier in Poland, family members may wish to withdraw from this level of closeness and seek peace in isolation as individuals. But if public child care provision breaks down (and despite some increase in unemployment for women, levels of economic activity for women with children are likely to remain high), family ties may yet remain vital as alternative sources of child care. Despite the emphasis on individual rights and liberties in the free market, underlying family values seem to be remaining strong (see Kurczewski, 1993). These values are strongly reinforced by supporters of the Catholic Church in Poland. As we shall see in Chapter 2 the Church's wishes to restrict divorce and remarriage and ban abortion are rapidly gaining ground. Divorce has been removed to the higher level of courts, which means a longer waiting period and increased costs for petitioners. And the long struggle in the Sejm to restrict the right to abortion succeeded in January 1993 by a narrow margin.

In the UK, in our predominantly secular society, discussion of the boundaries between the obligations of individuals to each other as individual citizens or as members of family groups, however these are defined, has less of a moral component and is usually debated in terms of material help given and received. In times of economic stringency there is a greater tendency to retrench on public spending and to stress the obligations of families to support their members. This is now countered by the desires of those speaking for the weaker members of families—women and children—to establish claims upon public resources in their own right as individual citizens irrespective of their family relationships. In the UK family structures have changed and diversified, partly as a result of the increased possibility of forming separate households when housing was more widely available in the late 1960s and 1970s. We have had a divorce explosion, followed by a plateau with a stable divorce rate, with nearly half the marriages contracted in 1993 being expected to end in divorce, and with more of the population never marrying and more not remarrying after a divorce. We have more older people forming separate households; we have more women in work, though often part-time, with ineffective provision for publicly organized child care. We still have a high rate of unemployment, particularly among young school-leavers who are being forced back into the family home by the reduced availability of welfare benefits for those under 25. Family ties, in the midst of discussion about the disappearance of the family, are being strengthened by the governmental policies designed to enforce private obligations. But there may be a considerable gap between governmental and private definitions of these duties and the accompanying rights. The family is strictly defined by the right as the repository of traditional virtues, and the chief locus for social control. The state is expected to withdraw from intervention within the family, except when it is compelled to legislate in order to enforce compliance with private obligations. Whether this constitutes privatization, reprivatization, or increased state control, it is difficult to say. The left on the other hand tends to accept more varying forms of family grouping, by being, for example, more willing to define lone parents and children as viable families (still drawing a distinction between heterosexual and homosexual partnerships), to be more aware of ethnic differences, and of the potential for exploitation and control of women and children within the family especially if the state draws a rigid line around the privacy of the family unit. From this perspective, state withdrawal from intervention in family life is perceived not as an increase in individual liberty, but of a failure to protect the interests of vulnerable family members. In the final chapter in this section Finch and Mason (Ch. 6) go on to discuss inheritance, or property transmission; an issue which will increase in importance in Eastern Europe as private property becomes both more widely owned and legitimate.

Part 3: Families and the Role of Law

We have looked at the political imperatives behind what can be described as the 'privatization of the family', within the East a drive towards increasing the freedom of the individual, and in the West a move to increase the operation of market freedom; and we have looked at the ideologies behind public and private expectations concerning the obligations of individual family members towards each other.

Now we turn to the intersection of these two social forces in family law. What is happening to the legal regulation of the family? In both countries we see rapid and extensive change. What are the goals and probable outcomes of these changes? In terms of our starting-point, can we see anything of value in the now rejected over-collectivism of the East, and what do we welcome or fear in the privatization or desecularization which is to come? In the UK do we regret the reduction of collective or state support for families, or do we applaud the reduction in the dependency culture and increased emphasis on enterprise and initiative in taking personal responsibility? Do we see privatization of the family as leading to increased individual liberty, or to less effective protection for the vulnerable? What part do we want the law to play in family life? Five models are suggested here:

1. Do we seek the enforcement of a religious code of behaviour on all citizens?
2. Do we seek secular guidance on moral decisions, as in the past when divorce laws were fault based and remarriage difficult?
3. Do we seek management of the outcome of freely chosen individual actions with respect to their consequences for others,

either individuals or the collectivity, either for everyday events, or at times of crisis when the individual has no experience to guide him?

4. Do we seek a more proactive protection of the broader interests of weaker family members?

5. Do we seek only a residual role, offering protection from physical harm?

The answers to these questions on a national level are largely determined by the political forces and individual values discussed above. On a personal level they are value judgements, and as editors we can give answers, but must make it clear that these do not necessarily accord with those of our contributors.

We would be very worried about the first option, portraying law as enforcing a religious code, though recognizing that it is clearly a possible strategy in Poland where 90 per cent of the population are Catholic believers. The second option, seeking secular guidance on moral decisions, describes the UK position until perhaps the early 1980s and would still attract considerable public support. Even in 1980, when interviewing divorcing couples a decade after fault had been removed from divorce, the vast majority talked in terms of guilty parties (see Eekelaar and Maclean, 1986). The third option, managing the impact of individual actions on others, would be hard to disagree with, whatever else might be chosen to accompany it. In fact we suggest that it is this option together with the fourth, which seeks to protect the vulnerable, that best describes the present UK position. Current policy debates in the UK are mainly concerned with choosing a position on the border of these two choices, that is, how far should the law intervene to protect the weaker party? Should it go beyond the role described in option 3, managing outcomes with the interests of weaker parties and the collectivity in mind, or should it go further and control the individual choices as well as the outcomes as implied in option 4. In the UK we seem to be moving in this direction in financial matters such as pensions (see Joshi, Ch. 16) and child support (see Maclean, Ch. 8) but not in relation to the interests of children which have a less direct impact on the public purse (see Richards, Ch. 17). It would be hard to disagree with the importance of the last option, which offers physical protection, except to argue that this is the province of criminal rather than family law.

The chapters in Part Three of this book debate the role of law in family matters. Szlezak (Ch. 7) describes the legal regulation of the financial aspects of separation and divorce, highlighting the increasing obstacles being placed between petitioner and decree by administrative means in order to implement the pro church policies which are now being substituted for the concept of 'the interests of the state' to justify the withholding of a decree. Maclean (Ch. 8) describes what from the West looks like good business practice in reducing public expenditure on welfare, that is the removal from courts of child-support matters and the establishment of the Child Support Agency which will assess and enforce what is, in effect, a negative benefit for absent parents. From the East, we are urged to treat with caution the question of what differentiates access to courts from access to administrative agencies and their tribunals.

The second group of papers in this Part are concerned with the protection of children. Sobiech and Kwak (Chs. 9 and 10) deal with two aspects of children's rights, the right to physical protection, and the rights of children *vis à vis* the rights of parents putting a child up for adoption. The elevation of the family under Communism has made it even more difficult than in the West to acknowledge the possibility of pathological behaviour within the safe family haven, particularly with regard to child abuse. Robert Sobiech outlines the dilemma, which is compounded by the current turning away from reliance on expert advice, of judicial discretion and proactive resocialization of problem-family members through the family courts. All the kinds of response to the problem current in the West are too closely linked in approach to the state paternalism and control of the previous regime, implemented through the family courts with their wide discretion to call in interested parties and devise a treatment programme. Strict reliance on the rule of law may make it even more difficult in the near future to accept and deal with the notion of a child's right to protection in a setting where problems of abuse in the past could be thought about only in terms of a medical problem. This situation resembles the current UK dilemma (see also Ch. 3), but in the UK we are less resistant to treatment plans and expert opinions, though our concerns about protecting parental rights *vis-à-vis* the state and its experts increased after the widespread removal of children from their homes as a result of suspected abuse in Cleveland. Our new legislation, the Children Act 1989, shows a tension between the aim of encouraging and enabling parents to exercise parental responsibility, and intervening when the boundary between being a good parent and a bad parent is crossed. This legislation, with the aim of empowering all parents, may disenfranchise a minority more completely.

The recent British legislation concerning children is discussed in Chapters 11 and 12. The first, from Judith Masson, brings in a new dimension to the role of family law, showing how its implementation affects the relationship between central and local government through the central government's role in managing the implementation of new legislation. Chapter 12 by Suzanne Gibson raises the question of the future of modern law-making, and considers the relationship between law and social work.

The Polish 'mirror' shows clearly how children's rights compete with the rights of others. Sobiech indicates the implications of historical experience and orientation for an apparently technical decision-making process in relation to the diagnosis and treatment of abused children. Kwak shows the paradox, whereby the unborn child receives such attention and support in Poland, where as the young child at risk is hidden within the family unit, the 'utopia christiana'. Meanwhile the British papers take an instrumental approach to the role of law, considering how the law affects the way local and central government work, and the relationship of law to the institutions of welfare.

When we turn to the protection of women, here too the differences in approach offer a marked contrast. It is always a surprise to West European feminists to learn of the women's wishes in Eastern Europe to secure the right, not to equal opportunities in the labour market, but to *stay at home* if they choose with their children. They already have general maternity leave and the right to return to a job up to three years after having a child—but this right is of little value in society where until recently every adult was required to work or be defined as a social parasite. Instead of the double burden described by Western women of paid and unpaid work in contrast with the single load on the man, in Eastern Europe everyone has one job, women deal also with the home, but the men will have at least one other paid job, probably with a private employer, as well as their main employment, usually with the state. The double burden is universal (see Fuszara, Ch. 13). The key problem in Eastern Europe is related not to employment but to housing shortage. Family life is dominated by the necessity to share an apartment with older relatives, siblings, and often strangers. On divorce, unless one partner is moving directly to a new partner, then the court's task is often to allocate space within their existing share of a communal flat to each party, sometimes by measuring where a curtain should be hung to divide a room. The political desire for individual liberty and personal freedom is not unrelated to the individual desire for privacy, or personal space. (See also Chapter 5, where Smigielska describes the wife's wish to leave the house as soon as she has put her man's food in front of him and escape to see a neighbour for private conversation.)

The main concerns of family law in the West, that is the allocation and enforcement of rights to property were of less importance in Central and Eastern Europe, where private property was less widespread and less politically acceptable (see Markowits, 1978). The Polish family justice system was grounded in a family-law code which stressed equality between the sexes but the codes were brief, and dependent in practice on the discretion of the family-court judges for interpretation. These judges are trained career judges, often women, without particularly high incomes or status, whose job is to intervene in a difficult family situation by making a plan to cure or improve anyone behaving in an antisocial manner. These judges are not senior lawyers of high rank and prestige, but capable women perhaps more like a senior social worker in the West. Their discretion is considerable (Fuszara, 1990) and indeed it is within their jurisdiction to refuse a divorce to a couple who both consent to it and seek it, if it is thought to be contrary to the interests of the children of the marriage or to society as a whole. Prevention and resocialization are the aims of family justice. In this context, the Church's insistence on the family as the 'utopia Christiana', with gender-based division into the mother's authority within the home and the father's authority outside, with marriage a sacrament and abortion a sin, all lie uncomfortably alongside the legal code's insistence on the equality of individuals and their overriding duty to the state.

Anne Bottomley (in Ch. 14) on women and legal rights to property in the UK presents a fascinating contrast. In the UK we lack the established acceptance that women will take a full part in all aspects of life, which in Poland springs in part from the participation of Polish women in the series of armed conflicts. In the UK women are still struggling to achieve full equality of opportunity in paid work, and this generation in particular are caught in the trap where divorce became common and acceptable *before* the full economic effects on women of having children and so damaging their earning capacity became fully understood. This 'damage' had always occurred, but became a problem when the effects were no longer concealed within a marriage where, although there was no guarantee that resources would be fairly distributed within the household, at least this was a possibility. After divorce, the woman finds it far more difficult to achieve a fair allocation of resources. Anne Bottomley deals with women's property rights. The family home and pension entitlements, are the chief assets of any UK family, and both tend to be lost to a woman on divorce (see also Joshi, Ch. 16).

Part 4: Family Law and Social Policy

In the final part of the book, we return to the boundaries between public and private interest, and raise the question of the point at which the state should intervene when private decisions have public consequences. The question of public interest in private family matters is addressed broadly by Łaciak in Chapter 15, and in the chapter on the public consequences of the private decision to divorce for women (Joshi, Ch. 16) and children (Richards, Ch. 17). So we have come full circle to reconsider the doctrine of the privatization of the family, to be accomplished by the retreat of state intervention and the elevation of family responsibilities. In the East this represents increased personal freedom, in the West the reduction of government expenditure. In both settings it fits well alongside the emphasis on a free market economy. But in the UK instead of family law rolling back to accomplish this shift we see increased regulation to ensure the fulfilment of these private obligations. The government must legislate to free itself of responsibilities. In the East a family-law code based on equality before the state (we must remember that this was an authoritarian state) is being revised in accordance with the views of the Church, for whom marriage is a sacrament, where the patriarchal structure of the Church is replicated within the family, and individual wishes and desires are subordinate to the greater good of not only the individual family but also the greater Christian family of the Catholic Church.

Conclusion

Comparison of two countries like UK and Poland is interesting in itself, but we wish to re-emphasise some aspects that may otherwise go unnoticed. Of course, there is the contrast between West and East, the East implying the modern experience of Communism. but this is a relatively recent phenomenon. At the start of the post-war period the differences were far less marked. Communism developed in Russia within its former imperial frontiers excluding Moldavia, Poland, Finland, and the Baltic states. When the Ribbentropp–Molotov pact was signed in 1939 the process of putting those countries under Soviet control began with East Germany, Hungary, Bulgaria, Yugoslavia, and Rumania coming under the new political regime. Central Eastern European countries like Poland were indeed different in family life and family law from the UK in 1939 as was UK from France, France from Italy, Italy from UK. In 1939 Poland had mixed family law, with civil marriage in some regions, denominational in others; women had had the vote since 1918 and feminist organizations were active in the upper middle class while the Catholic Church was defending the traditional moral order against modernization. The economy was predominantly private, with little provision of social benefits. In the countryside the traditional peasant family was often illiterate and patriarchal, though agrarian movements and organizations were raising the consciousness of women and young people. These characteristics would put Poland behind UK on any modernization scale, but on a par with the majority of less developed European nations at the time.

Communism brought something qualitatively distinct. Poland was perhaps more interesting to the British when it was an exotic Communist state than after the 1980 or 1989 discovery that 'the peoples of Eastern Europe are recognizably our kin, educated heirs to related languages and cultural experiences' (Dingwall, Ch. 1). Comparison between the two countries makes sense for Eastern Europeans as it shows what troubles may appear or reappear once they re-enter the basic market economy, democratic polity, and culture; it makes sense for Westerners if the Communist *ancien régime* underlying local and universal experience in the half century of the Communist experience can be understood.

The Polish chapters in this volume assess family policy, family law, and family life in Communist Poland. Naturally, the emphasis is changing from how things were under the previous regime into how they are now in the democracy that strives towards rule of law and free market principles. But the political hiatus between the two systems—pre-1989 and post-1989—does not necessarily correspond to a breakdown of social and legal continuity. Social benefits did not stop immediately, and paradoxically it is often the politicians from the most pro-capitalist party who administer the 'social cushion' (see Łaciak, Ch. 15). Family law is changing but only gradually, and not necessarily in an individualist direction (see Kurczewski, Ch. 2 and Szlezak, Ch. 7). In general, despite the rhetoric and goals postulated explicitly we can observe a process of gradual change, not abrupt transition, to another social reality. On the other hand, it is necessary to remember the distinct Communist system which lasted for decades in Poland and elsewhere east of the Elbe, which merits assessment, however difficult this may be as time passes.

Szlezak observes that Polish family law of the period was designed for the poor rather than for the rich; Łaciak observes that however imperfect the implementation of socialist social policy nevertheless it became firmly established in public opinion. These statements under-lie the most important political dilemma that confronts the politicians of transition—the syndrome of expectations often named the *Homo Sovieticus* mentality, following Alexander Zinovyev. According to this the totalitarian experience imprinted the expectation that not only should the individual *not* be active in pursuit of individual goals but also that he has no need to be active as the Party-State will provide whatever is necessary. In fact, this socialist theory was developed in the nineteenth century, and exposed by Anton Menger in his *Neue Staatslehre*. When applied in practice by the Communists, critics claim it leaves people with a Soviet mentality, devoid of any concept of individual self-reliance and responsibility. The Communist economy was finally demolished, according to this view, not so much by the impossibility of global rational economic organization based upon the principle of a unitary hierarchy of power, command, and submission, but by the lack of any spirit of free enterprise, that can only develop among those who feel both free and doomed to take responsibility for themselves. Economy without competition, politics without responsibility, social life without autonomy: this is the triangle of fac-tors that undermined the whole project.

The social policy of Communism was not bad because it provided people with various social and economic rights that even today are entrenched in public opinion and may counteract the development of the market economy. Full employment was real even if economically artificial. The key to the question is that in practice all social benefits were provided conditionally, even if promised unconditionally to everybody. Free kindergartens were available but there was always a shortage of places. And if there were a place available, what use was it for a working woman who needed to travel; for two hours of work, not to mention the time spent shopping and queuing? Janos Kornai described the socialist economy as the economy of scarcity. But the socialist economy made by Marxists was deliberately a political economy. Scarcity served the important political purpose of control by bureaucrats who administered each sphere of life. The right to a kindergarten place was not enforceable in a court—the socialist Party-State was not based upon the rule of law but upon administrative discretion—but dependent upon the availability of free places to be allocated by the political and civil administration. In this way citizens of the Communist Party-State became subject to structural blackmail. They had social and economic security guaranteed by the Constitution, but enjoyment of these benefits depended upon the arbitrary decision of those in power. Once political control was removed, society was unwilling to waive its rights, and there is a natural desire to have them enforced by law rather than to redefine them as mere aspirations, or goals to work towards.

To understand Communism in practice we need also to point out the interest of those in power in the creation of a new labour-force. Women, involved in the process of accelerated industrialization, had the double value of being not only a capable and disciplined labour force with equal opportunities and emancipation but also producers of the next generation of labour. Communism was a highly militarized system, with an imperial mission to seek international revolution, and so the Soviet, or Chinese, or Albanian leadership was interested in procreation as it provided the cheapest reinforcements. We need to recollect the sacrifice of Soviet people in the second stage of World War Two, after Stalin had been betrayed by Hitler, to understand how human resources were made use of without any humanitarian consideration. The amount of forced labour provided by the deliberately vague and arbitrary penal system is yet another illustration. Not only industrialization but also the mission of the totalitarian Party-State was most cheaply assured by the maximum exploitation of the available human resources. Imperial policy also seemed designed to acquire new pools of this human material that could do miracles with its bare hands (and feet) if available in sufficiently large numbers. Not surprisingly, revolutionary libertarianism was soon followed by strict control of abortion, and contraception was either forbidden, as in the war or post-war periods of the Soviet empire, or just encouraged as in Red China. Economic calculations governed policy. Thus the law was neither 'pro-choice' nor 'pro-life': the choices were made by those in power. The relaxation in international and internal Communist relations after Stalin's death resulted in changes as, with growing independence, each Communist Party-State could decide for itself whether to engage in building up 'human power' like Romania, or to improve the level of social satisfaction by allowing individual family control as in Poland. In Romania abortion was criminalized and pregnancy was monitored by the state, in Poland the liberalization of laws and practices developed, lamented by the Church which had survived the years of repression.

We also need to recognise that the social benefits provided by the Party-State were of two types: cash and kind. Provision of benefits in kind was conditional, and controlled through the mechanism of scarcity. Some, however, were freely available. Łaciak describes the high level of financial incentives for child-bearing, including family allowances. To assess the system, the functioning of the economy as a whole needs to be considered. In a socialist economy, money was not so much a mystic generalized medium of exchange between people, but rather the arbitrary medium of control by the state. Under Communism there was no independent Bank of England as there was no independent court of justice. Money was printed whenever needed and the whole system worked until it became isolated, as in the days of heavy-industry-plus-agriculture Communist autarchies at the time of the Korean War. There is also the fiscal aspect. In a socialized economy personal income tax seems an aberration. Why should the state tax the income it provides for employment in state banks, kindergartens, universities, mines, grocery shops, and taxis? During the late 1940s and early 1950s, private property in Poland seemed about to vanish, and wherever it remained, as, for example, in housing, it was circumvented by state administrative control to such a degree that it seemed almost obsolete. State grants under these circumstances amounted, according to the economic theory of the day, to an administrative decision to produce more money, while in practice it amounted to levying another hidden tax on the citizen whose remuneration was centrally pooled, allocated, and redistributed. All this because there are certain limits to the actual purchasing power of money in general and of cash benefits in particular. More benefits meant more money, which was easy, but more money also meant more pressure on the already under-provisioned shops. The Party decided, hesitantly, to slowly introduce luxury goods such as television sets, or cars, but the resulting creation of consumption contradicted the theoretical clarity of the heavy industrialization model. No wonder that Communism, as it departs, leaves the scene practically devoid of services. The systematic attempt to buy the loyalty of citizens by liberal distribution of social and economic rights in general and family benefits in particular failed because of the pressures such a policy exerts on the national economy, and because it reinforces the mechanism of political control by the blackmail of scarcity. More benefits mean more shortages and more social dissatisfaction that can be only temporarily placated by more benefits (see Łaciak, Ch. 15). This was the vicious circle of socialist Poland.

The chapters by Łaciak and Szlezak indicate well the change that is under way not only in Poland but in other ex-Communist countries also. The old system was based upon public schemes for shaping the material situation of families and of individuals. Szlezak observes that alimony decrees were surprisingly infrequent in the past. In a socialist economy it was well understood that everybody had a right to relatively safe employment. Poland was the last of the socialist countries to introduce (as late as the Marital Law period of the early 1980s) the so-called antisocial parasitism legislation, but women were still exempted from the duty to be employed. It was the self-imposed political duty of the administration to organize full employment. The labour law which, in the Stalinist early 1950s, had put the labour force under strict control, safeguarded by penal sanctions, gave way after the 1950s to another system where the employed, especially the breadwinner, was heavily protected against the managerial staff. Under these conditions the breakdown of marriage did not amount to the sudden loss of a breadwinner as both spouses were usually employed. The rich were always but few in this society. Earnings in the black and grey economies were often financially more important than the formal salary and the lack of personal tax made it impossible for the court to decide mutual obligations. Now, in the new economy, the family law provisions may remain the same but their meaning is likely to change. It is no longer the public but the private sector that is numerically dominant, the unemployment rate exceeds 10 per cent, women are fired more often than men, general personal taxation has been introduced, the state is cutting down its expenditures, the new business class is increasing. Some people are becoming decidedly poor, but others are acquiring both goods and marketable careers. In these conditions the economic aspects of divorce become steadily more significant. Before, it was the national economy that was imperceptibly adjusting itself to the mass effects of change in family life. Now the burden is put more and more on the family members themselves, and on their private resources.

Is that where East meets West?

This chapter began by pointing to the difference in the way the two legal systems face their problems at the beginning of the 1990s. On the one hand, we have Polish society re-entering the capitalist economy and leaving behind decades of a public welfare system that had not fulfilled its promises, but had left the expectations imprinted in the public mind. On the other, British society is cutting its public expenditure as well. In both societies major political forces stress the importance of the family for the proper functioning of the society. In Poland and in Britain there are forces, not only the traditional left but also the Church, that would like to stress collective responsibility for family well-being. But the privatization of the moral life of the family need not go hand in hand with the privatization of its economy. The Christian concept of the family would like to see the family as an indissoluble union, whose interest as a whole should override the interests of its individual members. The left accepts the individual freedoms within the union. Both expect public policy to support the family financially. Public policy which lays stress on the rights and duties of the individual and which places the burden of responsibility for financial independence on family members either explicitly as in Thatcherite Britain or implicitly as in post-Communist Poland is undermining the collectivity of family life. The two countries differ in their political philosophy *vis-à-vis* the courts also, Britain beginning to put matters in the hands of administrative agencies and tribunals, Poland stressing the need for rule of law and judicial decision-making. So much for appearances. But the concrete decisions on the gradual stage by stage restriction of family benefits are, in both cases, taken by the administration.

This brief introduction is designed to give the reader an indication of the orientation of this volume, which is not to compare factual details of Polish and English law, not to 'teach' the East how to achieve democracy and the rule of law in a market economy, nor even to warn of the worm in the apple, but to engage in the inspection and elaboration of the concepts and terms used in each place for the illumination of both: to use the cross-national mirror. We suggest that in the UK we may never fully understand the value of the rule of law unless we listen carefully to those who have lived without it. In Poland there is an urgent need to appreciate the economic costs of the rule of law in a market economy; an accessible notion supported by clear evidence in the UK.

We end as we began, with excitement at the speed and extent of change in both societies, asking to what extent private law can regulate the excesses of the liberal society and offer protection to the individual, and at what cost. We need to fill the vacuum between authority and the individual with institutions in addition to the private world of the family. The law is just a mechanism in both post-Communist society and in an atomized post-welfare society: a vital part of the web of obligations essential for societal cohesion.

REFERENCES

Eekelaar, J. and Maclean, M. (1986), *Maintenance after Divorce* (Oxford University Press, Oxford).

Fuszara M. (1990), 'The Judges Room' in J. Kurczewski and A. Czynczyk (eds.), *Family, Gender and Body in Law and Society* (Warsaw).

Galbraith, J. K. (1993), *The Culture of Contentment* (Penguin, London).

Glendon, M. A. (1988), 'Changes in the Relative Importance of Family Support, Market Work and Social Welfare' in M. Meulders Klein and J. Eekelaar (eds.), *Family, State and Individual Economic Security* (Story Scientia, Brussels).

Kurczewski, J. (1993), *Resurrection of Rights in Poland* (Oxford University Press, Oxford).

Markowits, I. (1978), 'Socialist v. Bourgeois Rights', *University of Chicago Law Review*, 45/3: 612–36.

Mount, F. (1982), *The Subversive Family* (Cape, London).

Van Houtte, J. (1990), 'Individualisation in Family Matters', in J. Kurczewski and A. Czynczyk (eds.), *Family, Gender and Body in Law and Society* (Warsaw).

2. Privatizing the Polish Family after Communism

Jacek Kurczewski

In a society so inadequately protected by institutions of order and public safety . . . the majority of the duties that should have been performed by the state, authorities and law fell upon the family. Even the most severe judge of the past should recognise that the Polish family fulfilled this great duty, that it was the strongest civic and national base, and that it remained so even in the worst times . . . The ethical strength of the family was the only salvation in public matters. The Family was also the most important, and perhaps the only sentencing institution in a society plagued by impunity and public tolerance (Lozinski 1902).

Communism, despite its promise, did not abolish the family either in Poland or elsewhere. This does not mean, however, that the family remained unmolested by the Party-State, nor that it did not play a peculiar role in the new configuration of social life which developed under real socialism. The Polish case might seem unrepresentative for various reasons, but close inspection reveals that Communist societies were as different as are democratic societies. To study the general type one needs to investigate the particular case and such investigation will not be meaningful unless the interpretation is made by reference to the general characteristics of social types. The society we speak about, was prior to World War II, still predominantly agricultural, though with pockets of industry which began to develop in the nineteenth century or earlier. Society was trying to modernize itself with the help of a state that had regained independence, and which, although far from the democratic-liberal ideal, was also far removed from the totalitarianism of its two great neighbours to the west and to the east. This society came under Communist rule as imposed by the victorious Red Army in the aftermath of World War II. This meant that, after the initial terror of the post-war period and the early 1950s, the Party-State political system developed with political control over all aspects of life, executed from behind the public agencies, as well as through them. Towards the end of this period, the First Secretary of the Party was afforded the highest salute in military protocol, but still could not be held responsible for the political decisions concerning the country. Real socialism, as it was called, meant political control of the economy as well as political control of advancement in positions held in the national organization of everything: the economy, education, the arts, or even shopping centres. If Poland survived the system that collapsed for good in 1989, many would give at least a part of the credit for that to the Polish family. This chapter is part of the political history of the Polish family under communism and afterwards.

Family and values

In the 1970s Polish sociologists were already pointing to the role of family in the hierarchy of values as having political importance. The fact that the family was described in various public opinion polls as being of the utmost importance was the starting point. During the 1970s the communists launched the official pro-family policy that emphasised the role of the family in the social organization of the country. From today's perspective, we might see that as an important moment of truth, when Polish Communists moved a step closer to social reality, and felt obliged to establish a political link between the Party-State and the family as the now officially recognized unit of social organization.

The stand taken in what follows is rather simple and far from original. I assume that there are no values but objects of various kinds—including ideal ones—that may have value or not. Thus I am using the term 'value' to indicate a certain feature of objects, namely that for some reason (the reasons being as various as human interests are varied) an object acquires a status distinguished in our eyes, thought, or action. A decision to include objects in a list of goods in the case of positive value depends on the sphere of the phenomena concerned. In the area of social life, two types of goods can be identified: those that have autotelic value, that is, their achievement and possession constitutes the final goal of our activities, and those that have instrumental value, that is, their possession helps to obtain the former. Since objects may have both autotelic and instrumental value simultaneously, and may have value in one respect and not in another there is a common tendency to speak of 'values' as objects. This, however, is neither necessary nor useful. Using these very simple distinctions therefore I attempt to outline a way of analysing the value-judgement system adopted in society.

In contrast to interpretations based on some list of 'real' or 'basic' needs adopted in advance, those using general (and therefore useless) concepts of 'reward' or 'punishment', detailed functional theories may display their explanatory powers by referring to a specific social phenomenon and analysing definite 'needs', 'interests', and moods. Findings from various opinion polls of the 1970s can provide such a starting point for the interpretation of Polish society in the later stage of real socialism. Apart from detailed questions and prearranged answers, those studies provide us with the basic information that health, a happy family life, and a small circle of reliable, close friends constitutes the list of goods treasured as being those that give meaning to human life. To explain attachment to these goods in terms of consumer orientation would be nonsense, unless we say that they are merely objects of consumer or, in other words, autotelic value. They are regarded highly for themselves, whereas the value of other objects depends on how instrumental they are in the achievement of these basic goods.

The assumption here then is that the value of goods treasured in society is determined by the extent to which possessing them facilitates achievement or uninterrupted possession of the basic good—the state of social rootedness—of which, I suspect, people are not clearly aware but sense it as a syndrome including health, harmonious marriage, satisfaction with children, and a sense of security coming from the trust one has in one's spouse, other family members, and relatives. Added to these comes the feeling of an adequate social position that manifests itself not so much in the need 'to be better-off than others' but rather in being 'not worse-off than others'. The 'others' are naturally different to different people, hence the level of 'fair living and prosperity' will vary with particular positions in the social hierarchy.

Where we discuss the social rootedness syndrome, we must touch upon several detailed issues the solution of which lies beyond our competence. First, instead of assuming social rootedness (SR) to be a primary good, a basic fact for the interpretation of Polish society, we may consider why it is that this very good seems to have autotelic value to most people. Let us note, however, that such regression in explanation can be carried on without end, therefore each theory, being a coherent system, has to be contained within specific limits. Secondly, a relevant issue is the structure of the relationship between the elements within the above-mentioned syndrome, that is to find out what dominates: the desire for trust or sexual harmony; the need for alikeness or prosperity, and so on. This requires very detailed investigation, such as, for instance, the study of choices people make among goods of various types. However, investigations of this kind assume in advance the existence of a clear-cut inner structure for the syndrome which to me seems to be quite different in nature; dynamic, and changing with the circumstances in which people are likely to give up the basic good. We do not presume SR to be an innate good, in the sense that it is necessarily common to all people and equally varied regardless of the context. SR is a good permanently present in the structure of choices. But protection of this particular good is not always chosen as examples from life and statements from survey research show. Along with SR there are also other goods of autotelic value, although their co-existence is only possible because they normally do not conflict. Thus, for example, the motherland is highly regarded as a good of autotelic value, and most people honestly declare their readiness to sacrifice their lives to protect their country. In periods of normality, the readiness to make this choice is declared, while at the same time the probability of the choice having to be made is low.

Research findings allow us to state that two basic goods were of autotelic value to Poles. One was the SR syndrome determining conduct in daily life. The other linked the individual with the wider community, security, so to speak, a reserve in social rootedness due to participation in a wider community, a 'substitute family' which in our situation was not a class or occupational community but the national one. Participation in it can be functionally explained as an additional factor strengthening the feeling of SR.

Functional analysis of the value system consists of revealing social actions and their structures as means to secure the possession of basic goods; those of autotelic value. These are not problematic. Their value, empirically tested, constitutes the basic fact, the starting point for the whole interpretation. As needs, interests, or moods are empirically tested they appear in the explanation of the functional interpretation. The interpretation adopted here refers primarily to processes of exchange and distribution of goods in society, since it is in these processes that the hierarchy of goods of a different type, namely those of instrumental value, is established.

The components of the SR syndrome are not all in the same position as far as their dependence upon the processes of exchange and distribution is concerned. Some are achieved through processes of microstructural exchange, while the attainment of others involves participation in wider chains of co-operation and competition in social life. However, no strict division will be made here in so far as the chances of success in both microstructural and wider-scale exchange are interdependent, for example, as success in the labour market depends, among other things, on successful family life and vice versa.

What are the basic requirements for achieving a happy family life? Erosion of traditional sexual norms, even though it has not brought about such radical consequences as in the north-western Protestant cultures, still creates difficulties. We shall find traces of this erosion when questioning about attitudes towards adultery, divorce, abortion, or contraception. In view of a clear attitude change in this field, a 'successful family life' acquired a new meaning, and became a 'harder-to-get' good, and therefore perhaps more valuable. Affective contact between the spouses becomes most important, and eroticization of conjugal life is not reduced to the area of sex only. Yet, eroticization—a culturally new phenomenon in contrast with nineteenth century traditions—comes into conflict with the stability of marriage and family. A right to conjugal love also implies that one has a right to divorce when this love is gone. This was observed by Durkheim and classified as domestic anomie. Thus, while in the traditional model both partners were in exclusive possession of each other, nowadays the exclusiveness of rights to the spouse is temporary, and restricted by the right of the other party to break the contract. Tolerance of extra-marital liaisons, however, supported by up-to-date ideological rationalization in terms of hygienic and psycho-hygienic needs, favours stability of the contract. On the other hand, mutual trust and loyalty between spouses have not lost value, and—as studies show—married life as compared with other types of social relationships enjoys relatively high evaluation in this respect in the eyes of the younger generation. The generation of Poles, aged 16 to 29, whom we studied in 1973 (Kicinski and Kurczewski, 1977)— that is the future generation of 'Solidarność'—attached great importance to love as a factor determining happiness, though not a necessary condition of it. K. Kicinski demonstrated that in this respect young people fell into two categories, depending on the level of anxiety: those who were more apprehensive, as Karen Horney has observed, were more likely to regard love as a value in itself bringing meaning into human life, whereas the less neurotic were more likely to claim that love is important but not the most important factor.

Compared with goods such as social position or prosperity in an open society, goods like a happy family life or the bonds of friendship can never be acquired through purely formal social exchange. Establishment of affective bonds involves a subtle process of exchange in face-to-face interactions, governed by its own rules and above all presenting at least the appearance of the will to risk investing in a relationship regardless of what will be gained from it. Certain personality traits may be regarded as more or less favourable to the achievement of these cardinal goods. Thus, the lists of personality traits desired in the self and in others that reappear in various studies constitute, I think, a list of exchangeable goods in return for which one can gain both the establishment and the continuity of emotional bonds with intimates. In the study by Stefan Nowak (Nowak *et al.*, 1979) carried out among secondary school pupils and their parents, the ability to get along well with others was ranked first, followed by intelligence and high intellect, will-power and strong character, and honesty. Ireneusz Krzeminski pointed out that apparent contradiction in the above, saying that:

> The ability to get along well with people has been included among the most desired personality traits both by young people and their parents. The personality traits the subjects were given to choose from included at least two that might be regarded—in a psychological sense—as instrumental in relation to the quality mentioned above. What I have in mind here is the ability to gain people's respect and willingness to help others. A striking fact is that these were ranked hopelessly low in the list of desired personality traits. (Nowak *et al.*, 1979: 294)

The simplest explanation is to assume that those 'instrumental' qualities were ranked lower because the list specifically included the most frequently mentioned ability to get along well with others, and this took priority.

Our argument then goes as follows. Of elements of the SR syndrome that constitute a good of autotelic value some, like 'a good life', prosperity, and an adequate social position can be achieved through the process of exchange in return for goods of instrumental value. In Communist Poland, the formal certificate of education became the commonest instrumental good leading to social advancement, to being 'not worse-off than others'. Education could serve this function because, like money, it has become a symbolic medium of exchange, since knowledge itself is not involved here but rather the formal certificate of individual effort and time spent in education institutions, leading to prestige and income that, in turn lead to the realization of SR. There is a difference with money, though. Money, which was once distributed by the Party-State among those who were entitled, even in the socialist economy may flow without control, and this is the pure case of a symbolic and generalized medium of exchange, while a certificate of education which is issued by public institutions under political supervision—for example, politically unworthy elements are now allowed to enter some types and some degrees of education—cannot be put in to circulation as such. and therefore remains under political control, as when someone is deprived of a right to perform a profession. For this reason, in the face of the inevitability of social differentiation in society, it is formal education that in Communist society, with the passage of time, acquires the dominant position in the hierarchy of goods of instrumental value. This is accompanied by education, or knowledge rather than education, which has an autotelic value to only a small group in society.

In all societies we know, the SR syndrome appears to be a cardinal good of autotelic value for the vast majority of people, which does not imply that there are no alternative goods of that rank—or even a higher rank, for example patriotism, faith, ideology, etc.,—nor does it exclude the existence of minorities for whom the SR syndrome plays no such role in the organization of thought and action, and loses or never acquires autotelic value among, for example, psychopaths, artists, desperadoes, and other deviants. Some societies, in particular periods of their existence, differ, however, in their hierarchies of instrumental goods in exchange and investment. But above all they differ in the distribution of opportunities to obtain instrumental goods and also, therefore, the distribution of profits gained from the exchange of investment goods in relation to those elements of the SR syndrome that are available through extended, 'macrostructural' chains of exchange. Access to upward mobility within the main hierarchical structures has so far been the basic source of social tension in contemporary Polish society. Such tension is imminent in every society that combines a rigid social hierarchy with the principle of open boundaries between particular positions. The demand for higher positions in such a society must exceed the supply, and social conflict arises when representatives of various social categories have unequal chances to rise. And what if such a society maintains that it is already classless and hides, with the help of censorship, the formal barriers that separate the incumbents of all decision-making and privileged positions from the rest of society? Interruption to the realization of the aspirations of active participants in social mobility, who were being prevented from getting ahead by the rapid worsening of average living conditions and the widening gap between those and the ruling élite, led to the revolution of the middle classes in the summer of 1980 (Kurczewski, 1981).

The legal form of the family

At first glance, the legal form of the family does not change under Communism. In the first years, the pre-war law was kept unchanged, but later in the second stage the secularization of marriage bonds began to develop. In pre-war multidenominational Poland marriage was performed before a religious official in both the former Russian and Austrian zones, and in the former Prussian zone there was a civil register. With the extermination of Jews under German occupation and the resettlement of Germans, Poles, and Ukrainians after World War II, the country became more than 90 per cent Catholic. The strengthening of Catholicism in Poland thus paradoxically accompanied the introduction of Communist power. Secularization meant, in this context, the decision to relieve the Catholic church of legal control over society. The Civil Register was introduced in former Prussia in order to have state control over all sectors of society, now that enlightened absolutism was to be followed by scientific socialism. The take-over was executed with the help of the introduction of the institution of divorce, which was previously possible only on condition of changing denomination from Catholic into a less demanding one.

'So, five to six years prior to the outbreak of World War I, the new problem of spreading disintegration of families emerged in the life of one of the largest Polish cities. In Polish circumstances this is thus a product of the twentieth century', comments an eminent Polish demographer. 'A process started that, with the passage of time, took the shape of a serious crisis for the family. In Poland its beginning goes back to the first decade of the twentieth century. After World War II, in the new political circumstances, secularization of the marriage law led on to the legal dissolution of marriages, that, *de facto*, had broken down. And not only this: the model of the Polish family itself underwent fundamental change' (Rosset, 1986: 42).

This new, secular institution of marriage is defined operationally in terms of the administrative action taken together by the man, the woman, and the state official. One needs three to make the marriage, but this time it is the gender-neutral state that is of importance. Art. 1 para 1. of the Polish Family and Tutelage Code currently in force states that:

A marriage is made when a man and woman, simultaneously present, make before the chief of the civil register office, the statement that they enter into their marital union with each other.

The marriage should be made publicly and solemnly, in the presence of two witnesses. Only for 'important reasons' (as the law says in Art. 1, para. 2.) may the marriage be made outside the office. Under the condition of immediate danger to life of one of the future spouses, the marriage can be made before the chief of any civil register office or before the local councillor without presentation of proper documents (Art. 9).

For the purposes of the present paper it will suffice to say that, according to the Polish Family and Tutelage Code of 1964:

1. 'if there is a full and permanent breakdown of cohabitation, each of the spouses may request that the court will dissolve the marriage through divorce' (Art. 56, para. 1);
2. 'spouses have equal rights and duties in marriage; are obliged to cohabit, to give mutual help and fidelity, and to co-operate for the sake of the family that they have established through their union' (Art. 23);
3. Legal arrangement of the family is under judicial review, as Art. 24 states that: 'spouses should decide together about essential family matters, and in case of disagreement each of them may apply for a decision by the court';
4. Marriage creates a community with common property administered by both spouses jointly, unless decided otherwise by contract or by the court;
5. Offspring of a female spouse within the marriage count as part of the family unless objected to by the male spouse and this objection is supported by the court;

6. Joint parental authority over the children continues until maturity unless the court limits or abolishes it;

7. Family relations are composed of the mutual rights and duties of parents and children to each other that are enforceable by law before the court.

To this one should add the constitutional character of the family as recognized in Art. 79 of the Constitution:

1. *Marriage, maternity and the family are protected by the Republic of Poland. The State takes special care of families with numerous offspring.*

2. *It is the duty of parents to raise children with virtuous awareness of their duties as citizens of the Republic of Poland.*

3. *The Republic of Poland safeguards the fulfilment of maintenance rights and duties.*

4. *Children born outside the marriage have the same rights as the children born in the marriage.*

5. *To take care of the welfare of the family, the Republic of Poland aims to improve the housing situation and with the participation of citizens to develop and support various forms of housing development, especially co-operative housing and the rational management of housing resources.*

This text comes from the Constitution as amended in 1976 and italics mark what was added to the original 1952 formulation of the constitution modelled on the Stalinist Soviet model. It is interesting to note that it was under the most peaceful and prosperous Communist regime of Edward Gierek that the article on the family and its protection was amended. As the next section on the position of the Catholic Church in Poland will show, the amendments were a result of the mutual pressures exerted by the Communist Party and the Church. The family in Poland became secularized in its legal form. The civil marriage did not, however, eliminate the religious one. Even communists submitted their children for baptism, were confirmed, and went through religious marriage rites in church. In this way the double allegiance was sustained throughout the whole post World War II period. Things were rather different under Stalinism in the early 1950s, but even then the Church was not delegalized and participation in religious services was not in itself an object of police counter-measures. Liberalization from 1956 onwards meant that the double standard and dual allegiance were from then on accepted by the Party-State. To this one should add that this did not mean equality of rights were enjoyed by believers and professed non-believers. It was against the practice of the Party-State to acknowledge the existence of religion in public. Religious people were in practice given secondary status and lower changes of job promotion. Religious marriage belonged to the private sphere, and was non-existent from the perspective of the late Communist Party-State, which was preoccupied with keeping the public sphere clean of any hints of the religious life as practised by the predominantly catholic society. Things like the secularization of marriage law and opening family life to outside intervention by the state administration and by the state court are by no means peculiar to the Communist organization of society. I would like, however, to stress three points here; first, that in Poland as well as in most other Communist countries, the Communist take-over coincided with the enforced modernization of family law and life, and that Communism was a specific type of modernization with results far from the original message of quick progress; second, that in the overall context of Communism as a peculiar form of social life, the secularization of family life was a crucial component of the totalitarian system of control of social life by the political authorities; third, that the general neglect of the political organization of society makes it impossible to judge control of the family by reference to intrinsic legal standards.

The social reality of socialism

I would like now to elaborate the last two points. Social life in all societies develops in symbolically mediated space. Social life in a socialist society is characterized by socialist housing, which is by no means a uniform system, and differs from country to country, and may differ according to region within one country. In Poland, three types of space could be listed: (1) the village that typically consisted of separate household dwellings clustered in a nucleated neighbourhood or arranged along the road; (2) the areas of family housing with adjacent gardens that form a small town, or residential areas typically in suburbs or enclaves in the urban area; (2) the urban living space with multi-family housing of old, nineteenth-century rows of adjacent houses or housing estates composed of hundreds of multi-storey, prefabricated apartment buildings. Two factors made the housing crisis that was partially relieved at the turn of the 1960s and 1970s but which has reappeared and is in its most acute stage at present. First, there was significant war damage, especially in Warsaw, which was systematically destroyed by the Germans after the 1943 Jewish insurrection and thereafter in 1944 after the Gentile Polish insurrection. The whole city became deserted, and in 1945 resettlement started under strict administrative control. Home ownership was abolished, the rebuilding was dense, with enforced residence titles according to the norms of residential density which were one of the most important normative structures in the everyday life of socialist society. Second, the rapid industrialization of the country was accelerated in the face of the Korean War and global confrontation and this led to migration from the countryside to old and new urban areas at a rate unprecedented in the country's history. The housing industry, having being nationalized like every other branch of the economy towards the end of the 1940s, kept output at the minimum level that was necessary. Homelessness was eliminated with the help of increasing the housing density in such a way that, at times, two or three unrelated strangers were given residence titles to share one of the rooms belonging to a particular family. Those residence registration titles were non-negotiable, free of charge, and distributed at administrative discretion. Knowing the political obsessions of socialist regimes one should not be surprised to learn that political loyalty was one of the factors taken into consideration when granting such a title. On a small scale, in the early 1950s politically hostile families were resettled, following the exodus from the countryside of the families who had owned land which became subject to the post war land reform, soon to be followed by the attempted collectivization.

Theoretical discussion of socialism as a centralized economy led Petrazycki to develop the following model: everybody has a right to have his or her needs satisfied by the collective and at the same time everybody is obliged to work in an assigned post either as manager or as a subordinate. Thus, protection of families and of the non-productive members of society is the duty of the collective. At the same time, there is no private property and no private inheritance. In effect, there is a lack of unbound legal motivation of an ego-altruistic character. Two other types of motives are important instead; first, work in the interests of the collective is performed out of the internalized duty of social service (called by Petrazycki immediate legal motivation); and second, the auxiliary legal motivation to work is developed through appropriate sanctions, through upward and downward mobility on the social ladder according to personal contribution to social goals.

Now we are in a position to conduct safely the mental experiment omitted by Petrazycki, and to ask what would happen in the centralized system if private inheritance and the economic autonomy of the family were retained. The unbound ego-altruistic motivation would surely reappear but this time with negative social consequences. People tend not only to secure their own and their family's position, but also to improve their own lot as much as possible in comparison with others. If all property was communal then it would be a total nonsense to conduct such an experiment. Still, there are many things left which make people differ, for instance, the gift of leadership. And Petrazycki, amongst others, predicted the necessity of some social ladder unless legal motivation prevails and the relevant disposition is imprinted in the legal mentality of citizens. The total effect of all these trends would be for families to develop a constant urge to increase their social position through the accumulation of social positions by their members, and through exploiting as much as possible the economic functions they perform in the society. It is possible that people will try to take as much as they can from the common pool of goods and give as little as possible in exchange. This is the practice of real socialism under Communist rule.

The Catholic Church and the Family

It would be a gross misunderstanding to reduce the Catholic family philosophy and policy to matters such as sexual restrictions and protection of the unborn child, even if this may be the popular view in Polish public opinion. From the beginning Christian moral theology has been torn between ascetic condemnation of mundane matters and the ideal of the well-ordered family within which the natural instincts that reflect the essence of mankind can be fulfilled. The outcome is the moral concern with sex and family relations.

Apart from this historically developed doctrine, additional stress was put on the family by the Church in post-war Poland. In its struggle with the Communist Party-State the Catholic Church began to develop a quite specific social philosophy in the context of which one should read the particular precepts and policies. In his 1976 Holy Cross Sermons, a Polish primate Cardinal Stefan Wyszynski most authoritatively developed this Polish interpretation of the universal Catholic teaching:

In Poland the permanent reality is Family, Nation, and Church; society, national culture, and religious culture. Whoever enters the territory where this reality dominates, if he seeks peace and wants to make easier the realization of his programme, must not destroy this reality. One cannot destroy family, national culture, church, the religious life of the people of Catholic, Protestant, Orthodox, or other faith. Those are the values and forces solidified and grounded with citizenship rights in the Nation. One cannot abolish them. Anyone who would make such an attempt, would make difficult the fulfilment of his own programme, for instance, in the socio-economic sphere. The programme would develop with the utmost difficulty. People would have too many reservations concerning the defence of national and religious culture, and would react with distrust to even the most justified undertakings. There are many proper plans, for instance, in the area of social or economic transformation. Speaking about it in the most general terms, we hold it was and is necessary in Poland. And if it is arranged according to the family, national, cultural, and religious reality then conflicts will not arise. (Staszewski, 1976)

One should not underestimate the political significance of this statement. The speaker was the legendary priest who in the late 1940s had been attempting to build up a historical compromise between the Church and the new power in Poland and then was interned for several years, to be freed in 1956. Primate Wyszynski was the leader of Polish Catholicism until the Solidarity Summer of 1980–1, and under his guidance the experience of people like the present Pope John Paul II developed. For decades before the dissidents, revisionists, and workers began, he was the only public speaker who represented non-Communist Poland before international public opinion as well as before the Communist government. A fact of considerable comparative interest is the difference between the post-war developments in two, apparently similar Central-Eastern European countries, Poland and Hungary. Hungary experienced full scale revolution against Communism, Soviet military intervention in 1956, and the subsequent self-isolation of the invincible and uncompromising Cardinal Mindszenty; in Poland there was the Party-led liberalization of October 1956 followed by a lenient counteraction led by the same politician who symbolized the break with Stalinism. Cardinal Wyszynski was, despite all attempts by the Party, not an isolated symbol of resistance but the head of a strong Church, very busy integrating its believers and entering into contacts with the Party-State whenever possible. The statement quoted above is perhaps the best documentation of the policy that gave the Church final success. The

Church was not fighting socialism as such. On the contrary, the need for social transformation was accepted. But the emphasis was put on the form of these changes, and above all on the need for recognition of the Church as well as of the family and nation the Church politically represented before the Communists. This took place in the middle of Gierek's era and during the last moment of economic success. From 1976 onwards the economic crisis developed due to the poor investment of foreign loans. It was at the moment when Communist power in Poland was at its greatest that the Cardinal offered a truce: Support the Church, family, and national values in exchange for recognition of the political realities of power. 1976 was also the year of the Brezhnevite amendments to the 1952 Polish Communist Constitution. The Church opposed the amendments that stressed socialism as the official ideology of the state, and the Church's opposition was successful. The final formulation recognized the 'leading role' of the Communist Party in the state, but the ideological element was reshaped into the more neutral language of social-solidarity and functionalism. The Constitution clearly recognized the role of the family in social life, and paid tribute to national virtues. 1976 was also the year of the food-price riots in Radom and Ursus and uncontrolled social unrest started to threaten the Communist élite anew. The role of the Church in pacifying the public was open, and the Communist authorities stressed the positive role the Church had to play in fighting social pathology, work ethics included. Even during the summer strikes in 1980, Cardinal Wyszynski in a censored sermon, reminded the workers of the need for restraint and social compromise.

In the Holy Cross Sermon of 1976 Cardinal Wyszynski spoke as leader of the Catholic, Polish, and family-oriented majority who were downgraded by the Communist establishment. The political realities of Communism made possible the equation Church = Nation = Family. One needs to be reminded that the family only slowly became an element of the official ideology of the Communist party in power. This was the party that came to power in the name of class conflict and war, and not for the sake of organic co-operation between family cells in the social fabric. The uneasy truce that was made *de facto* between the Communists and Polish society through most of post-war history was based upon recognition of the role of the family. But only the Church was able to elevate the family to the forefront of social ideology, as in these words of the document expressing the official Church's position in the 1976 constitutional debate:

The state has a duty to promote respect for the rights of the family and to assist it in fulfilling its innate obligations. The family is the basic social cell, the smallest but the most permanent, with the socio-biological creative force that provides nation and state with citizens. Without this assistance the state could not exist. The family is the natural ally of nation and state, and it is necessary for nation and state. No considerations can justify anti-natalist state policy. The state needs to care for and respect the innate rights of the family, and to help it in such a way that the family will be able to perform its innate educational, socio-moral, religious, and national obligations. Therefore, the position of the family in the political community should be privileged. The state should do everything to enable a family to enjoy fully, within the scope of its rights and duties, the social and economic goods as its natural right. Even if the family may not be able to fulfil all its duties to the political community, it cannot be deprived of all that would safeguard its existence. The Constitution should therefore safeguard all family rights, defend its wholeness and create conditions for its normal biological and social development. The family is the biological foundation of the nation. The family should be given priority before the professions or other social or political groups. Its rights should be taken into consideration in the organization of work, production, and the distribution of goods. (Staszewski, 1976)

The Catholic doctrine of the family is the natural-law doctrine. In contrast, lay sociology sees in sociological reality pure types such as the small groups that are exemplified by families, and in the theory of real social entities, family and state are the two most important. At this point we should make the distinction between the collectivism that would presuppose the priority of the collectivities like family and state over the individual, and Catholic sociology where family and nation are not glorified above the individual. Individual rights *are* stressed as *not* to be subordinated to family rights. 'Human rights cannot be taken over by family, nation, or state! These are also respected by the Church' adds Cardinal Wyszynski in the Holy Cross Sermons, and by this he meant the sacrosanct right to life. It is refreshing to read about the pro-life philosophy in such a context. Whatever one thinks of the dilemma between the right to life and the right to individual freedom of decision, as the debate on abortion is typically construed, it is necessary to take into account another perspective also. The Church, from the point of view of innate individual freedom of decision, is perceived as anti-individualistic, but it *is* individualistic when confronting the demographic policies that states may like to impose upon citizens or the family understood as the supra-individual entity. To call it individualism would be as misleading as to call it collectivistic, because this Catholic sociology, philosophy, and policy is above all theology, and makes sense in relation to the concept of the metaphysical meaning of life, acts, and life events. A different meaning might be attached, however, to Catholic politics. I would not call the Catholic doctrines collectivistic but I would call the Catholic polity collectivistic when legislating on metaphysics, as the consequences are collectivistic. Paradoxically, the defence of the unborn infant represents defence of an individual only when undertaken by someone who is not the secular power. The unborn infant in fact needs to be represented by someone already alive. A politician who makes decisions on behalf of the unborn infant against the living person is making a decision for himself or herself. The invisible constituency of those yet unborn grants politicians unrestricted authority against those who are in this world already. In order to legislate for the interests of those who are not full citizens yet, one needs to impose their interest upon the will of those who are actually participating in civic life. It is in this leap from supernatural sanctions to the penal law that the sudden transformation happens. This is why political Catholicism might be termed collectivistic.

Why are those in the East afraid of collectivism? For quite simple reasons, such as freedom for making family decisions on procreation. So far we have been listening to the voice of the rulers, spiritual and political. What about society itself? There is an abundance of empirical data accumulated throughout the years by Polish sociologists that supports the general characterization of Polish public opinion—or, if we want to escape the difficult problem of defining public opinion in the old system of Polish society—as being inclined towards individualism, or as Leon Petrazycki remarked at the beginning of the century, ego-altruism which is represented by thinking in terms of one's own and the good of one's immediate family. Here the syndrome of the SR, social rooting comes into play and puts the average individual somewhat at odds either with the Communist Party-State or with the Church. Finally, the individualism of the unrestrained market makes people satisfied in their psychological inclinations. In fact, it seems to me that there are four points of reference that make sense of the complex relationship between the Polish family and Polish politics of the past, present, and future:

Catholic Church _____ Communist Party

INDIVIDUAL

Living Family _____ Liberal State

The Catholic Church represents the metaphysical perspective that recognizes the value of individual life, as well as the instrumental value of the family, as the natural structure that procreates and supports life. As I have already mentioned, this perspective, when translated into the political plane, changes into an instrument for political domination of the individual citizen by the political collectivity, and in this sense it is collectivistic. The Communist Party-State started as an instrument to achieve the realization of the aspirations of mankind on earth, the collective character of human life being taken as the natural base for political dogma with all the well-known totalitarian consequences. To recognize the family from this perspective means changing the substance of Communist collectivism from class-oriented to family-oriented. Polish Communism under Gierek in the 1970s was based not so much upon the theory of class as upon the doctrine that was expressed by Cardinal Wyszynski: that nation and family are natural social entities·that any government wishing to survive, not to speak of managing societal development, needs to recognize and co-operate with. Add the Church to this. Class policies ceased to exist in the 1920s, and were reintroduced by the Communists at the take-over in order to legitimize the dictatorship and develop co-operation and passive acceptance by society. Later on, the administrative command of society developed with the organizational hierarchy of direct dependency and supervision hidden behind the veil of Marxist rhetoric. Society was ruled by administrators advanced to their position as a result of their political skills and loyalties. To involve the family in this 'scientific management of the society', as communist socio-technicians started to call their own expertise, was a necessity. But the living family, the family taken as a natural social fact differs from the theoretical arrangements and philosophical arguments. Everybody who has studied everyday life under Communism stresses that the family was the elementary structure for adjustment of the individual to the system. It was through the family that the individual was able to survive on underpaid official employment. It was through the family that almost everybody was able to engage in the unofficial, illicit, legal, or semi-legal exchange of goods and services that constituted the real social economy under conditions of permanent shortage. The family performed thus not only a procreative, sexual, emotional, educational role, but also, or perhaps above all an economic role. Take periods of formalized food rationing, for instance. (Fuszara, Jakubowska, and Kurczewski, 1988) It was in the family that coupons were pooled, and the composition of the household determined the rights of individual members to a share in the pool of food redistributed through universal rationing. Each individual had a right to a coupon, but the content of those coupons was determined in the context of the rights of other household members, and the actual redistribution was made within the family itself to everybody according to needs and merits. From the Communist point of view the family was normatively concerned with the proper upbringing of loyal citizens, and from the Catholic perspective with the prolongation of the divine gift of human life, but the social meaning of the family was the survival of those individuals already in existence.

Within this context an ethos has developed which, as usual, is difficult to describe in face of the difficulties involved in tracing the differences between various levels of maintaining a façade, resolving cognitive dissonance, and so on. Many studies have been made on the subject and I relate here some of those in which I took part and which were pioneered in Poland by Adam Podgorecki. For instance, in 1966, our survey revealed that though bigamy was still taboo and condemned by 70 per cent of a national sample, adultery was found to be sometimes justifiable (69%) in contrast to those who thought either that it was never excusable (26%) or generally permitted (17%). (Podgorecki *et al.*, 1971) The summary of the 1987–8 surveys ended with the conclusion that: 'The more often people think that one has the right to use one's body in this or another way, even if they themselves find it personally improper or even disgusting, the more evidence it is of privatization of the body that had been for centuries under the direct control of the rulers, the masters of the state, or the masters of the family or house. As society, a term which is in effect a metaphor for people and the agencies in power, becomes willing to remove controls from the expression of a political anima of the citizens and the privatization of political views becomes a fact, the same happens in the sphere of social controls over the body: it gets privatized too'. (Sojka-Zielinska, 1971) In the 1990 national survey of a random sample of 898 people the results were similar, this time after one and a half years of life in the post-Communist system with full freedom of speech, including exposure to all types of ideologies, especially the Catholic one. In this sample 60 per cent were religious practitioners, 29 per cent claimed they were practising Catholics though irregular, 9 per cent said that they believed but were not practising, and 2 per cent were non-believers. This distribution is similar to results of many surveys conducted over the last few decades. It should not mislead us into thinking that the overwhelming majority in Polish society supports the doctrine of the Catholic Church to which they are affiliated. The majority (74%) thought that sexual life should be governed by some common moral rules. Relations between parents and children were also held to be subject to strict rules as 75 per cent rejected the right of children to not support an old father who had not cared for them in the past. An even larger majority, 92 per cent, thought that the Sixth Commandment and 91 per cent that the Ninth Commandment applied to them. Cynical comments apart, it is important to stress that in the same surveys open dissent from official Catholic teaching was manifested, as 82 per cent supported freedom of abortion at least under certain circumstances (1990) and 77 per cent supported the teaching of contraception in secondary schools in order to prevent unwanted pregnancy (1988). The common thread is that people are ready to pronounce moral judgement on family relations, but their judgement, as they proclaim it themselves, is most often made in consideration of the social meaning and function of the acts. Individual freedom of decision is negotiated with collective duties such as the obligation to support others in the family, or of fidelity. Life itself is a series of negotiations and most people do not assume that a compromise, even if attained, will last for ever. The judgements made by others as well as the external normative frames of reference such as religion, customs, or law, are taken not as absolute but as providing the guidelines to assist people in making decisions for themselves and by themselves. The Polish ethos, not surprisingly, seems thus to be a working compromise between the basic principle of individual pursuit of happiness in life, and the objective collective structures such as family that are instrumental in achieving the SR, social rooting. The actual process of this negotiation is, however, kept private in one's conscience.

Instead of a conclusion

In 1989 the Round Table negotiations paved the way to political compromise between the ruling Communist élite and the opposition. The compromise was obtained with the help of mediation by the Church which was the only institution to have survived Communism in good shape. It soon became clear, and this was predictable for those who knew the scope of Communist political influence prior to World War II, that in the northern part of the former Communist Central-Eastern Europe, Communist power was based upon the direct support of an alien power. The compromise collapsed, even though it still survives in the antiquarian composition of the lower house in the Polish parliament. Resurgent Solidarity is much weaker than ten years ago, and lack of support for the drastic economic policies that Solidarity-based governments run by no means helps to strengthen the position of the anti-Communist trade union. Another mass organization of Communist trade unions is handicapped by its past political record. Parties are either old and compromised or new and unknown to the public. Politics is parliamentary only in the literal meaning. Of the two major pinnacles of authority, only the President has achieved full democratic legitimacy through unrestricted elections, which makes the situation vulnerable to attempts at excessive increase of the role of the executive. The Catholic Church remains in this landscape as the unchallenged pillar of social order, the symbol of historical continuity and the last resort in case of political troubles. Not surprisingly the Church reiterates its old position, attacks the constitutional principle of separation of state and religion, supports the ban on abortion in the name of natural law, and the Catholic majority influences the legislature as well as the administration.

All this means that today and in the near future, family issues will continue to be the focus of political controversies. Politicization of the abortion issue is well known everywhere. But this is only one element in the wider complexity of issues. The Church continues to defend the individual, the family, and the nation according to its doctrine, and in the aftermath of Communism this seems to be the only ideology that makes life meaningful in the disorganized world of transition to a capitalist economy and political democracy.

The definition of the family is, like definitions of human life and of the human body and its functions, a political issue of the utmost importance. Let me quote again from the 1976 sermons of the Cardinal of the Millennium as Stefan Wyszynski is called in Poland:

One can speak about the attempts to secularize society . . . made to substitute the sacraments of the Church with lay rituals for the citizens. It reminds us somewhat of the ritual of the masonic lodges which was widespread, especially in lay France. It would be somewhat below our national dignity to borrow from the secularized French masons and create, following their pattern, some lay rituals and rites to substitute for our full sacramental experiences of baptism, confirmation, or marriage. This is why for the sake of God's Peace and an increase in the credibility of the political community this also should be surrendered.

This statement was made against the Communist Party-State at the peak of its power, and this remains the political programme of the Catholic Church in today's democratic Poland. The Church teaches Cardinal Wyszynski's doctrine and takes it as a legacy to be upheld and implemented.

It is hard to imagine the length of the history of resistance of Polish Catholicism to the secularization of family law. The first attempt dates back to Napoleon's rule as, in the part of Poland he resurrected from the alien yoke under the name of the Duchy of Warsaw, French legislation had been introduced as in other parts of a Europe being forced to modernize. The Code Napoleon retained the revolutionary legislation that introduced secular marriage as the sole procedure necessary for a legal marital union. To this the exclusive jurisdiction of the common courts in family matters as well as the dissolution of marriage through divorce was added. However, although the code regressed a little by comparison with the early revolutionary enactments, the basic changes introduced by the constitution of 1791 were retained. Marriage and the resulting family were now secular institutions under the control of the public authorities. The family was separated as much from religion as from the state. The strict division of family relations into legal and illicit, that was best manifested by the severe discrimination against children born of adulterous unions, demonstrated the fact that since then the family has not become liberated from social control but simply removed from the control of the religious corporations that were previously acting in co-operation with the sovereign under the control of the lay state. Napoleon entered Poland as liberator and as revolutionary. As usual he introduced revolutionary legislation, and this was opposed by the clergy who were part of the establishment of the country he had helped to re-establish in some form. Opposition was strong, particularly when, in the face of a shortage of local administrators, the clergy were entrusted with the task of running the civil state register, a task that put priests in conflict with Canon Law. A general boycott by the clergy resulted in a special decree of 23 February 1809 that entrusted the clergy with the civil register duties, but these could be followed by appropriate religious rites. This was supplemented by the provision that clergy acting simultaneously as clerics and public officials would be allowed not to publicize the divorce decreed by the courts, as well as to refuse marriage to those who had previously divorced. The effect was that, in the whole Duchy of Warsaw in 1808–18 only 'a handful' of divorces were granted by the courts and a 'dozen or so' civil marriages contracted. The following decades marked the struggle between the Catholic Church and that part of the administration in the Kingdom of Poland established temporarily by the Russians in some of the territories of the former Duchy of Warsaw. The clergy boycotted the liberal rules by which the public courts retained jurisdiction in family matters, according to the denominational status of the spouses.

Five legal systems were inherited by the newly independent Poland in 1918: Russian, Russian Kingdom of Poland, German (in the former Prussian provinces), Austrian, and Hungarian. Except for the German secular system of contracting marriages that had been efficiently introduced by von Bismarck against Catholic opposition throughout united Germany during the Kulturkampf, those systems were either fully religious or of a mixed character as in Austria, where non-believers were offered civil and believers religious marriage. Not until the early 1930s were the criminal and civil law and procedure codified in a unified way.

However, many provinces of the civil law had not been successfully unified. Especially controversial was the issue of the marriage law. The draft, prepared mainly by Prof. K. Lutostanski, had been completed in 1929, and was published later. It had provided for optional civil or religious marriages, civil divorces, equality of spouses, and judicial jurisdiction in family matters. The draft was not put into effect mainly because of the resistance of the Catholic Church. The Government neither presented the draft to the Seym nor issued it in the form of a presidential decree (Leszinski and Rozwadowski, 1980: 396).

Instead of summing up what has gone before, let me conclude by stating where we are in Poland now. The historical paradox is that the problem of the relationship between sacred and secular approaches to marriage, sex, and procreation has emerged as the most controversial issue in the political life of free Poland. The political aspect of the debate on abortion has been spectacular, and has been well described in its earlier stage. Less well-known is the width of the interest that organized Catholicism—sometimes it is difficult to say whether the given stand is the official policy of the Church as such—has had in changing the legal regulation of those matters in Poland. Already, under the government of Tadeusz Mazowiecki, religious teaching in schools had been reintroduced by simple ministerial instruction, a move that was contested by the Ombudswoman but finally approved by the Constitutional Court. The Minister of Justice in the recent government, Prof. W. Chrzanowski, leader of the Christian-National Union was certainly behind the recent change that made the granting of a divorce more difficult by moving it to the upper level of the courts in Poland. In an interview he also expressed interest in preventing divorce by relevant modification of the law. The Church is not alone in its condemnation of freedom of divorce. The Polish authority on population policy and demography, Professor Edward Rossel characterizes the light-hearted entry into and breakdown of marital ties by young people as '*sui generis* moral crime' and supports the view that the only way to stabilize family life is through a ban on divorce. Professor Adam Strzembosz, President of the Supreme Court, has expressed the opinion that though 'in Poland concubinage is not a legally regulated institution . . . It does not seem that it is in the interest of the state to support concubinage. It is better to create legal conditions to strengthen the family. The situation in which one of the partners may, without any difficulties, break the union is demoralizing and dangerous for a child. In every marriage, though crises happen, several legally defined conditions must be met to get a divorce.'

Recently the government introduced a draft legal regulation to bring the institution of separation across from Canon into Civil law, a motioń that provoked me and my party colleagues in the Polish Seym to express concern for the future of the right to divorce, and the need to complement separation with no-fault administrative divorce by consent. The liberal draft Charter of Rights and Liberties introduced by President Wałesa into Parliament is to be supplemented by a Charter of Family Rights promised by the National-Christian deputies. Some politicians in contemporary Poland stress the need to retain national peculiarities, and want to find a third way between the decadent West and the decadent Communist East. Not surprisingly, Poland has been chosen by the Pope as the starting point for the rechristianization of Europe. The legal changes we speak about are kept away from public attention, and even in the case of abortion, democratic parliamentarians when informed about public opinion polls decided that a public referendum would not be appropriate in reference to a matter of principle (Fuszara, 1991). It is interesting that small technical modifications that are negligible in the face of the hundreds of legal Acts going through the Polish parliament might be of quite decisive importance in the matter. With changes in the administration of graveyards that are returning to denominational rule, the resacralization of family law seems a real possibility.

As an indicator of future attempts to achieve this, one may quote recent press information about the priest who performed a religious marriage ceremony in a case where one of the spouses had already been in a civil marital union. (As a post-script let me note that on 6 November 1992, Deputy K. Tchorzewski introduced an Interpellation to the Ministers of Justice and of the Interior asking what legislative action was needed in order to grant legal validity to church marriages. The Minister of Justice answered that this issue had not been contemplated by the Civil Law Reform Commission at the Ministry of Justice.)

This resulted from the 1989 Law on the Relationship of the State to the Catholic Church that abolished the duty to go through religious marriage rites after a civil marriage had taken place. Most likely, all that this would amount to would be the reintroduction of the mixed system that is in force in some north-western non-Catholic countries, and constitutes in itself nothing peculiar from the British point of view. In the context of the previously presented information on contemporary Catholicism in Poland it is evident, though, that religious registration of marriage will serve the purpose of increasing control of believers by the Church. Until today in the almost exclusively Catholic society, there was a significant minority of those who registered as Catholics through church weddings, and other sacraments, but who held views independent from those of the Church on a variety of issues. The issues of marriage, sex, and procreation are of foremost importance. Religious education in state schools, however voluntary, constitutes pressure on both parents and their offspring, especially those who are lukewarm in their religious outlook. Until now, a church wedding was a social must, easily waived in case of remarriage after divorce. Under the mixed regime, as before the war, divorce, though possible, would amount to a public and formal breakdown of relations with the Church, which in socialist reality amounted to private penitence under ecclesiastic sanctions. In the context of the rechristianized State and predominantly Catholic society, even the free choice between religious and civil marriage would offer the Church an opportunity to exert direct control over the millions of Polish families who are now living in various degrees of Catholicism. This new paradigm will be strengthened economically due to the recognition by the state of religious institutions. Catholic establishments are going to be financed from public taxes, the Catholic University of Lublin being the first test case of the kind. The Church is going to receive back the buildings in which the institutions of support for the elderly, etc., nationalized under Communism, were housed. It does not mean that there will be no houses for the elderly or for children in need of special care. The Communist budget had already become too poor to attract a sufficient number of personnel to those places, and the role of the religious staff had been recognized a decade ago. Now those services will be staffed by people with religious enthusiasm, managed with more economic discipline by the Church, and supported from the public budget. This is the economic meaning of the privatization of public services.

The alternative to religious marriage would not be civil marriage but the alternative life-style of free copulation, cohabitation, and coeducation of those children, born despite attempts at birth control through illicit means such as contraception and abortion. The formalization of affective and sexual ties would be postponed by those who saw life as continuous free choice, and not as the inevitable consequences of the free choices once made. It seems that at the moment there is quite a large pool of those who think in this way in Polish society. This seems to be correlated with the entrepreneurial spirit and economic activism, the virtues praised and reinforced in the transition to a market economy. But one may doubt whether the new society is really going to be that of the individualistic market economy, or whether it will be rather the continuation of the previous trend that combined elements of the ego-altruistic drive with mutual assistance and the collective security system that the

Communist politicized economy provided. The idea of popular capitalism under the control of Church, state, and trade unions may result in something different from what the liberals envisage who run the country at present and provide the direction for economic reform. The answer is thus not so much in the ratio between the fundamentalist and libertarian factions of Polish society, but in the social consequences of the economic change now under way. Within the process, the family may dissolve in the same sense as in Western Europe, or it may be reinstitutionalized as the constitutional unit of society and be the major unit of economic responsibility and solidarity it was in the past.

The paradox of the Polish family is that the collectivistic Party-State introduced modern family legislation which in many aspects was ahead of that of the West. This legislation secularized marriage and individualized family relations but the family nevertheless survived due to the stress of the economic, political, and social conditions of real socialism. The new republic, based upon the principle of the rule of law, works to develop the individualistic market economy and institutionalize the safeguards of individual liberties. The family legislation, however, now opposes the privatization of family life making it dependent upon publicly recognized and supported corporations such as the Church. The distinction between public and private was blurred under Communism; it seems that it is blurred in the new system as well. There is no better social privacy than the intimacy of love, procreation, and bringing up children and the new legislation and policies for the family tend to subject this area to institutionalized social control. It is hard to imagine that, following the reinstitutionalization and resacralization of marriage, negative discrimination against illicit unions, chance encounters and the offspring of these will not develop. The institutionalization of the divide between the secular and sacred has this corollary as the price to be paid. Privatization in the sense of fewer duties and rights of the state does not necessarily mean the privatization of individual life. The advocates of the society in which there are no boundaries between the people in their human form and people in their formal civic role will thus have another chance to check the merits and faults of a polity in which the distinction is removed. But the economic success of recent policies is not excluded, and the privatization of economic life, by no means a simple and unambiguous process, may mean the separation of the public domain from business. If so, and this is the scenario everybody seems to be busy following, then the two processes go in opposite directions: the Polish family may soon be composed of spouses enacting together their public civic duty at night and opening by day their separate banking accounts under private and sacrosanct bank secrecy. The paradox of being a citizen as a family member and being a private individual in business cannot resolve itself without further social disturbances, or the dualism of adjustment which Polish society has experienced already under Communism.

REFERENCES

Fuszara, M. (1991), 'Will the Abortion Issue Give Birth to Feminism in Poland' in Mavis Maclean and Dulcie Groves (eds.), *Women's Issues in Social Policy* (Routledge, London).

Fuszara, M., Jakubowska, I., and Kurczewski, J. (1988), 'Justice in Time of Rationing', *Tidskrift for Rettssosiologi* (Oslo).

Kicinski, K. and Kurczewski, J. (1977), *Poglądy etyczne mlodego pokolenia Polaków* (Ethical Views of the Young Generation of Poles) (Warsaw).

Kurczewski, J. (1981), 'Dawny ustroj i rewolucja' (The Old System and the Revolution), *Res Publica* 7.

—— (ed.) (1985), *Umowa o kartki* (Rationing) (UW, Warsaw).

Lesinski, B. and Rozwadowski, W. (1980), *Historia prawa* (History of Law) (PWN, Warsaw).

Nowak, S. *et al.* (1979), *Ciągłość i zmiana tradycji kulturowych* (Continuity and Change in Cultural Traditions) (UW, Warsaw).

Petrazycki, L. (1955) translated by H. W. Babb as *Law and Morality*, vol. vii in 20th Century Legal Philosophy Series (Harvard University Press, Cambridge, Mass.).

Podgorecki, A., Kurczewski, J., Kwasnieskie, J., and Los, M. (1971), *Poglądy społeczeństwa polskiego na moralność i prawo* (Moral and Legal Attitudes of Polish Society) (KiW, Warsaw).

Rosset, E. (1986), *Rozwody* (Divorces) (PWE, Warsaw).

Sojka-Zielinska, K. (1971) in Juliusz Bardach and Monika Semkowska-Gluck (eds.), *Historia państwa i prawo* (History of Legal Attitudes of Polish Society), (KiW, Warsaw).

Staszewski, M. (1976) (ed.), *Kościół o konstytucji* (The Church on the Constitution) (Warsaw).

3. Dilemmas of Family Policy in Liberal States

Robert Dingwall

It has become a commonplace observation for Western social scientists that the transition to democracy of the former Communist states of Eastern Europe has created a unique laboratory for the study of social change. For the first time, a process which we can recognize contemporaneously as historic is taking place in societies which are relatively accessible and pose few of the personal risks run by students of regime transitions and modernization in the Third World. The peoples of Eastern Europe are recognizably our kin—and heirs to related languages and cultural experiences. Notwithstanding present economic difficulties, their countries have a measure of public order, the elements of a welfare state, and an infrastructure for the exchange of goods and services between the agricultural and industrial sectors. What distinguishes them from us is the legacy of Lenin's revolution, as disseminated by his successors behind the Iron Curtain created at Yalta.

State socialism has revealed itself as a cul de sac. The result, however, is not the end of history but a new beginning as Eastern Europeans seek to recapitulate the post-war experience of their Western cousins, in the belief that this will bring the same material conditions and entrench the same personal freedoms. In so doing, however, they challenge the adequacy of our analyses as accounts of our own societies. Can the models and theories developed by Western social scientists, and peddled alongside the Marriott hotels and McDonald hamburgers, provide a basis for the reconstruction of these sibling states? To the extent that they succeed or fail, we should, in turn, be provoked to review the extent to which we have really understood our own conditions of life. At the end of our journey, we find ourselves.

Family policy is a key site for the exploration of these questions,

An earlier version of this paper was presented at the ESF Coloquium on Social Representations of Justice, Geneva, Switzerland, 1991. I am grateful to Robert Sobiech, Andrzej Szlezak, and Anna Kwak for encouraging me to think about Poland and to John Eekelaar for his colleagueship over many years.

not least because of its tendency to express the core values of a society. The successful accomplishment of reproduction and socialization is what we used to be unembarrassed to call a functional prerequisite for the maintenance of a society through time. There are many ways in which these tasks may be accomplished, but they cannot be avoided.

The foundational character of reproduction and socialization has made it a central issue for social reformers throughout recorded history. Any proposal to reconstruct the real world on Utopian principles necessarily carries implications for the perpetuation of the change whether in the Shaker faith that conversion would provide sufficient recruits to maintain a celibate community, in the attempt of Meiji Japan to resist domestic modernization as the bulwark against the threat of economic and technical modernization to the traditional order, or to the direct attacks on established family relationships which have accompanied Communist revolutions from Lenin to Mao. The values embedded in the institutions of reproduction and socialization simultaneously constitute the definitions of pathology, of social problems. 'Value judgments define certain conditions of human life and certain kinds of behavior as social problems: there can be no social problem without a value judgement' (Waller, 1936: 922).

The case of Poland is particularly interesting because of its parallels with Western experience. Family life could not be a problem in Communist Poland because the millennial official ideology dictated that the regime had abolished all social pathologies. Actually existing socialism was Utopia, a society which accorded extensive formal rights to men and women, offered easy divorce and abortion, and provided ample support for child care so that women and men could pursue their individual interests without compromise. This claim left no official space to respond to the abundant evidence of poverty, oppression, and injustice, between genders and generations alike. The Catholic opposition cast the family in a heroic role as the one site where everyone could resist. Whatever the external pressures, here was a space in which God's will could be given effect. If there were injustices, these reflected human aberrations which could be corrected by greater personal devotion. Again, a familist ideology left no space for a critique of the institution itself. No organized group put forward and mobilized around a value judgement that the justice with which family members treated each other might be seen as problematic. After democratization, the influence of Western libertarian thought became a further bar to public concern for private welfare. The new official values assumed that the market would provide the relevant incentives and motivations for family members to treat each other in an appropriate fashion. If some parents treated their children or their partners badly, the results would encourage others to behave better.

This is, of course, a superficial account of the last forty years of social policy in Poland. Nevertheless, it is indicative of the sources of official indifference to family matters in many developed societies in the post-war period. For almost a generation it was assumed in Western Europe that the welfare state had solved most family problems through its policies of Keynesian economic management and public provision of social insurance, health care, and education. Nothing provided for the family to be treated as a social problem. The 'rediscovery of poverty' in the 1960s and the accumulating evidence that the middle classes had been the major beneficiaries of state welfare undermined this Panglossian complacency. In some ways more shocking though, was the realization that economic justice was not enough, that even a sufficiency of income, housing, and other welfare provisions could not ensure that all members of a family would share equally in their benefits. The family remained a domain of violence, coercion, and injustice to degrees that would not be tolerated in the relationship of its members to strangers.

There was, however, no consensus on the appropriate responses. Some argued that it was a matter of improving the efficiency of social interventions by administrative reform. Others claimed that the whole endeavour was misguided: family problems would not be solved without some more general social transformation, either in the communitarian version of the late 1960s or the feminist version of the 1970s and 1980s. State welfare was merely a means of propping up an unjust social order. Finally, a third voice was heard arguing that these failures were essentially the result of human wickedness which would not be changed either by the interventions of the welfare state or by the overthrow of patriarchal capitalism. Government policies should be directed solely to the maintenance of public order and the protection of property rights: family pathology would ultimately be eliminated by natural selection.

This last, libertarian, argument has played a large part in the thinking of governments in Britain and the USA over the last ten years or so. Its attractions for Eastern Europe are understandable given the recent historical experience of those societies. Nevertheless, it is a theory of social organization which seems to have a number of significant flaws. The analysis of these may contribute to a 'post-liberal' approach to family policy.

The Family and the Liberal State

One recently influential analysis of the position of the family in liberal states has come from Jacques Donzelot (1980). He starts from an orthodox sociological claim: that a qualitative change occurred in European societies around the end of the eighteenth century with effects that could be seen in both culture and social organization. The rationalization of productive labour by the Industrial Revolution was matched by the rationalization of the human mind and body. In the course of this transition, the status of the family came into question.

Under the *ancien regime,* Donzelot argues, the family had been the most local manifestation of the state. Absolute economic and legal power was delegated to household heads who were, in return, accountable to the Crown for the conduct of their kinsfolk and servants. The family was a microcosm of the state and the justice with which its resources were distributed or its members treated was a matter for the character and discretion of its sovereign patriarch. While the abuse of power might attract disapproval, and might be overridden by the equally capricious commands of a feudal superior, there was no formal basis on which it could be challenged any more than could the whims of a monarch.

Because the family had such a basic role in this system of social organization, the Enlightenment's challenge to the legitimacy of royal absolutism almost inevitably extended to its microcosm. Utopian writers argued that the family was as obsolete as absolute monarchy and looked forward to its replacement by new collective institutions. Both the absolutists and their critics, however, shared a model of the family state, where a conception of the good life would be imposed on all citizens, either through the Divine inspiration of the king or through the rational authority of the Enlightenment philosopher.[1] In

---

[1] Guttman (1989: 71–2), discusses, for example, Socrates' rejection in the *Crito* of arguments, resurrected, ironically, by Rousseau in *The Government of Poland*, that the law and constitution of Athens had the right to his obedience simply because they had cre-

neither case was the justice of family life a problem because of the identity of private and public actions. In the former, there are no external standards of justice against which private actions can be measured: in the latter, the new institutions of collective living were expressions of the perfected society, rather like the official ideology of Poland's Communist rulers. As such, there were, again, no relevant benchmarks against which they might be evaluated.

In reality, though, the family proved remarkably resilient. The liberal states which succeeded absolute regimes in Western Europe and North America constructed legal boundaries around the family and denied themselves the ability to encroach on this space beyond the law. Donzelot suggests that liberals promoted this policy because they saw the family as an important check on the possible excesses of state power. The legal and social boundaries around the family guaranteed a sphere of privacy in which every citizen could exercise their own preferences provided these did not impinge upon the public domain.

Of course, this unregulated sphere was also a site for much oppression and injustice as numerous critics of the gender and generational order have pointed out. However, rather than lamenting the failings of the model, and of so many attempts at reform, Donzelot asked how it had been made to work so successfully for so long and what its positive contribution to the viability of the liberal state might be. Although there are considerable problems with both the evidential basis and the theoretical coherence of his answers (Van Krieken, 1986; Dingwall and Eekelaar, 1988; Dingwall, 1992), these questions did move the debate onto new ground and take some account of the persistence of the family through the many changes that European societies have experienced in the last two hundred years.

Donzelot directs us to a more serious reading of liberal political thought. Classically, this views society as the product of a series of free contracts between responsible individuals. The role of the state is limited to that of an ultimate guarantor of the conditions under which contracts can be made. However, even early writers like Adam Smith recognized that this model became highly problematic as the division of labour increased. When individuals and their contributions became more differentiated, they became more interdependent.

ated the conditions for his birth and raising. Socrates points out that this would require obedience to any regime, however repressive, and the proper basis for loyalty lies in the possibilities for freedom offered by a state.

The growing differentiation of knowledge and skills meant that people were less able to evaluate the goods and services which they depended upon and had to trust each other's good faith in many transactions. At the same time, the spread of trading relationships meant that more of them became anonymous and impersonal so that people had many more opportunities to deceive each other without fear of the sanctions that could be mobilized in traditional communities. A great deal of nineteenth and twentieth century social thought has been devoted to the search for a resolution to this paradox.

With the residual role accorded to the state in liberal thinking, the first preference is for the regulation of relationships by individual initiative. The distinction between private and public spheres is one of the ways in which this is made possible. In the private sphere of small-scale, continuing, face-to-face relationships, it is thought that the incentives for deviance are attenuated by the prospect of repeated action over a period of time and that it is practicable for each participant to assess the character of the other through close observation. Family justice rests on the self-interest of its members. In contrast to the autocracy of the family state, whether absolutist or collectivist, this 'state of families' assumes that individuals left to their own devices will treat each other well because their relationships depend upon it. Parents, for example, will invest in the care and education of their children because they expect some return in the form of economic security in old age. Consequently, there is no reason or justification for state intervention.

In contrast, relationships in the public sphere are mainly segmented, transient, and anonymous so that it is more difficult to individuals to carry out their own regulatory actions. If the large-scale social organization associated with the division of labour is to flourish, some substitute form of regulation must be developed. The importance of such regulation was recognized by, for example, the authors of *The Federalist Papers*, in rejecting the radical libertarianism of the New England states in favour of a strong central government for the United States (Madison *et al.*, 1987). The Articles of Confederation, America's first constitution of 1776–7, did little more than provide for a loose association of states without a centralized executive or judiciary and with minimal power vested in the legislature. The result was a series of commercial and territorial disputes between the states with no obvious mechanisms of resolution short of armed conflict. A number of states risked degenerating into populist despotism, since the absolute sovereignty of state legislatures could easily lead to the tyranny of majorities in, for example, the relative treatment of creditors and debtors. Madison and his colleagues promoted the 1787 constitution as a means of restraining what they saw as an excessive and self-destructive zeal for liberty. The strengthening of federal authority, albeit restrained by the separation of powers, and the entrenchment of the Constitution as a source of legitimacy beyond state governments, were the keys to creating the conditions for a liberal state.

The Federalists were concerned mainly to prevent economic anarchy, although some of their comments on the freedom of religion touch on the implications for social policies. The dispersion of powers and the broader sweep of the federal government would make it harder for any faction to impose its will on the whole country, as it might in a county or state. But it is important to be clear that the protection for minority rights both flows from, and is limited by, the constitutional use of federal power. The system is designed to incorporate as many interests as possible and to check arbitrary behaviour by a majority. Once that majority has been constructed, however, its power can be used to declare certain types of action legitimate or illegitimate to the extent that they compromise the sphere of public life.

There is, though, always a risk that the state's operations will extend beyond the terms on which that regulatory power has been granted. Regulation or policing is also a weak solution to the problem of trust because it tends to react to breaches rather than creating the conditions for confidence in the appearances or promises of others. Compliance reflects the degree of certainty which attaches to discovery or punishment, which may be quite low in a highly differentiated society, rather than the principled rejection of the possibility of misconduct because of its wider threats to the social fabric. The kind of 'total policing' advocated by some eighteenth and nineteenth century writers has rarely received the scale of practical endorsement that much of the writing on social control might imply.

The main alternative, then, has been a detailed concern for the moral socialization of the citizenry. This was, for example, Adam Smith's preferred approach (Smith 1976). He saw that the benefits of liberal economic organization would only be realized with a strengthening of personal morality so that the pursuit of wealth would not be self-defeating because of the way in which it damaged or degraded others. This was a genuinely proactive strategy: liberalism would survive because people were so thoroughly imbued with appropriate moral principles, or presented with incentives to behave as if they were, that they chose to constrain their own actions in such a way as to permit the social order to survive. By the 1830s, for instance, similar sorts of arguments were being voiced in the USA where the ideals of the founders of the republic were seen as having been subverted by the moral inadequacies of the population which could only be remedied by improvements in child nurture (Wishy 1968).

As Guttman (1989) has pointed out in a recent discussion, this is a difficult point for liberal theorists. There is a fine line between the transmission of liberal ideals and the Platonic model of socialization for the family state, where education is equated with governance, teaching all citizens to live the good life defined for them by the philosopher kings. Nevertheless, she argues, it is just as unacceptable for the State to abandon any claims to influence the conditions of its own reproduction and to afford parents absolute liberty in the education or, in more sociological terms, the socialization of their children.

It is one thing to recognize the authority of parents to educate their children as members of a family, and quite another to claim that parental authority may serve as a shield against exposing children to ways of life or thinking that offend their parents. The state of families—a state that cedes parents sovereignty over the education of their children—mistakenly conflates the welfare of children with the freedom of parents when it assumes that the former is best defined or secured by the latter. Just as a substantial realm of parental authority is essential to both the freedom of adults and the welfare of children as members of families, so too is a substantial realm of political authority essential to the future freedom of children and their welfare as citizens (Guttman, 1989: 73).

The generational order is a point of endemic conflict between the *laissez-faire* values of self-determination and the civic values of self-restraint. The family is constituted as a territory of private regulation, surrounded by strong boundaries in both domestic and international human rights law. While this insulation may be synonymous with liberty, however, it also creates a space for license. Public indifference to the inner life of families involves a tolerance of gender and generational injustice. These will not necessarily be eliminated by some evolutionary process. Patriarchy works rather well for men and the rewards for investment in children may be so distant and uncertain that they do not seem worth pursuing.

But these actions have public consequences. A society which denies itself the public contribution of women impoverishes itself and one which neglects the normative socialization of children hazards it public order and its prospects of reproduction. Indeed it is the argument for conscious social reproduction that Guttman sees as the prime basis for State regulation of education, a case which might be made about child care more generally. The state of families makes children the captive property of their parents. The liberal state is a state of individuals, which recognizes, with John Stuart Mill, that those whose capacities for autonomy are impaired or undeveloped require particular protection from abuse and guidance in cultivating the character and intellect to adopt liberal virtues as a matter of choice rather than imposition. The family plays a key role in that process. It is, however, a role which it is difficult for public bodies to influence without destroying the benefits of its privacy, the fact that there is an opportunity for individuals to experiment with ways of life and to maintain a basis for social diversity. Yet without such influence, the chances of preventing trust-eroding deviance in public actions are severely limited.

Much of the history of nineteenth and twentieth century social welfare provisions can, as Donzelot shows, be understood as successive attempts to square this circle, to produce practical organizational solutions to the problem of prevention. He points, in particular, to the decentralization of responsibility for preventive work to private philanthropy as the result of 'a search for a calculated distance between the functions of the liberal state and the spread of techniques of welfare and administration of the population' (Donzelot, 1980: 55). Intervention could be carried on autonomously of the State, thus avoiding the risks of centralized power, while closing the breach in the liberal system of regulation or control. Guttman makes this point in slightly different terms when she hints at the importance of professional autonomy in the provision of education, an analysis which links to some of the recent writing in the sociology of the professions by people like Halliday (1987) and their attempt to explore the reasons for the *supply* of regulation by the state in the form of licensing. Professionalization is a decentred form of social intervention, which derives authority from the state without being directed by it.

Donzelot traces a movement from moralization through normalization to tutelage or wardship as successive attempts to penetrate the boundaries of family life in order to anticipate and prevent, rather than merely react to and contain threats to the public order.[2] In the process, the organizational base of intervention shifted from private philanthropy to the State.

Again, there are points of detail on which his analysis may need some modification, but the broad thrust seems persuasive (Dingwall and Eekelaar, 1988; Dingwall, 1992). In effect, the liberal states of Western Europe evolved systems of family regulation which made it possible for public agencies to intervene in family life. John Eekelaar and I would extend the analysis of techniques mainly by pointing to the way in which family intervention has been fragmented by constituting different agencies to emphasize different aspects of the moral structure of the market economy and by diffusing power between those agencies so that no single one can venture far down a coercive path on its own. The whole is further divided by the varying weight given to professional and bureaucratic forms of organizational governance. The art of government is to prevent the formation of monopolies or cartels between these regulators and to protect the loose coupling that is the citizen's guarantor against unwarranted intrusion on his or her privacy (Dingwall and Eekelaar, 1988).

By this point, of course, many political theorists might question whether we are really talking about a liberal state at all, although our analysis still recognizes the classic principles of pluralism and competition. Most of the societies being considered here might be more commonly described as social democracies. It could be argued that we should look to the contemporary United States for a more authentic model of liberalism, where the celebration of privacy has long restricted family intervention to a much greater degree. It is possible, however, that the USA may be better understood as displaying the incomplete development of the liberal state rather than as its showpiece. Its very abundance of human resources has insulated the country from the policy problem of managing them in such a way as to sustain a successful liberal order. That task, however, is now massively complicated by the sheer ethnic diversity of the society and the deep passions aroused by any non-relativist response.

Some aspects of this problem were explored by Karl Mannheim

---

[2] Moralization involved the imposition of behavioural requirements as conditions for assistance; normalization, the deliberate propagation of specific norms and values; tutelage, the systematic creation of opportunities for individuals to display their respectability and acquire moral credit in advance of any need.

(1943) in a series of lectures given during the Second World War. Writing as a refugee from Fascism, Mannheim attempted to analyse the basis for the fragility of social order in contemporary societies and to describe the basis of a response in the form of what he called 'militant democracy'. He argued that all *laissez-faire* societies risked disintegration as a result of the effects of the changing scale of social organization, of technology, and of cultural contact. Their order rested on forms of justification which diffused authority and denied the role of moral judgement. Consequently, the means by which fundamental normative conflicts had previously been mediated had either been overwhelmed by the size of the task or had begun to wither away for lack of support.

In a society where disintegration has proceeded too far, the paradoxical situation arises that education, social work and propaganda, notwithstanding highly improved techniques, become less and less efficient because all the values that could guide them tend to evaporate . . . What is the good of developing child guidance, psychiatric social work and psychotherapy if the one who is to guide is left without standards? (Mannheim, 1943: 25).

Mannheim was not, of course, advocating 'a regimented culture and an authoritarian education'. He sought a third way between *laissez-faire* and totalitarianism which he called democratic planning. The struggle against Fascism created a climate for the explicit elaboration of democratic virtue, particularly the importance of self-discipline.

But this self-restraint will only be produced on the parliamentary scene if the same virtues are being exercised in everyday life . . . Only if in daily contacts the habit of discussion produces reconciliation of antagonistic valuations and the habit of co-operation produces a mutual assimilation of each other's values can it be hoped that a common policy can be hammered out in parliament (Mannheim, 1943: 27).

Apart from encouraging the means of resolving and managing social conflict, however, Mannheim also noted the need for the legitimacy of these institutions to be positively nourished, for all the intervention agencies of a society to be infused with the virtues of social justice and peaceful dispute resolution.

The long economic ascendancy of the USA has obscured the limitations of its celebration of *laissez-faire* privacy as a basis for social organization, while encouraging the dogma that a remodelling of any society in an American form will result in the same material achievement. This is a belief which has found some support in Western

Europe over the last dozen years and which seems to be casting the same spell in Eastern Europe at the present time. But the emergence of interest in moral liberalism among American political theorists is an indicator of the dissatisfaction of at least the intelligentsia with that account.

Liberalism's defenders . . . do not meet contemporary charges of moral deficiency by recapitulating the traditional argument for a sacrosanct private sphere . . . Increased notice is taken of the concrete social and institutional contexts, both actual and possible, for developing moral habits and expressing moral values (Rosenblum, 1989: 9).

This movement rejects the claim that democracy takes priority over philosophy, that what citizens decide to be right should be preferred to what can be justified as right; the claim in fact which the Federalists sought to resist in preferring representative republican government to radical libertarianism. While neither philosophy nor sociology can give people a good life, since this is something which must come from inside, which people accept and identify with as an expression of their own nature, and which necessarily manifests a degree of individual discretion, such analyses can identify the conditions of possibility in the public and private realm which make the liberal state possible. There are important tensions here and conflicts of principle: what is important is that these should be directly faced and explicitly traded (Gutmann, 1987; 1989).

One of these is the conflict between family autonomy and civic virtue. Liberalism entails a space for self-determination, but only to the extent that this does not diminish the freedom of others. The family is a site where the moral conditions for liberalism are reproduced. If its internal regime is unjust, then not only are the freedoms of some members diminished, but public life is also threatened because of the impairment of members' capacities to participate in the institutions of liberal democracy. It is here that the argument for intervention rests, that no group can be permitted to disable those under its control for participation in civic life. John Eekelaar and I (Eekelaar, 1987; 1989; Dingwall and Eekelaar, 1984) have expressed this as a theory of trusteeship. Parents are not the owners of children, any more than wives are the property of husbands. The privacy of the family rests on the condition that the practice of its members will promote the general values and goals of a society. Where this trust is breached, the family may properly become the object of intervention.

A state which abandons any concern for the home life of its citizens in pursuit of a mistaken ideal of privacy is colluding in the perpetuation of everyday oppressions and inequalities which are ultimately likely to subvert its public order.

This may be one of the great tragedies of events in Eastern Europe: that the uncritical adoption of a narrow version of liberalism, for understandable historical reasons, undermines the effort to trace its limitations as a form of social organization and to examine the compromises that are necessary to reconcile material prosperity and human freedom. Reactive policing cannot create those conditions. The disorderly tendencies of *laissez-faire* must be contained by careful regulation of the social conditions under which relationships develop. The challenge, to East and West alike, is to reassert and re-elaborate the legitimations which will make this possible.

REFERENCES

Dingwall, R. (1992), 'Family Policy and the Liberal State', in H.-U. Otto, and G. Flösser (eds.), *How to Organize Prevention* (de Gruyter, Berlin).

Dingwall, R. and Eekelaar, J. M. (1984), 'Rethinking Child Protection', in M. D. A. Freeman (ed.), *State, Law and Family* (Tavistock, London).

Dingwall, R. and Eekelaar, J. M. (1988), 'Families and the State: An Historical Perspective on the Public Regulation of Private Conduct', *Law and Policy*, 10: 341–61.

Donzelot, J. (1980), *The Policing of Families* (Hutchinson: London).

Eekelaar, J. (1987), 'Family Law and Social Control', in J. M. Eekelaar, and J. Bell (eds.), *Oxford Essays in Jurisprudence: Third Series* (Oxford University Press, Oxford).

Eekelaar, J. M. (1989), 'What is "Critical" Family Law?', *Law Quarterly Review*, 105: 244–61.

Gutmann, A. (1987), *Democratic Education* (Princeton University Press, Princeton)

Gutmann, A. (1989), 'Undemocratic Education', in N. Rosenblum (ed.), *Liberalism and the Moral Life* (Harvard University Press, Cambridge, Mass.)

Halliday, T. (1987), *Beyond Monopoly: Lawyers, State Crises and Professional Empowerment* (University of Chicago Press, Chicago).

Madison, J., Hamilton, A., and Jay, J. (1987), *The Federalist Papers* (Penguin, London), (first published 1788).

Mannheim, K. (1943), *Diagnosis of our Time* (Routledge and Kegan Paul, London).

Rosenblum, N. (1989), 'Introduction', in N. Rosenblum (ed.), *Liberalism and the Moral Life* (Harvard University Press, Cambridge, Mass.).

Smith, A. (1976), *The Theory of Moral Sentiments* (Clarendon Press, Oxford), (first published 1759).

Van Krieken, R. (1986), 'Social Theory and Child Welfare: Beyond Social Control', *Theory and Society*, 15: 401–29.

Waller, W. (1936), 'Social Problems and the Mores', *American Sociological Review*, 1: 922–33.

Wishy, B. (1968), *The Child and the Republic* (University of Pennsylvania Press, Philadelphia).

PART TWO

Family Obligations: The Empirical Evidence

4. Private Law and the Post-Totalitarian Family: Keeping Promises and Giving Help

Iwona Jakubowska

Our subject is the situation of the family, or to be more exact, the family in post-totalitarian countries. Posing the problem in this way suggests that we have assumed in advance that this has a specific nature in such countries. This assumption seems well-founded, as sociological studies for many years have shown that Poles value the family most highly, followed by a close circle of friends. A great variety of studies produced such findings, and furthermore similar findings were obtained just before August 1980, which gives rise to difficulty with interpretation in view of the subsequent political developments. Why do family matters seem so very important in the context of totalitarianism? The answer is rather simple, I believe.

A totalitarian system aims to acquire full control over the lives of individuals, including their private lives. To achieve this, it also strives to break up the family as a potentially dangerous social group. The most extreme example of such actions recently, lies in the decrees of the Chinese Communist authorities which forbade spouses to work in the same place at the same time. On the other hand, such actions can have exactly the opposite effect. The incessant struggle in which all totalitarian societies are permanently involved results in a polarization in the consciousness of individuals, who start dividing people into 'the good' and 'the bad'. The good ones are those who share the individual's socio-political opinions, the bad ones are the people who have different views. So, quite contrary to the actual intentions of the totalitarian authority, ideological communities are formed which come together in opposition to a common enemy. The family can be such an ideological community. Family members have very good opportunities to create a sense of safety and mutual trust. The family is where values and traditions can be handed down most easily from generation to generation. The family is the 'secret place' where one can say all one thinks: the place that is least liable to suffer from outside interference. As a result, the family has every chance of becoming isolated from the outer world and creating its own life style and perception of reality, which can be as independent as possible from external conditions.

The economic conditions of life in Communist countries draw our attention to another aspect of family life. Due to the permanent shortage of consumer goods, which was particularly felt in the days of rationing, the family can be treated as a hunter and gatherer group. The rationing system forced family members to make decisions within that family about how to consume the goods available. Some such decisions seem ridiculous today, as for instance, whether to buy chocolate for the children or a bottle to celebrate a family feast. But few people who have never experienced such shortages can ever understand the feelings of joy and pride of someone who manages to acquire such unattainable goods as chocolate or coffee with cream.

This function of the family as a group of hunters and gatherers not only led to stronger ties between close family members (parents, children, and possibly grandparents) and greater awareness of a strong community and interdependence, but also to the tightening of bonds, though perhaps not as tight as before, with more distant family members.

While writing this, I am particularly aware of the extent to which sociological texts deprive reality of its everyday character. Writing about the tightening of bonds with the more distant family members, which took place in the vast majority of families in Poland under Communism, I am thinking of my own numerous but more or less distant cousins living away from Warsaw. Throughout the period of rationing, these cousins supplied myself and my family with soap, washing powder, and other such articles knowing that it was absolutely impossible to acquire those goods in Warsaw. Exactly how they managed this in small towns is a separate sociological problem. With normalization of the market, my contacts with the aunts has grown less intimate again, but I am still grateful to them today for having provided me with soap to wash myself. I know I can count on them when in trouble, and I hope that they feel the same way.

Perhaps such private stories would be more appropriate in a private letter than a scientific study. But sociology is after all a science that deals with life; and aims at understanding social mechanisms. It is easier to understand the statement that in a situation of limited access to goods and with a common enemy—the authorities—the bonds of interpersonal solidarity are tightened and the incidence of so-called pro-social acts increases if you have in mind a man running like mad, with his hair blowing in the wind, informing every passer-by that 'the shop next to the church is selling eggs'.

With that incident in mind, it is also easier to understand the finding obtained in our earlier study which was concerned with the sense of threat. From the findings of a 1981 and 1982 study, the sense of threat reported by the inhabitants of Warsaw was very low, which is rather surprising in view of the socio-political situation at that time. It was only a detailed analysis of the data that made it possible to explain this question. Namely, the individual sense of threat was strong *vis-à-vis* authority–citizen relations, but was weaker than ever as far as direct personal contacts were concerned, particularly those between one's closest family and friends.

The above reflections are general in nature, but are based on experience resulting from participation in social life, and on an attempt at understanding the world around us. I carried out regular research into the problems of family life in 1980, while also investigating the structure of ethical thinking. Using the findings of the above-mentioned study, I attempted to characterize the incidence of specific ideal types of perception of the individual's relationship with others with respect to rights and duties. The notional apparatus used is derived from the theory of Leon Petrazycki (Petrazycki, 1955). It is beyond the scope of this essay to reiterate the basic assumptions of his theory; let me therefore just characterize the four basic types of perception of the 'myself–another' relationship he uses with respect to rights and duties.

The point of departure here is the following question: what rights and duties does the individual allot to himself and to 'others', that is, to his partners in interactions in different social situations?

The following situations are possible:

I. *Legal regulation.* This is characterized by imperative-attributive thinking. The individual imposes on himself the duty to behave in a definite way, at the same time granting to others the right to demand that he behave in that particular way. An example here is the situation of a debtor who grants his creditor the right to demand payment of the debt. This is therefore a perception of the myself–other person relationship in a social contract which defines precisely the rights and duties of each of the parties.

II. *Moral regulation*. This is characterized by imperative thinking. The individual imposes on himself the duty to behave in a definite way, but does not grant to others the right to demand that particular behaviour from him. It occurs, for example, when a passer-by sees a beggar and feels obliged to give alms, even feels an inner constraint to do so, but would be outraged if the beggar rose to his feet and said, 'you must give me alms'. Thus we are dealing here with the perception of the self–other relationship in voluntary duties towards such others, the duties that are nevertheless free to the extent that nobody can demand their fulfilment.

III. *Absence of legal regulation*. Here the individual neither imposes on himself the duty to behave in keeping with a norm, nor grants to others the right to expect from him such behaviour. Here, therefore, the self–other relationship is perceived in categories that go entirely beyond the social contract.

IV. The fourth situation is one that seldom happens but is interesting from the theoretical point of view. The individual grants 'another person' the right to demand a definite behaviour but at the same time does not impose on himself the duty to meet that demand. This situation is of theoretical interest for the reason that, according to general belief, each right to a claim granted to one party must necessarily involve a duty imposed on the other party to the interaction. Giving more thought to this situation, however, we reach the conclusion that two aspects of this problem are possible. First, by granting another person the right to a claim, we can transfer the resulting duties to others. Second, in the situation of competitors or contenders we grant to the adversary the right to strive after triumph but do not impose on ourselves or on any other person the duty to fulfil that right.

The discussion of the above four models was lengthy, but pertinent. I believe an attempt at understanding the respondents' perception of reality with the help of those models may be very productive. Starting my research, I anticipated that the perception of the legal reality in everyday life would be entirely different depending on who was the individual's partner in the interaction. That proved to be true.

I examined 477 Warsaw children in three age groups: 7–8; 14–15; and 17–18. The sample was stratified: first the schools were selected at random, then the forms, and finally the children to be examined. The method employed was a questionnaire.

What interested me in relation to the problem discussed was the following question: to what extent does the child's attitude towards the mother as the closest family member differ from that towards friends and persons who are practically strangers? I expected the incidence of perception of the nature of interaction with others, as defined above, to differ according to the identity of the partner in that interaction, and to depend on the child's age. What I found most important was the fact that contacts with the family, especially with the mother, are compulsory and unavoidable to some extent in the case of children, while friends can be chosen by the child independently. I therefore expected an increase with the child's age of the incidence of imperative-attributive thinking in contacts with friends, and a decrease of the incidence of this perception of the self–other relationship with the mother as partner in the interaction.

I told the children stories which contained two situations, rather generally outlined, related to the principles of disinterested help and of keeping a promise. Neither situation should be thought of as extreme. In neither would the object of the action suffer any considerable loss if the behaviour was inconsistent with the principle concerned, nor would the subject of the action bear too large an expense if behaving in accordance with that principle. It was my intention to confront the respondents with precisely these kinds of situations. First, psychology or sociology should not investigate situations which depart in any way whatsoever from the 'norm', a term I use in the sense of approximating to everyday life. This statement seems a truism; yet many researchers into social life show a truly admirable persistence in confronting their respondents with dilemmas such as the story of three persons on board a sinking boat. One of those persons has to be thrown overboard, and the question is, who is it to be? The other reason is that both intuitive knowledge and knowledge from the sphere of social psychology lead one to the conclusion that people tend to think in different categories and to pursue different values in extreme situations from those in everyday situations. Thus one can hardly expect the information about moral opinions concerning such extreme situations to lead to accurate conclusions about the whole of an individual's moral experiences.

The story which concerned the principle of disinterested help was as follows. A woman was ill and could not go out. She asked someone to do her shopping for her, and then to go to her office and tell her boss about her illness. That person did what he was asked to do despite the fact that he had to leave unattended various important matters of his own. I asked four questions about this story:

1. Who was obliged to help the woman: her son (daughter), her friends, or a person she hardly knew (a neighbour)?
2. Do you think the woman would have a right to complain if she failed to receive help from: her son (daughter), her friends, or a person she hardly knew (neighbour)?
3. Do you think you are obliged to help if the person who needs your help is: your mother, your friend, or a person you hardly know (neighbour)?
4. Would you complain if the person who failed to help you were: your mother, your friend, or a person you hardly know (neighbour)?

This part of my study deals with an individual's perception of himself and certain others in respect of rights and duties.

The first of my models, 'legal regulation' (imperative-attributive thinking), was found most frequently in the consciousness of the respondents if the partner in the interaction was their mother. This was the case irrespective of their age. The second most frequent was when the partner in interaction was a friend, and in third place was the situation where a person the respondent hardly knows was involved. The distribution of answers is reported in the following tables. It is worth stressing that the perception of the self–other relationship in a social contract develops with age in situations where the partner in the interaction is the mother or a friend, but decreases when the situation concerns a person the respondent hardly knows.

The second of my models, called 'moral regulation' (imperative thinking only) functioned most frequently in the consciousness of my respondents if the partner in the interaction was a person they hardly know. The second place here was taken by a friend, and the third by

TABLE 1:

Question 1. Who is obliged to help?	Age		
	7–8	14–15	17–18
mother	84%	94%	93%
friend	50%	57%	68%
stranger	24%	6%	8%

TABLE 2:

Question 2. Should she complain if the person who failed was:	Age		
	7–8	14–15	17–18
mother	18%	5%	8%
friend	41%	33%	24%
stranger	47%	54%	43%

the mother. Here is the distribution of answers: The perception of the self–other relationship in the categories of duty without the corresponding right to a claim granted to the other person decreased with age if the partner in the interaction is the mother or a friend, and remained stable in the situations that concerned a person the respondent hardly knows.

The third model discussed, that is absence of normative regulation, occurs most frequently in the consciousness of respondents if their partner in interaction is a person they hardly know. In practice, this model functioned in the respondents' consciousness only in relation to persons they hardly know, its incidence increasing with age. This finding agrees with our expectations to the extent that it hardly requires a commentary. To summarize: 90 per cent of the oldest respondents perceived their relationship with the mother as a social contract which combines rights and duties, and this type of thinking increased with age. At the same time, the perception of the relationship with the mother in the categories of imperative thinking decreased with age. It can be guessed from this finding that with age,

TABLE 3:

Question 3. Are you obliged if the person is your:	Age		
	7–8	14–15	17–18
mother	1%	1%	2%
friend	8%	8%	6%
stranger	26%	39%	47%

imperative thinking in relations with the mother gives place to the imperative-attributive one. The process is identical if the partner in interaction is a friend. What is important, though, is that the number of respondents who perceived interaction with their mother as a social contract was about one third higher than the number of those who applied this type of thinking to their interactions with friends.

This finding is inconsistent with my initial hypothesis. I expected friendship, as a voluntary partnership, to be a stronger stimulant of interactions with respect to rights and duties. This, however, proved not to be the case.

What seems rather alarming is that nearly half the respondents in the oldest age group excluded relations with persons with whom they have no emotional ties from normative regulation. More alarming still was the fact that the incidence of legal regulation in interactions with such persons dropped with age from one quarter to a mere 8 per cent of respondents. This, in my opinion, proves that with age, the 'privileged' position in the individual's consciousness is taken first and foremost by the family, close friends coming next. Persons with no emotional ties with the individual have no rights whatever in the opinion of that individual. (Let me stress again: a mere 8 per cent of respondents in the oldest age group felt any obligation in relation to such persons, although such duties involved no claims).

I have already mentioned that the other story I told my respondents concerned the principle of keeping one's promise. The model of legal thinking was repeated in this case with great precision.

I find the picture of the individual which appears from the findings to be negative from the social point of view. It is, however, in keeping with the theoretical discussion in the first part of this paper. Due to the functions it performed in the totalitarian system, the family takes the central position in the individual's consciousness. If we realize that the conception of justice which functions in that consciousness is based mainly on consideration of one's own and other persons' rights and duties, as has been explicitly shown by my study, the difficulties become quite clear in connection with the transition to the type of thinking that takes the rights of others into account—the one upon which democracy is based.

These findings are tentative and exploratory in nature. They are, however, explicit enough to be treated as a strong indication of the importance of considering the above statements. I also believe that my method of investigation of the structure of legal consciousness is useful to the extent that it may provide the base for further comparative research.

REFERENCES

Petrazycki, L. (1955), *Law and Morality*, translated by H. W. Babb, 20th Century Legal Philosophy Series vol. vii (Harvard University Press, Cambridge, Mass.).

5. What do Family Members and Friends Expect from One Another at the Transition to Democracy?

Joanna Smigielska and Artur Czynczyk

Despite the minuteness of detail and comprehensiveness of sociological and psychological family studies, the picture of the family that emerges remains shadowy. We realize how very difficult it is to show how the family functions on a day to day basis while at the same time preserving the quality of representativeness. Specific simplifications or exaggerations cannot be avoided. The study reported here is an attempt to describe the functioning of the family: both the everyday activities and the opinions voiced by the family members studied, and addresses the question: what do family members and friends expect from one another? The study is based on the authors' systematic observations of family communities. The material was collected during the seven years (1984–91) when Smigielska lived in a workers' district of Warsaw, renting a flat in one of its housing estates. At the beginning, as the new neighbour, people told her the history of the estate and of the individual families living there. She learned about the fates of whole families, their friends and relatives. When taking her own children out for a walk, she met members of her new local community in playgrounds and parks. With time, contacts grew closer and closer and soon she got to know all about the problems of her new acquaintances. This was easier because the neighbours treated her as something of a psychologist. They often came to her for advice on family matters, asked for help when writing applications to the authorities, and finally began to invite her to their homes on the occasion of family feasts. During those seven years, she had several hundred conversations concerning family matters. The material she gathered is derived from those conversations, and also from several dozen interviews concerning family life carried out in the years 1987–91. Thus the picture discussed in this study is not representative but a fragmentary description of reality.

Material assistance

The basic principle by which a Polish family functions is mutual help, and this is treated as self-evident and quite natural. It is rendered in many different ways, financial matters being a most important area. Let us first consider material assistance rendered by the family to the children, particularly those who already have families of their own. Several different forms of assistance are possible. Financial help may consist of giving the children a considerable sum several times a year, that sum being, however, assigned for a definite purpose: 'The parents give us money some three or four times a year. Sometimes they say, buy yourself a rug or a radio, or go for a holiday.' Parents also give money to their son or daughter only, specifically stressing that it is their child only and not that child's spouse who is to spend it: 'We gave our daughter the money for a fur coat. She has her needs, too. Let her at least have a decent coat, and we bought her a gold watch last month. One has to help one's children, right?' But more often financial assistance consists in giving the children a definite sum of money every month or providing them with food. Many parents pay the rent and other expenses, such as the cost of driving lessons or language courses: 'I'll take a course in January. Father's going to get a bonus then, he's sure to pay for me.' In many families, such assistance is based on the principle, 'I never had such things, I want my child to have them. I don't need much for myself.' As this statement indicates, self renunciation on behalf of one's children is quite natural. The parents' own needs seem to be reduced to the bare minimum. An extreme case is as follows: 'I don't need it any more. I'm an old woman and can do without it. Let the young ones have a good time.' These are the words of a woman of 85 who regularly gave a part of her pension to her daughter, 67, and son-in-law, 70.

Another example of assistance is the situation where the grandparents help the young couple who have children of their own by subsidizing or even fully providing for their grandchildren. This involves buying clothes, toys, and sporting equipment; paying for holidays and language courses; giving expensive presents, and so on. The children accept such assistance as natural on the one hand; but on the other, they are grateful for it, realizing that their young family would not be able to function normally without it. This is a dramatic fact, apparent in the discrepancy between young people's level of earnings and the amount they must spend in order to meet their basic needs. Let us imagine a situation where the parents or grandparents simply refuse all financial assistance to their children (which hardly ever happens): then one would expect questions such as, 'What's come over them? How shall we manage now?' As a threat to the living conditions of the young couple, this situation would give rise to many negative emotions. In the specific Polish family situation, over the past forty-five years, the suggestion that the parents should only accept financial responsibility for their children until those children set up their own families lacks all justification. The extensive assistance rendered to children is considered perfectly normal by both parties. '. . . they have to be helped with settling down comfortably. We don't want them to start from nothing'; 'Parents help their children because they don't need much themselves, they already have enough.' The reverse situation, financial assistance rendered by the children to their parents (apart from the legally sanctioned duty to pay alimony), happens much less frequently and is usually a temporary measure.

Help with getting accommodation

This is just as self-evidence as financial assistance. The housing shortage in Poland, both the lack of opportunity to buy a flat for cash or with a loan, and high rents, lead to a situation where the adult children still live with their parents, grandparents, siblings, or as entire multi-generational families. Setting up one's own family is not associated with leaving the parents' flat. It often happens that two separate families share a flat consisting of two or three rooms:

The seven of us share a floor area of 43 square metres: two rooms, a kitchen and a bathroom for my parents and brother, my husband, our two children, and myself. It's worst in the mornings when we're all in a hurry to get ready to go to work, and the children must be taken to the kindergarten. We had to prepare a schedule of visits to the bathroom. I make up my face at work. We haven't the ghost of a chance of our own flat yet. My brother's moving out soon, though: he's getting married and he'll live with his wife's parents . . .

This sharing of flats often gives rise to many conflicts. The lack of any prospects for their own flat results in frustration for young couples. On the other hand, the fact that the parents or grandparents cannot get the peace they deserve because of their age is hardly conducive to harmony. Thus is often happens that those who live together under one roof are not on speaking terms with each other as a result of many quarrels. 'We don't talk. We don't care what each of us is doing and planning to do. There's no alternative as we have nowhere to go. It's not that I'm waiting for them to die—I just treat them as strangers.'

Many years spent together sometimes result in quite the opposite, however: 'We had been living together for ten years when they finally got a two-room flat of their own. But we got so used to having the children and grandchildren with us (and so did they) that we spend nearly all our Saturdays and Sundays together. The grandchildren are with us more often still—they stay overnight. As soon as they were in that other flat, they kept crying, "We want to go home".'

Sharing a flat is related to other forms of help within the family. This includes above all the care of grandchildren, which in turn is so diversified that it would make no sense to proliferate examples. In extreme situations, the grandparents practically act as substitute parents by taking over the parental roles. It is sometimes the parents who help the grandparents to take care of the children: 'We practically brought my grandson up. My daughter and son-in-law work long hours and only come home late at night when the child's asleep. I'm retired; I can help as long as I'm in good health. Let them earn money in peace.' Such help does not always go so far. Grandparents usually take their grandchildren out for walks, bring them to kindergarten and to school, and play with them. Such assistance is sometimes rendered on a regular basis even if the grandparents do not share a flat with the young couple: 'I get up at 5 every day and take a train to my daughter's to get my grandson to school at 8. My daughter starts work at 6 and cannot get the boy ready before going out. It takes me an hour a day to commute. It's worst in winter. But I have to help my daughter, I feel sorry for the boy.'

Queuing

As recently as two years ago, when there was a shortage of many basic articles in the shops, the average Pole also spent a lot of time queuing. The situation in this respect developed according to the following pattern: 'It takes a lot of queuing to buy anything, and sometimes you stand in line but what you need is sold out before you reach the counter.'

Incessant struggling to acquire basic foodstuffs was primarily the task of grandmothers and grandfathers, cousins and friends. The permanent hunt for necessary and basic supplies such as washing-powder became a natural part of everyday life. It became a matter of course in times of rationing that whenever a family member or friend had the opportunity to buy an attractive article (cheese, shampoo, cigarettes) in unlimited quantities (meaning that the quantity of goods purchased was not limited by the shop assistant), he or she always bought more than actually needed in order to share with others. To buy meat, one had to struggle and stand in line for many hours. This resulted in bringing into action literally all family members, particularly 'privileged persons': that is pregnant women, women with children aged under 2, disabled persons, ex-service men, and people aged over 80. This led to situations where there would be two gigantic lines in the shop: one composed of people without any special rights, and the other one of the privileged. The shop assistants often introduced extra rigours, e.g. they served only every second or third person from the 'ordinary' line. Consequently, those from this line often got only the lowest-quality meat.

This situation gave rise to a network of specializations and connections within the family: one person bought meat, another cheese and butter, still another, whose workplace was situated strategically next to certain shops, would be on his or her guard all the time not to miss any attractive article that might be delivered. Besides the emergence of a specific shopping jargon, the irregularity and small size of deliveries resulted in people remaining alert and in a continual state of expectation. Long queues stood patiently in empty shops hoping for a delivery to take place. This situation, where many hours of queuing were required, led in turn to the emergence of a new job, in that pensioners could be hired for a specific fee to stand in line. Parents of children under 2 who were entitled to extra provisions used to hire the children out to friends for shopping. A specialized network of informers was set up in a given apartment house or within the family which told the others about deliveries or unlimited sales of goods. Similar specialized networks in accordance with the special opportunities or contacts of particular individuals (giving a nudge, speaking to a shop assistant one knew, or organizing medical drugs) could be observed in all spheres of life. It was a matter of course that, if you applied for something in an office in which your friend or relative was employed, your case was settled much more efficiently. What is meant here is not just vague hopes but definite expectation of help. 'She's got to arrange that for me, working there as she is. It makes no difference to her who she helps, me or another person. This way all that work of hers will at least be useful.' Gratitude for such forms of assistance would be expressed by way of gifts—coffee, brandy, envelopes with money, and so on, but this kind of gratitude was usually shown outside the family only.

Ways were developed of settling matters 'at the bar' or 'under the table', and a number of idioms developed to describe how everything could be arranged for a consideration. These developed because it was obvious that all problems could be solved through channels of access, that is the existence of the possibility of informal exchange within the group's reach. This kind of assistance should however be distinguished from corrupt practices, where the sums involved were many times higher. Everyday life, under the slogan, 'Finding food and fixing things are our main aims', was not the only arena where mutual help could be found. There was another area of mutual support. Family members and friends often performed the role of therapists, and were expected to give advice or just to listen to another person's complaints and to sympathize or share happiness. Here, also, it was not necessary to discuss the fact of expecting help. Almost everyone realized the principle underlying the functioning of society to be: how can I help you? Engagement in the problems of one's family or friends was a matter of course: 'I'm looking for a specialist for a sick child of my friends'; 'I'm trying to find the way to help a girl I know to get a flat'; 'I'm arranging for my brother's wife to get a job in my firm.' Many problems would remain unsolved in spite of all these efforts, but the fact that one could share them with others and hear their opinions created a considerable feeling of safety and security.

Joint celebrations

Participation in family life was inseparably connected with joint celebrations, occasional meetings of the family and friends to celebrate weddings, name days, birthdays, baptisms, or first Communions. Church holidays were usually spent with one's family. Traditionally, such occasions involved the giving or exchange of presents. In times of crisis, such gifts were usually socks, toothpaste, or a bar of soap. As the situation improved the gifts became less basic, but were still usually practical in nature. Participation in the family community created a very strong obligation to function within this scheme. The pattern is difficult to overcome. To say 'we won't be together for Christmas this year. We're going to the mountains' would cause surprise and even offence in most families.

Between family members and among friends, borrowing and lending money is quite natural. 'We borrowed money from our friends to finish the repairs in our flat.' The debts are usually paid back without interest or extra sums for inflation. What is more, they can be paid back in instalments at the debtor's convenience.

Relationships within the family and among friends were extended to include neighbours. Neighbours participated in mutual services, from small but frequent loans of salt, bread, or eggs, to taking a sick person to the doctor in one's car, helping with transporting furniture to a flat, or to the situation where a neighbour is asked to baby-sit for several hours. Neighbourly help based on reciprocity makes everyday life easier, and promotes feelings of security. Besides the measurable service, there were other expectations from one's neighbour: a neighbour is quite often the only person with whom one could spend time talking or just 'being together'. This is particularly important for the elderly and single.

Rights and duties within the family

The discussion so far has been concerned directly with a narrow view of family, that is the relationship between husband, wife, and children. The rights and duties in such a family are most interesting. How far-reaching is the process of democratization? What do the spouses expect from each other; what values do they treasure? As shown in our interviews, a stable family with a good standard of living is of great importance for both workers' and intellectuals' families. Financial security is guaranteed by work which the workers' families regard primarily as the means of acquiring money, while for the families of intellectuals, work is expected to offer opportunities for self-fulfilment. Many women take a job in order to improve the family's economic situation. This is no doubt advantageous for the household economy, but many of these women complain about being grossly overburdened. Therefore, they demand that their husbands lend them a hand in household chores and participate in the upbringing of the children.

Following our observations, we suggest that the husband is expected to provide for the family, and the wife to run the household (whether she has a job or not); the children are expected not to make any trouble. This is of course a most general formulation, as the scene of family life is by no means homogeneous. The arrangements between husband and wife are mainly concerned with the economic aspects of family life. At the same time, the wives expect their husbands to give them housekeeping money. The husbands are consulted in the case of larger household purchases, and the spouses plan the holiday expenses together. Questions from outside the financial sphere are not settled by consultation between the spouses. The description most frequently given of the husband by the wife is as follows: 'He provides for the family, gives me what he earns as housekeeping'; 'Comes home from work, has dinner, has a rest, reads a bit, takes a nap, watches the film on TV'; 'He throws the garbage out, helps a bit with the kids.'

Asked what the husband expects on coming home from work, a vast majority of wives, as well as husbands answer, 'dinner'. Dinner is an important moment of the day: it is also what both the husband's and wife's expectations focus on. The husband expects to be served dinner, while the wife expects dinner to be duly eaten. This way the woman feels she has fulfilled her duties as a good wife. The preparation and serving of dinner does not necessarily lead to it being eaten together, as shown by one woman's statements, 'I served his dinner and went to see my friend, to talk a bit.' Our observations show that the husband is not the person for many women with whom they could talk as they talk with friends. The conversations with friends are the wife's sphere of privacy within the family: 'Some days, as soon as he's back from work, I just serve him dinner and hurry to my friend or she visits me. We have coffee in the kitchen and talk about our own matters. I'm entitled to this: dinner's cooked, the flat's tidied up—what else should I do?'

The husband expects the wife to run the household: to cook, tidy up the flat, care for the children. It is also important for men that the wife create a warm family atmosphere: 'What I need is a wife, and not some offended female dragon.' 'I come home from work tired, I need some pleasant atmosphere in the evening, not all those problems and problems.' 'A wife should be a good cook, and she should run the household, too. I'm giving her the money for it, aren't I?'

While the wives have privacy in the form of conversations with their female friends, the husbands satisfy that same need by meeting their male friends 'for a beer', repairing the family car, watching sports broadcasts, or indulging their particular hobbies. In the families of intellectuals, a greater need to read and participate in cultural life is apparent. Both in these families and in the families of workers, many men admit to having given up a hobby for the benefit of the family. The husbands try to help their wives with at least some of the housework by, for instance, shopping or playing with the children. The men are of the opinion that their wives have a much easier life than their mothers, not only because of the greater mechanization of housework, but also because they themselves take a greater part in the household chores and have greater respect for their wives.

Extended co-operation

This picture of the family, fragmentary and random as it no doubt is, has emerged as a result of the family's adjustment to the conditions created by the system. The threat to the family presented by Communist rule no doubt increased the importance of the family's interpersonal functions. Yet with its members forced to live together—which does not mean close to one another—the family could only survive thanks to the extended co-operation between its separate members. The efforts to survive and the performance of mutual services were a necessity which prevented a total disruption of family functions. In spite of the recent change in the political system and with the new legal system still unclear, the situation is likely to remain as it was before: protection of the family will require of its members no less effort, services, and mutual respect for the aspirations and needs of others.

If we consider the future of the family as we enter the new political and economic conditions (an apparent cure for all troubles), is it at all possible that one day, the answer to the question of what family members and friends expect from one another will be, to be left in peace?

II. Why do family members and friends expect so much from one another?

In the second part of this chapter, we discuss the conditions of daily living for the Polish family. We seek explanations for the present state of affairs in the economic, political, and legal spheres, and to a lesser extent, in those of culture, tradition, and history. These particular spheres have been chosen quite consciously: the aim is first to find out to what extent the attitudes and life-styles discussed above can be understood and accounted for in the context of everyday living conditions. During the last forty-five years, those conditions were most specific, largely determined by politics, and quite unlike those in West-European societies. This may be at least one of the reasons why family life takes a different form in different parts of Europe.

Shortage of supply

First, the situation in Poland was characterized by a permanent shortage of supply of goods. That shortage particularly affected food, but also clothes, furniture, consumer durables, and many other goods. Some date the beginning of the problems from the late 1970s; this, however, seems unwarranted. Throughout the postwar period, the situation remained very much the same with shorter or longer breaks. What did change was the stock of goods in short supply. 'It wads precisely the market crisis,' writes J. Kurczewski in the introduction to his chapter on rationing in *Resurrection of Rights*, 'the shortages, prices and the system of sales, that led to the succession of outbreaks of social discontent in 1970, 1976, and 1980' (Kurczewski, 1993).

Dissatisfaction with food supplies is confirmed by the findings of public opinion surveys. In a national survey carried out in 1974 by the Centre for Public Opinion Surveys and Programme Studies attached to Polish Radio and Television, 34 per cent of respondents described the supply of food stuffs near their home as very good or good, 32 per cent as 'not too bad', and 30 per cent as bad or very bad. At the same time, over half the respondents were unable to buy articles such as beef (65 per cent), ham (62 per cent), inferior-quality beef (60 per cent) and high-quality smoked sausage (51 per cent). Articles such as chicken, sea fish, eggs, liver-wurst, lemons, honey, meat preserves, inferior-quality sausage, oranges, pork, fresh-water fish, and higher-quality meat and meat products were 'in constant supply' for less than half the respondents (Szostkiewicz in Kurczewski, 1993).

Rationing

Shortages grew worse over time until, finally, rationing was introduced for many articles, in response to public demand. The first article to be rationed (and the only one for the next five years) was sugar. In 1981, rationing was extended to include meat, butter, flour, cereals, rice, washing-powder, cigarettes, alcohol, chocolate, soap, and a variety of baby products (semolina, milk powder, cotton wool, soap, baby oil) (Fuszara in Kurczewski, 1993). While early in 1981 the rationed goods affected a mere 2 per cent of household expenditure, one year later as much as a quarter of total expenses and a half of the money spent on food was included. But rationing failed to bring about the expected improvement in supplies; nor did it make shopping easier, particularly as far as meat was concerned. 'The number of people who were actually issued with coupons greatly exceeded the number of those entitled to the rations', K. Hagemejer writes. Whole groups of those entitled were given rations larger than originally expected. According to the author's estimates, about one million persons more than planned were issued with coupons in 1981; at the same time, due to the fact that larger rations were granted to many, the average ration per capita went up by about 0.1 kg (Hagemejer in Kurczewski, 1993). Therefore, with unabated demand and strong pressure to preserve the former level of consumption, the market situation improved slightly. Economists point to the unexpected financial resources of the population after 1982, which 'reflected the surplus demand of Polish families which production was unable to satisfy' (Piasny, 1990: 79). A shortage of many goods kept making itself felt, and queues continued as a universal everyday phenomenon.

Catering for the family

In this situation, catering for one's family became a time-consuming and arduous task, as well as a person's basic occupation. 'Our slogan is: provisions are the main job.' This is how one mother described the situation of her family in the 1980s. One person alone would never be able to cope with that task; all family members did shopping to a varying extent. The greatest assistance was rendered by those who stayed at home: women taking care of small children, and retired grandparents. Many families found this help indispensable, as both parents were usually employed even though only a few families could afford domestic help. In this way the permanent market shortages forced many members of the nuclear family to co-operate, as well as creating a system of help among the grandparents and more distant relatives. Against expectations, rationing reinforced the system of mutual help. Helping one another with buying rationed goods, giving surplus coupons to others and exchanging coupons (chocolate for cigarettes, etc.) all added to the interdependence of various members of the extended family on one another and made them take an active part in the system of exchanges.

Material destitution

What also forced co-operation was brought about by material destitution. Here the absence of widespread private property and the resulting dependence of most of society on the state as employer was decisive. The lowering of living standards was particularly noticeable in the 1980s. The proportion of total household expenditure on food increased greatly in that period. This affected first of all the families of employees, where the ratio went up from 35 per cent in 1981 to 48 per cent one year later. In the case of disabled and retired persons, it usually exceeded 50 per cent. In some years, wages were only just enough to meet basic needs. Hence the second aim, of equal importance with providing for the family was in most cases 'to survive until pay-day'. Those who had been employed for some time (at least several years) managed somehow; but most young couples were doomed to financial dependence on their parents. Parents assisted young couples for a period of up to a dozen years, their help assuming a variety of forms: direct financial help, providing food, or help with furnishing the flat.

Difficult housing situation

The difficult housing situation also reduced the independence of the younger generation. Polish flats are small. In 1984, nearly two thirds of all flats had a floor area of not more than 59 square metres: 61 per cent had three or fewer rooms (MSO, 1988). A comparison of the British and Polish housing situation is rather interesting. While in 1966, two-room flats constituted 54.2 per cent of all flats in Poland, they amounted to a mere 4.6 per cent in Great Britain in 1961. In Great Britain the majority of flats had at least five rooms (57 per cent) of which there were just 4.2 per cent in Poland (MSO, 1972).

As a result of the small size, the flats are badly overcrowded. In 1984, as few as 7 per cent of Poles had a room of their own; about half shared a room with another person, and one quarter with two persons (MSO, 1988). If we consider only the habitable rooms the situation in Poland was nearly twice as bad as in Great Britain, where the average was 0.8 persons per habitable room in 1970, compared to 1.4 in Poland (MSO, 1975). Somewhat earlier, in the first half of the 1960s, the flats with under 1.5 persons per room amounted too 57.1 per cent of all flats in Poland and to 97 per cent in Great Britain (Data for 1960–1; MSO, 1972).

First and foremost, many families could not and still cannot get a flat. In the 1980s, nearly three million families were waiting for a flat. At the same time, the number of flats in newly built houses was not even equal to that of newly contracted marriages. In the years 1980–7, the author has calculated that an average of 673 flats were built per 1,000 newly contracted marriages. Only a few young couples could hope for a new flat from a housing co-operative; fewer still could afford to buy a flat on the free market. The prices of flats have always been very high in Poland and far beyond the financial reach of most families.

The accessibility of flats is well illustrated by the present situation, which is similar in principle to that of the last ten years. In the advertisements of an estate agency published in one of the country's chief daily newspapers in mid-June 1991, prices range from 161 million zlotys for a single-room flat with a floor area of 25 square metres to 750 million for a three-room flat with a floor area of 91 square metres (£7,800 and £36,750 respectively) (*Życie Warszawy*, 17 June 1991). In the same month, the average wage in the five basic branches of the economy was about 1.7 million zlotys (somewhat less than £80).

Employment situation of women

Family bonds are greatly influenced by the employment situation of women, the wives and mothers in particular. In the years 1970–87, women constituted from 45 to 48 per cent of the work force (i.e. 'those who perform work that yields earnings or income'). In that same period, the author calculates that the percentage of all women of child-bearing age in employment rose from 77 per cent to 85 per cent (*Statistical Yearbook*, 1988). A comparison of the proportion of employed married women with all women in employment in the years 1931–67 shows that women's employment as a mass phenomenon is characteristic of the Communist period in Polish history. In 1931 married women amounted to 16 per cent of all women employees; in 1950, 18 per cent; in 1960, 55 per cent, and in 1967 as much as 70 per cent (Lobodzinska, 1974: 83). Women constituted an extensive labour source in the state sector. In 1950 they amounted to 30 per cent of all employees in the nationalized sector, and twenty years later to as much as 40 per cent. Many studies show that women's chief motivation in taking a job was the need to contribute financially to the family. In 1962 when asked by the Centre for Public Opinion Surveys, 'What induced you to perform paid work?', 56 per cent of respondents answered, 'The need to earn extra money because my husband's earnings are not enough to provide for the family.' Only 16 per cent reported liking the job, and 5.8 per cent spoke of the wish to have social contacts (Drozdek and Zajdowa, 1974). Economic motives also come first when the women take jobs after childbirth. Of eight thousand female manual workers in over 1800 factories examined in the mid-1960s, 70 per cent continued in their jobs after childbirth. As many as three out of four of the respondents (female manual workers) stated that their reason for returning to work was the need to help with providing for the family or with buying and furnishing a flat (Kurzynowski in Lobodzinska, 1974: 88).

Thus many women were away from their family duties for a considerable part of the day. Someone else had to substitute for them. Some duties were taken over by the husband and older children, others by the other family members. Neighbourly help was also necessary sometimes. The money earned by the wife was as a rule included in the family budget and used to provide for the family and to satisfy basic needs. In most families, the husband's wages were not enough to provide for the household. Nearly 90 per cent of the earnings of both spouses were allocated to that purpose. In employees' households, the average monthly earnings in 1985 amounted to 12.795 zlotys per capita, while the monthly sums spent on food, clothes and shoes, rent, energy, hygiene, culture, education, free-time activities, and transport were 11.042 zlotys (MSO, 1988). After basic needs had been satisfied, less than 14 per cent of income remained. So, while complicating the woman's family life, her paid work did not even give her financial independence.

Legal regulations

Financial independence for individual family members is also limited by legal regulations. The Family and Guardianship Code, Article 32.2, provides that the spouses' joint possessions include 'remuneration for work and other services rendered by either of the spouses' as well as 'the income from their joint property, and also from the separate property of each of the spouses'. Adopting this solution, the legislator was motivated by the belief that 'in our society, remuneration for work is the basic source of maintenance. Therefore, were that remuneration excluded from the statutory joint property of spouses, this would result in practice in an actual impairment of the very principle of joint property' (Winiarz, 1980: 211). In most Polish families, neither of the spouses in practice has his or her own money, if small sums for cigarettes or for beer are left out of account. This, however, seems to result not from the legal regulation quoted above but rather from the economic reality. It seems that the lack of economic resources for material independence is one of the main reasons for the communal nature of family life in Poland. The mutual financial dependence of the separate family members is hardly conducive to independent decision-making as all of the more serious purchases have to be discussed with the rest of the family in advance, nor to the emergence of individualistic attitudes. The economic barrier cannot be overcome.

Rights and duties of parents in relation to children

These interdependences are even more explicit in the sphere of mutual rights and duties of parents in relation to children. 'Parents and children are obliged to assist one another.' 'That duty', the author of a textbook on family law comments, 'is interpreted most broadly by the statute . . . It follows from the very fact of finding oneself in the legal parent–child relationship and persists until a person's death' (Winiarz, 1980). This general formulation of the Family and Guardianship Code is of great importance in practice although it is not supported by any sanctions. The code treated broadly the parents' duty to maintain children, a duty which continues even after the child comes of age (Article 133, point 1). 'The parents' duty to provide for their child', to quote the above-mentioned textbook once again,

arises at the moment of that child's birth and ceases when the child has been adequately prepared for professional work in accordance with his talents and preferences . . . The actual duration of that duty can also be influenced by the parents' financial and earning abilities, the nature of the child's preferences and interests, his or her diligence, vital interests, etc. . . . The fact of the child coming of age does not in itself lead to the expiration of the parents' duty to provide for that child

This means that, during education, mature offspring may feel entitled to financial assistance from the parents. This happens in practice.

The system of scholarships and the principles for deciding the amount of the grant transferred a significant share of the costs of living for students on to the shoulders of the parents. Scholarships paid by the university amounted to the difference between the income per capita in the students' family and the social minimum necessary to survive during the studies. Scholarships were thus granted only to those from the poorer families, and in the remaining cases parents were covering the costs. Such a solution deepened the financial dependency of children upon parents, and extended it in time as university education was completed at the age of 23 to 25 years. The students themselves were freed from the necessity to earn their living and their entrance into independent life was delayed. But the imposition of the duty by the legislator upon the families to support students was in some sense a political move, to help the state to be free of the significant financial burdens related to university education. The state was also freed from creating other types of solutions, such as, for instance, bank loans.

In addressing the question of why family members and friends expect so much from each other, we have tried to point out some of the external causes of the collectivization of family life in Poland. The difficult economic situation and the mutual financial dependency of the members of the family on each other seems to be crucial from this point of view. We appreciate the limitations of such a perspective. Perhaps the Catholic tradition that forces parents to 'forget their own comfort, and parental concern and assistance to the limits of possibility even at the moment of commencement of family life' (Witek, 1983: 339) was also an important source of such a shape for the Polish family. Perhaps the characteristics of daily-living factors were of importance. It is difficult to develop an individual personality when living most of the year with the whole family in one heated room, which for economic reasons is still common practice in many peasant families today. One should also remember the planned attempts by the Communist authorities to create the fully socialist family.

The current shape of the Polish family is certainly the result of several concurrent factors. Focus on family life is both a reaction against attempts at the collectivization of the whole society, and also an efficient instrument in dealing with the everyday troubles of the family. This is why collectivism seems, *sui generis*, an economically calculated manner of escaping poverty: five persons will always eat more cheaply when cooking together than when making their meals separately. The economic approach is the most widely neglected in current Polish thinking among the many approaches to social behaviour.

REFERENCES

Drozdek, A. and A. Preiss Zajdowa (1974), *Kobiety wobec pracy zawodowej* (Women in the Face of Employment) (OBOPiSP, Warsaw).

Fuszara, M. (1993), 'Prawne aspekty reglamentacji' (Legal Aspects of Rationing) in Kurczewski, 1993.

Hagemejer, K. (1993), 'Ekonomiczne i społeczne funkcje reglamentacji' (Economic and Social Functions of Rationing) in Kurczewski, 1993.

Kurczewski, J. (1993), *Resurrection of Rights* (OUP, Oxford).

Kurzynowski, A., 'Ciągłość pracy a macierzyństwo' (Employment Continuity and Maternity), paper cited by B. Lobodzinska (1974).

Lobodzinska, B. (1974), *Rodzina w Polsce* (The Family in Poland) (Warsaw).

Main Statistical Office, *Statistical Yearbook 1972* (MSO, Warsaw).

—— *Statistical Yearbook 1975* (MSO, Warsaw).

—— *Statistical Yearbook 1988* (MSO, Warsaw).

Piasny, J. (1990), 'Tendencje zmian w poziomie życia rodzin polskich w latach osiemdziesiątych' (Trends of changes in living standards of Polish families in the 1980s) in Zbigniew Tyszka (ed.), *Stan i przeobrażenia współczesnych rodzin polskich* (The State and Changes in the Contemporary Family (Poznan 1990).

Szostkiewicz, S. (1993), 'Zaopatrzenie żywnościowe w opinii społecznej' (Food Supply in Public Opinion), OBOPiSB, in J. Kurczewski (1993).

Winiarz, J. (1980) *Prawo rodzinne* (Family Law) (PWN, Warsaw).

Witek, S. (1983), *Chrześcijańska wizja moralności* (Christian Vision of Morality) (Poznan).

6. Family Responsibilities and Inheritance in Great Britain

Janet Finch and Jennifer Mason

Inheritance and family responsibilities: defining the issues

The topic of our chapter is inheritance—the transmission of assets (property, money, personal belongings) within families after someone has died or, sometimes, in anticipation of death. Though people may, and do, chose to leave assets outside their families—to charities, other organizations, friends, or neighbours—inheritance has always been regarded essentially as a family issue. Our chapter focuses exclusively on transmission of assets between relatives. In the past inheritance may have been regarded as a matter of interest only to a small minority of wealthy citizens, but no longer. Rising standards of living, and the spread of home ownership in particular (two-thirds of all households are now owner-occupiers), have ensured that large sections of the UK population belong to families where there is something significant to be bequeathed when a death occurs.

Each chapter in this book is considering—in different ways—the following two issues:

(1) What do we expect family members to do for each other?
(2) What do we expect for families from the law?

We shall address these questions in relation to inheritance and in the British context, using data from a recently completed study (1). Though the study itself looked at family responsibilities across a broad spectrum, in this paper we are concentrating on the specific issue of inheritance. Before we do that we need to unpack these two questions, since they raise some complicated issues of definition and interpretation. Essentially they are questions about *public* expectations ('what do *we* expect . . .'), yet no discussion of public expectations about family life can afford to ignore people's *private* experiences, definitions, and understanding of what is appropriate within their own families. The law must somehow relate to both public and private definitions.

To present this rather complex picture more systematically, we would argue that public and private definitions can be further sub-divided. In all there are four levels on which responsibilities within families can be analysed. We refer here to any type of obligation which may occur between relatives: to give or lend money, to give practical help, to offer someone a temporary home, to look after a relative's children on an occasional basis, to pass on some of your assets after your death, and so on. The four levels are:

Level 1. Public definitions (a) What the British population, at the present time, generally see as appropriate responsibilities and obligations within families. This level is sometimes referred to as social norms.

Level 2. Public definitions (b) What the law says (or does not say) about family responsibilities; legal rules.

Level 3. Private definitions (a) What I actually do (or do not do) for members of my own family; the help which I give them in practice.

Level 4. Private definitions (b) What we understand to be appropriate forms of help in *my* family; the common understandings which we have evolved which tell me, for example, that *my* parents or children would never expect me to lend them money in a crisis, whereas in other families this definitely would be expected. These might be thought of as norms specific to each family.

We would argue that these four levels can and should be kept analytically separate, and that we always need to be clear which level we are talking about when we speak about responsibilities within families, and about expectations of what family members should do for each other. Of course there are overlaps between the four levels, but there may also be mis-matches. From the perspective of social science, this is where many of the interesting questions lie. For example, what is the relationship between publicly acknowledged norms and people's private understandings of what is normatively appropriate within their own families (Levels 1 and 4)? The two are not necessarily the same.

Other comparisons lead us to consider the role of the law (Level 2) in relation to other levels. For example, how well do the two levels of public definition (Levels 1 and 2 above) align with each other? This comparison is interesting, in that British legal systems have traditionally treated as paramount the principle of testamentary freedom—the idea that anyone should be free to dispose of their assets exactly as they wish, without being tied by the law to expectations that a spouse, or a child, or anyone else has the right to inherit from them. Though this principle has been modified in the course of the twentieth century in particular, it remains important, and may be at odds with the idea that social norms about family responsibilities can or should be built into inheritance law (Davey, 1988). In relation to legislation on both inheritance and intestacy, the changes have tended to be based on the idea that the law should try to follow changes in prevailing social norms. Where public expectations have clearly changed (for example, about the right of women to own property), the law ultimately has followed this. In relation to intestacy, the whole logic of the law has been that the distribution of property follows what would have happened had the deceased made a will, again drawing upon social norms about what is reasonable (Law Commission, 1989).

So the British legal system has moved into a situation which acknowledges that the law should reflect social norms, at least to some extent. In this context, the minimum which can be expected from the law—in relation to inheritance or any other issue of family responsibilities—is that it does reflect prevailing social norms with reasonable accuracy. However a further complication arises at this point, since the law can only do this if those social norms are clear and accepted reasonably widely amongst the population. But it is quite possible in principle—and happens in practice, as we show below—that social norms about family responsibilities are *not* clearly held in common amongst the majority of the population. People may well hold a variety of different ideas and beliefs about the family, with little obvious common ground. In this case, the issue for the law is: how much flexibility can be built in, to accommodate variation in people's private definitions of appropriate behaviour in their own families?

This consideration of general questions about public and private definitions about inheritance sets the scene for the main focus of this chapter, where we are going to draw upon our empirical data to discuss questions about inheritance and family responsibilities. Because of the nature of our data, we have to focus on Levels 1, 3, and 4. We have not made any direct study of the role of law in this context, but we are aware that the kinds of questions posed about the law can only be answered fully if we do have a reasonably reliable empirical data about both public norms and private definitions.

Essentially our data enable us to answer two types of question. First there are questions on the nature of social norms about inheritance at the level of public definitions, and how they link with private definitions. *Are* there clear social norms, which are understood and accepted by the majority of the population, about what should happen when someone dies, about how assets should be passed on and to whom? Is there clear normative agreement that people do have an obligation to bequeath to certain members of their family and, conversely, that any of us has a right to expect that we will be beneficiaries from the estates of certain relatives? If there are clear norms about this, between whom do they operate—spouses, parents and children, grandparents, and grandchildren, or more broadly within families? Are there norms about *what* should be left within each category?

Second, there are questions about how far inheritance operates in a vacuum within families. Is it interlinked with people's actions and beliefs about other responsibilities, or treated as an entirely separate issue? Are matters of inheritance treated as a 'black box' within families, quite unconnected with any other aspects of family relationships? If this is the case, we might expect to find that people treat the distribution of assets as something which happens by virtue of a particular genealogical tie (someone is entitled to inherit simply because she is a daughter), rather than seeing it as connected with the particular relationships which have been formed between individuals (one daughter inherits the house and the other gets nothing, because the former has a closer relationship with her father, or because she has given him considerable practical assistance in the past).

If inheritance *is* treated as a black box—that is, if it is reasonable to expect inheritance simply on the basis of a genealogical tie—then presumably any child, or grandchild, or niece, or whoever, has the same right to expect inheritance as any other. If, however, people do link inheritance with other aspects of family relationships, and with other responsibilities accepted within the family, this opens the possibility that inheritance is something to be earned. In that case, one child or grandchild might reasonably expect their closer relationship with the testator, or their greater commitment to assisting the testator in the past, should be reflected in a greater share of the testator's assets. It is interesting to note that the Law Commission report *Distribution on Intestacy* (Law Commission, 1989) did not quite get to grips with this issue of whether past actions might alter the way people evaluate the right of an individual to expect to inherit, but concentrated simply on rights which flow from the genealogical tie— implicitly accepting a black box view.

These points, about whether inheritance operates as a black box, are particularly important in the light of other contemporary social pressures, particularly an ageing population and the costs of caring for them. Social policies now presume that public funds cannot cater for all the practical and personal needs of the whole elderly population (Wistow and Henwood, 1991). The pressures are certainly there for older people either to turn to members of their family to care for them in old age or to use their financial assets to finance their care from other sources. In either case, what part does inheritance play in this equation? Is it likely that someone who cares for an elderly relative will receive their 'payment' through inheritance?

The data available in our own study of family obligations enables us to address some of these issues. We shall present two different types of data, which are complementary. First, we shall present some normative data, taken from a survey of a random sample of the adult population, and which enables us to address Level 1 questions. Then we shall discuss some cases examples of responsibilities in practice, taken from an in-depth study of a small number of families, which enables us to focus on Levels 3 and 4.

Public norms about inheritance and family responsibilities

Our data on public norms about family responsibilities (our Level 1 above) come from a survey conducted in the Greater Manchester region in the autumn of 1985. Respondents were sampled from the electoral register, which means that they were a random sample of adults in this region (aged 18 and over) and a 72 per cent response rate was achieved. In total we interviewed 978 people.

Respondents were asked questions about a wide range of issues concerned with family responsibilities, and an over-view of the main findings of this survey can be found in Finch and Mason (1991). Many of the survey questions came in the form of vignettes. This means that we told a story (some of these were quite complex) about people who had to face questions of responsibilities within their own families, and asked respondents to say what should happen. Thus we were trying to discover whether a random sample of the adult population would broadly agree about the proper course of action within a family, when presented with a given set of circumstances and given some detail about them. We were not asking them to say what would happen in their own families, or what they themselves would do in such circumstances. We were trying to tap publicly acknowledged social norms by asking them to say what third parties—the people in the story—should do. A more detailed discussion of this vignette method can be found in Finch (1987).

One of the vignettes included an issue about inheritance, and how it is tied into other family responsibilities. It was quite a lengthy vignette about a family called the Harpers. It was presented in five stages, with respondents given more information and asked a new question at each stage. The full wording of this vignette, plus response frequencies, are given at the end of this chapter. The vignette tells a story about an elderly woman and her relationship both with her daughter and with a granddaughter. The essence of the vignette is to explore the nature of their responsibilities towards each other, given the particular circumstances of this family. The particular circumstances are as follows. The elderly woman, Mary Harper, has quarrelled with her daughter Valerie and subsequently cut Valerie out of her will. Valerie is aware of this. Valerie's daughter, however, has maintained a good relationship with her grandmother, and this has had important consequences for her. Her grandmother has given her a large sum of money to help her to buy a house of her own, and also has bequeathed her own house to the granddaughter in her will. Thus we have a complex set of relationships across three generations, in which questions of money and inheritance are bound up closely with the nature of those relationships.

This is the background information which we gave about the family in the course of the vignette. However the specific decisions on which we asked our respondents to make judgements have arisen because Mary, the grandmother, has become very frail and no longer can live on her own. What are the responsibilities of her daughter and her granddaughter in this situation, given the particular nature of their relationships with Mary? We began with her daughter Valerie's responsibilities, asking whether she has some responsibility to help arrange her elderly mother's care, either by taking her into her own home or in some other way. We also asked whether, should she decide to bring her mother to live with her despite their hostile relationship, it would be reasonable to ask her mother to change the will so that she, Valerie, would now benefit from it. This poses, in a rather sharp form, questions about whether inheritance should be tied explicitly to other responsibilities in the family. The implication was, if Valerie was going to look after her elderly mother despite the fact that they have a very poor relationship, does she have a right to expect some kind of recompense for this, in the form of inheritance?

When we were asking questions about Valerie's position, we had not yet mentioned the existence of the favourite granddaughter to our respondents. As we moved on to asking about the granddaughter's responsibilities, we focused upon two issues. Should the granddaughter offer a home to her grandmother? Should she give up her job in order to look after her grandmother? Whatever answer was given, we then asked respondents to say why they thought that the granddaughter should, or should not, give up her job. Though inheritance is not an explicit bargaining counter in this part of the vignette, respondents were told that the daughter had already received a generous sum of money from her grandmother, and that she was set to benefit substantially from the will. So questions of inheritance formed part of the background against which respondents were forming their judgements of the granddaughter's position.

The first point to note about the pattern of responses is that the views of our survey population are split on most issues. It was true generally in the Family Obligations survey that there were very few issues about which we have clear agreement amongst respondents (Finch and Mason, 1991), and this question about the Harpers was no exception. The strongest agreement comes in part (b) where 82 per cent of the sample give the same answer. But in general the survey population is split in its judgements about what constitutes the proper thing to do in the circumstances which we outlined. This in itself is an important finding, since it calls into question the idea that social norms about family responsibilities are a simple matter, or that they can be readily identified. In turn this challenges the argument that the law should seek to embody the prevailing social norms in matters of this kind, since in reality there are no easily identifiable prevailing norms.

Given this split pattern of responses on most parts of the vignette, one obvious question is: are there different groups of respondents answering this question differently? Might it be, for example, that one set of social norms is endorsed by men, and another by women?

We are not giving a full breakdown of the data analysis in this chapter, but the simple answer is that none of the obvious socio-economic variables (gender, age, social class, educational qualifications) makes a consistent difference to the way people answer these questions. There is no significant difference between the way in which men and women answer on any part of the vignette. Age of respondents is the only factor which does appear to make some difference on most parts of the vignette, but its effect is not always in the same direction. In some parts of the vignette (e.g. part (c)) it is older people who are more likely to emphasize the responsibility of family members, whereas in other parts (e.g. part (a)) it is the under-30s who seem to take a strong view of the responsibility of relatives. In respect of (b), which is about inheritance specifically, the likelihood that a respondent will chose the Change Will option increases with age. In this part of the vignette, older people are more likely than younger ones to take an instrumental view of inheritance, and see it as reasonable for the daughter to bargain over it.

Interesting though these patterns are at one level, they do not give the kind of consistency which one would need if socio-economic variables were to account for the split pattern of answers to our questions. We conclude therefore that people's normative ideas about these questions do vary, perhaps partly as a consequence of experiences within their own families (though our data do not enable us to be sure of that). However, those variations cannot be accounted for by gender, age, or social class.

In focusing more explicitly on questions concerned with inheritance we will consider first parts (a) and (b) of the vignette, which are concerned with the responsibilities of the daughter, Valerie, to her mother, Mary, with whom she had quarrelled. In part (a) when we posed the question of Valerie's responsibilities in this situation, 37 per cent of people said that Valerie should offer her mother a home, and 51 per cent said that she should arrange for her mother to go into a nursing home. On the surface this pattern might suggest that the poor relationship between the two women has led respondents to tend to favour the nursing home option. However this pattern of answers is very similar to other questions in our survey where we asked about the 'relative's house versus nursing home' option for a frail elderly person, but where there was no mention of a hostile relationship. Thus, in our view, responses to this part of the question about the Harpers indicate that most people took no account of the poor relationship between Mary and Valerie when forming their judgements about Valerie's responsibilities. They simply responded as they would do to any question about whether a daughter should take a mother into her home (slightly more than a third thought that she should, about half thought that she should not). In that sense people seem to be saying that the quarrel, and the fact that Mary had cut Valerie out of her will, should make no difference to the daughter's responsibilities to her mother.

This seems to imply a 'black box' view of inheritance—a view that decisions about who is going to be a beneficiary should be kept entirely separate from other family responsibilities—the one is not a relevant consideration in respect of the other. This black box view is further reinforced by answers to part (b) of the vignette, where we did have a high degree of agreement among the survey population, 82 per cent of our respondents said that Valerie should not seek to renegotiate the terms of her mother's will, even if she did take the step of bringing her mother to live in her own home. Instead, they thought that Valerie should offer her mother a home without conditions. This is the issue on which we have the clearest agreement between respondents in the whole vignette.

Thus it seems possible to interpret our data as showing a black box view of inheritance, and a belief that the distribution of assets after death should be held quite separate from other questions about responsibilities in families. To put it another way, the right of the testator to dispose of her assets as she wishes, without feeling constrained by any other expectations, is apparently upheld by the responses to these questions. On this interpretation, it seems that the principle of testamentary freedom operates at the level of social norms, as well as being central to the law on inheritance.

However, we think that this interpretation of our data is too simple, for two reasons. The first concerns the way in which we worded part (b) of the question ('would it be reasonable for Valerie to say that her mother must change her will, and leave her the house?'). Our wording suggests that Valerie might take the initiative and lay down terms to her mother. We have reason to believe that many of our respondents may have been reacting against this aspect of the story specifically. In other survey questions, and in our qualitative data, it seems clear that people often disapprove quite strongly of anything which looks like making demands, or even simply asking for some help or financial assistance from a relative. The right to offer or withhold help (of all kinds) should remain with the donor, it seems. This is the message which emerges from our work on family responsibilities generally (see Finch and Mason, 1992). We think therefore that, had we asked the question the other way round ('Should Mary *offer to* change her will in favour of Valerie?'), or simply suggested that Mary might make this change without discussing it, we might have got a different pattern of responses. We may well have found quite a lot of people putting the onus on Mary to offer to change her will, as part of the arrangement whereby Valerie was going to look after her. In other words, people were not necessarily rejecting the idea of an implicit bargain, whereby care given in old age is recognized through bequests. What they were rejecting is the idea that the potential beneficiary should suggest this, or even that she should expect it.

There is a second reason for arguing that our data are not a straightforward endorsement of the principle of testamentary freedom. This arises from considering responses to the rest of this vignette. In the parts which concern the granddaughter, the black box approach does not seem to operate. Here we have a situation in which the granddaughter *is* going to benefit substantially from her grandmother's will, as well as having received money in the past, and the implied question is: should that have an effect on her responsibilities to her grandmother in old age? The message from our respondents here is quite complex. They seem to be saying yes, but only up to a point. 74 per cent say that the granddaughter should offer her grandmother a home, and presumably thereby should take some level of responsibility for her care. This is twice as many as thought that Valerie should give her mother a home, and much higher in general than the proportion of respondents who say that frail elderly people should be taken into a relative's home. It represents a reasonable measure of agreement among respondents that this particular granddaughter does have clear responsibilities towards her grandmother.

Thus knowledge about inheritance, *inter alia*, seems to have had some effect on people's judgements about other responsibilities: the inheritance question is not kept in a black box in respect of the granddaughter. At the same time, respondents mainly seem to want to place limits upon the granddaughter's responsibilities in this situation. Whilst 74 per cent said that she should offer her grandmother a home, only 29 per cent thought that she should go as far as giving up her job in order to care for her grandmother. In giving their reasons for this (part (e)), respondents mostly emphasized the grand-daughter's youth, the importance of her long-term future, and the need to retain her independence. In other words, they seem to be saying that even in a situation where a granddaughter has a great deal to be grateful for, including being a major beneficiary of her grandmother's will, there are limits to the extent to which this should create reciprocal responsibilities. Some prices are too high to pay in this particular type of bargain and, for most of our respondents, giving up as job is too high a price for this young woman.

We think, therefore, that our survey data show two main things, related to the questions which we posed earlier in this chapter. On the question of social norms about inheritance (our Level 1), we have shown that there are few clear points of agreement on specific responsibilities between the generations, including questions about how inheritance should (or should not) be tied in with other responsibilities. In most parts of the vignette we can point to a majority of respondents opting for one type of answer, but there is usually also a sizeable minority who chose another normative option. This split between respondents is not explained by any obvious social or economic characteristics.

On questions about whether inheritance should be tied into other responsibilities in families, our respondents seem to have presented us with a fairly complex picture. In some parts of the vignette, the majority of answers seem to stress testamentary freedom, and envisage no direct link between inheritance and other issues. In other parts of the vignette, we appear to have the message that inheritance, or the promise of inheritance, *should* create a different situation between testator and beneficiary, which should properly be reflected in other responsibilities which they acknowledge towards each other. It should not, however, completely over-ride other considerations.

Negotiating around the Black Box?

The meaning of the patterns we have outlined is interesting, if complex, and can best be taken further through the consideration of some family case studies. These case studies are taken from the second, qualitative stage of our Family Obligations project, which was designed to explore the ways in which people negotiate their kin relationships and support in practice, and the role of concepts, like obligation, in that process.

By focusing on these data in this part of the chapter, we are moving the discussion towards our Levels 3 and 4 of family responsibilities. This means we are addressing questions of what people actually do in relation to members of their own families (Level 3); and also how they understand and construct what is or is not appropriate in their own family interactions (Level 4).

Our data on these aspects of family responsibilities are drawn from a pool of 120 semi-structured in-depth interviews conducted with 88 people, carried out during 1987–8 (2). We interviewed people about their own current and previous experience of family relationships and responsibilities. We approached this in a very open-ended way, trying not to lead our interviewees too much and allowing each of them to determine what experiences *they* saw as relevant to understanding responsibilities in their own families. This means that questions about inheritance were not asked routinely of all our study population. In all, 30 of our 88 interviewees volunteered information of family experiences in which inheritance was a factor. This means that we can only really begin to open up some of the interesting issues concerning inheritance and kinship here (3).

We have selected four case studies which help to shed some light on questions raised in the first part of the chapter, and also which help to identify some of the complexities which characterize the way inheritance is handled in practice in families.

1. Ethel Phillips

Ethel Phillips was in her early 70s when we interviewed her, living in comfortable (if not affluent) circumstances and owning her own home. She was a widow, with a son and a daughter, both married with children. Ethel had given considerable thought to the question of how she should manage the issue of inheritance in her family, and was particularly concerned about the position of her daughter-in-law, with whom she had shared a mutually supportive relationship for some years:

> *Ethel.* She's, she's a good girl. She phones me every night to see how I am. I mean to say, there's not many daughter-in-laws like that . . . and then she'll say, er, 'don't sit on your own, come down for your tea' at weekends you know and, oh yes, she's very good. She sends me things, you know, she sent the boy with a pint of milk the other night [laugh].

Ethel perceived this relationship to be rather special, and is clearly stating that her daughter-in-law does more to support her than one might reasonably expect of a daughter-in-law. For Ethel, this presented a dilemma concerning how to handle inheritance in relation both to this daughter-in-law and also to her son-in-law, with whom she was also on good terms. She had made a will, using the standard formula whereby the estate is divided between one's own children and, in the event of their predeceasing the testator, their children. But Ethel explained that—although she had written her will in this way—she did not consider it entirely satisfactory:

> *Ethel.* I made a will out but I feel as if my son-in-law, my daughter-in-law, are being left out of it. And I've explained to my daughter, so she said, 'oh they won't be'. I said, 'not unless you'll give them something', and now I feel . . . like it's my daughter-in-law's birthday next week and I feel as if I want to give her something to make up for what she won't be getting when anything happens to me. But you see I've provided for my grandchildren, and my son and daughter, hoping that they'll give their . . .
> *Interviewer.* Share it?
> *Ethel.* Yes.

2. *Mary Jackson*

Mary Jackson's case is actually very similar to Ethel Phillips's. Mary was in her late 60s, married, with three married sons, all with children. Mary and her husband, Richard, coincidentally had made wills about a month before we interviewed them. They had arranged that once they had both died, the proceeds from their house would be divided equally three ways between their sons, with £1,000 from each of the thirds to be given to each grandchild. But Mary reported disappointment that they had felt unable to provide for her daughters-in-law. Their solicitor had discouraged them from doing so, pointing out that should any of their sons predecease their wives, then the wives—and possibly a subsequent husband—would benefit as 'next of kin'.

> *Mary.* We felt awful about this you know. So Richard said 'it doesn't seem right'. Anyway, it's left that way. So I had a word with our June [daughter-in-law] when I went up and I said 'we feel awful about this June', because we think a lot about the girls you see. And, er, I said 'would you feel that we weren't bothered about you?' She said 'oh no, why?' I said, 'well, if it was the children that got it', you see if anything happens like that and the children do get the money, then if *they need* the money *for* the children, the daughter-in-law, she could get some, but you can't go and have it all. So she said 'well, you don't worry about us because', she said,

'I'm alright, because we're insured and Tom's insured'. You know, the house is her's if anything happens to Tom. It's done that way, and they also have an insurance. But I haven't seen the other boys to talk about it. I've *seen* them, but you don't sit down and . . . say 'oh well, when anything happens to us, Jennifer and Elizabeth won't get anything' [*laugh*].

What can the cases of Ethel Phillips and Mary Jackson tell us about our black box question, that is, about how far inheritance is kept separate from other considerations in families? In both these cases our interviewees felt unable to make direct bequests to their children-in-law, partly as a result of advice from solicitors. That both wanted to do so, seems fairly directly related to the close and mutually supportive relationships each had with at least some of their children-in-law in their own right. Their desire to bequeath to their daughters-in-law was not a simple consequence of these women being the spouses of their own children, but was seen as part of the on-going pattern of their relationships with these specific individuals.

This runs counter to the black box model, and indicates a strong link—on one level—between inheritance and other family commitments and relationships. Both these women wanted to be able to make personal bequests, based on individually negotiated relationships with specific in-laws. But there is a paradox here, since neither had actually defied her solicitor's advice, and named a daughter-in-law in her will. Thus, by implication, in her actions each was accepting that decisions about inheritance should be kept separate from her own feelings about specific individuals—though neither felt entirely comfortable about acting on this principle.

In effect both women were making attempts to rectify the situation, or to compensate for it. They were trying to find ways of negotiating around the black box. They were trying to find ways of extending their control after their own death through informal as well as formal means. Making a will is the formal means for doing this, but both Ethel and Mary were dissatisfied with the amount of control which it gave them in practice. In seeking other means of extending their control, both sought reassurance that their own children would respect their wishes that their inheritance should be shared with their spouses. Another informal mechanism which was considered was the use of life-time gifts, compensating children-in-law with larger gifts than they might otherwise have received, in recognition that their position in formal inheritance terms was less favourable than the testator would have liked. We are describing this as 'negotiating around the black box' because informal means of control represent a way in which both Ethel Phillips and Mary Jackson could continue to assent to the idea that inheritance should be treated as a black box within families, whilst at the same time finding ways of acknowledging their appreciation of specific individuals who were important to them.

By referring to this as negotiation we do not mean round-the-table talks. Clearly it did not happen in that way. Rather, we speak about negotiation in a more indirect sense—working out how you can best resolve paradoxes and dilemmas in relationships, how you can reconcile competing principles and competing demands, and how you can convey your intentions and the meaning of your actions to other people without necessarily opening up the subject directly. This type of negotiation is a central characteristic of family life, we would argue (Finch and Mason, 1992, ch. 3). In the case of these negotiations concerning Ethel Phillips and Mary Jackson, the negotiations certainly included initiating some discussions with both children and children-in-law. The purpose of discussion with the children seemed to be to try to increase their own control over what would happen after they died, above and beyond the formal requirements documented in the will. The purpose of discussion with children-in-law was essentially to explain their actions, to ensure that the formal provisions of the will were not misunderstood, that these were not taken as indicative of a lack of affection or family responsibility on the part of the testator. But none of these discussions were formal negotiations designed to result in explicit agreements. They were more indirect attempts to resolve the dilemmas which the black box approach to inheritance—represented by the law as they experienced it—imposed upon their own family relationships. They were not rejecting the black box model completely but, in its simple form, it did not enable them to live easily with issues of inheritance in their own families.

3. *Avril King*

Our next case raises further issues which help us to question the simple black box model, and also to understand a slightly different range of moral concerns about appropriate ways to handle inheritance. Avril King was a middle-aged woman who had nursed her mother through a terminal illness several years previous to our interview with her. She was married, with one son. Avril, by her own account, had received little or no help from her two married brothers in caring for their mother. Avril's mother had not left a will. In the following extract, Avril explains what happened after her mother died:

> *Avril.* Well, actually, they didn't have their own house, it was rented, so there was no problems there . . . obviously father had that. But, um, anything that there was, we brought the whole lot, split up furniture etc., etc., any money was split three ways.
>
> *Interviewer.* Mm, so you all dealt with that quite amicably?
>
> *Avril.* Oh yes, my eldest brother did all the dealings, you know, obviously. But there was, no, um, well, not really, but there again, Emily [cousin] stepped into the breach, because she was annoyed at the way I was treated, you see, um, because we'd arranged to meet at the house to sort all this out, and I was working at the time and I got to my mum's and it was all sort of 'well, I'm having this'. Avril was left with, er, what was, I got the three-piece suite, I think, like a cottage suite, and, um, Emily went mad, Emily bought that off me actually, and she said 'all that you've done for your parents, they've done nothing', um, 'cause I did, I looked after them, you know, even when they were well, as regards money and buying things, what have you. And she said 'they've had the cheek to come and sort all what they want out.' My sisters-in-law were there as well, you know, and I said to Emily, 'I'm not interested, that doesn't interest me.' All I wanted was my parents there.

One way of interpreting Avril's account is that it represents an outright rejection of the black box model, at least at the normative level. Avril's account of her cousin's indignation that she was not better rewarded for all the support that she had given her parents by comparison with her brothers, is a clear example of someone saying that the black box model should not have been operating. In other words, the special nature of Avril's relationship with her parents should have been counted when it came to inheritance. The stronger commitments between Avril and her parents, by comparison with her brothers', should have been taken into account when assets were being distributed. If the parents themselves did not do this, it is implied, then the brothers should have. In this case, it seems that we are being told that inheritance should not be treated as a black box.

But we can also go further in interpreting Avril King's case. In presenting her account, she is telling us some important things about moral aspects of the way in which inheritance is handled in families. By moral aspects we do not simply mean ideas about right and wrong, though clearly such ideas are an important feature of Avril's account. We also refer to the judgements being passed on the people concerned; on what their actions say about their moral and social identities. Just as both Ethel Phillips and Mary Jackson were concerned that members of their families should understand what they were trying to do, that the way they had written their respective wills would not damage their standing in the eyes of their close relatives, so Avril King is telling us that her actions show her to be a person who has moral integrity—unlike her brothers, whose actions show them to be morally flawed. This interweaving of moral questions with practical and material issues is another important characteristic of family life, we would argue (Finch and Mason, 1992, ch. 5).

We can best make these points about the moral issues by posing the question: why did not Avril make sure that she got a larger share of her parents' assets? Why did she not point out to her brothers that she deserved more than they did? The answer is that, in her eyes, it is not morally appropriate to expect an inheritance, still less to demand one. Therefore a person who does demand rights over inheritance is behaving in an unacceptable way. This comes across in her account in two different ways. First, Avril's brothers are being censured for their rather greedy or demanding behaviour after the death of their parents ('well I'm having this . . .'). Secondly, and perhaps most importantly, Avril is saying that *she* did not act in a demanding way. Her use of the voice of her cousin Emily to tell the story tells us a lot about this theme. Avril herself evidently disapproves of her brothers' behaviour, and supports Emily's view that she herself was badly done by. However, in making these points to us, she used a reported conversation she had had with Emily, in which—although she had not denied the validity of Emily's account—her own comments were 'I'm not interested'. Avril actually repeated this sequence of conversation to us several times in her interview, each time adding a comment like 'I'm not interested', or 'I've got these few things and I'm quite happy with that', or 'it doesn't bother me'. Using the voice of a third party and her own response to that third party allowed Avril to make these points— specifically about her brothers' greed, and her own deservingness— which otherwise she would have found difficult to make without running the risk of appearing to have been *expecting* an inheritance herself.

In the way that she told this story to us, Avril tried to establish herself on the high moral ground, even if she had lost out in material terms. She had evidently taken the same approach at the time when the events occurred. In this she is not unusual. In general, people try hard to establish themselves in a good light when handling their family relationships, as data from our study show (Finch and Mason, 1992, ch. 5). In relation to inheritance, it seems that one's demeanour in times of family crises like death and inheritance is actually very important in this respect—certainly, it seems likely Avril King's brothers have committed serious sins in the eyes of at least some of their relatives, which will not easily be forgotten.

The basic ground rule which Avril's case points to is that it is morally inappropriate to expect or demand the right to inherit. It is equally inappropriate to act as if you have such expectations. This holds even when someone seems to have a prima-facie case for special consideration. Even where there have been special commitments which could be acknowledged through the medium of inheritance, it is still wrong to expect this to happen.

4. Tilly Trotter

Our final case reinforces the message which comes from the Avril King example, especially on the issue of 'expecting' inheritance. There are others from our data set which we could have chosen to illustrate the same theme, but we have selected the case of Tilly Trotter, who, like Avril King, is a middle-aged woman, but living in council accommodation rather than an owner-occupier, and generally enjoying less advantageous material circumstances. Tilly is divorced, with children and grandchildren. She has three married brothers who all live nearby. Tilly's widowed father, who lives a few streets away, is beginning to need quite a lot of practical support and some personal care. Tilly currently visits him daily, and is trying to persuade him to move in with her so that she can look after him. She and her father often talk about inheritance:

> *Tilly.* He [father] always goes on about 'my will' so that I said 'who's bothered about your will, why don't you have a holiday? Why don't you?'

However, one of her brothers also discusses inheritance with her father, but Tilly is less approving of this:

> *Tilly.* My middle brother Stan's always saying, 'you want to make a will out dad'. You know how they are, I mean he's very, we call him a pen pusher, he's office worker and all that, where my other brothers are like labourers. And he [father] said, 'I know our Stan's after my money.' And I said 'don't be *stupid*'. He doesn't *need* it, you know, our Stan's at him

because he'll say my eldest brother, our Jack'll get it. He's always been sort of an ale-can like, he likes going in the pub and, he works hard, and drinks hard. And I said to him 'don't be silly, he's just frightened in case there's any animosity', you know.

Tilly Trotter's case reinforces the message that expecting, demanding, or asking for an inheritance is regarded as inappropriate. This case indicates that there is a risk, for a potential beneficiary, in even mentioning the subject—as her 'pen pusher' brother has done—since this may well be construed as being 'after' the testator's money. By contrast with her brother, Tilly is very clearly defining herself as someone who is not asking for, or even expecting to get, an inheritance. The way in which she approaches this in her interview has much in common with Avril King. Tilly also uses the technique of reporting a conversation with a third party to illustrate the ways in which both she and her relatives are handling inheritance, and the contrasts between these. Again, as with Avril, her account interweaves issues about the division of material assets with strong messages about the moral identities of the people involved, and how they can be damaged by the way in which each person positions him or herself in relation to inheritance within the family, and the way in which their actions appear to others.

In common with all the other individual cases considered here, we see that the issue of inheritance is much more complicated than the black box model would allow. Whilst on one level the significance of inheritance to potential beneficiaries is deliberately de-emphasized ('Who's bothered about your will? Why don't you have a holiday?'), it is equally clear that the possibilities for inheritance both affect relationships in the present and could potentially change them in the future. In these senses, inheritance clearly is not an issue which is divorced from other areas of family life.

Conclusion

In this chapter we have used both survey and more qualitative case-study data to show some of the complex ways in which inheritance might be linked to other family responsibilities both at abstract normative levels, and in practice. Our aim in doing this has been to explore some of the links between inheritance and other family responsibilities. This is an interesting issue in its own right but also, we have argued, it affects questions of how the law can incorporate prevailing social norms about appropriate patterns of inheritance. We focused, in particular, on the question of whether people generally endorse the view that the right to inherit should be based simply on genealogical ties, unconnected with any other patterns of responsibility within families (a model which we called the black box), or whether people generally think that the right to inherit to an extent can be earned through special commitments acknowledged and fulfilled.

Our general conclusion is that the black box idea does not quite work. In our view it is not the best way in which to understand and interpret how people really handle inheritance in families. Within our study, sometimes people did seem to operate within this model, at other times they did not. And sometimes people's actions accorded with the black box model, but they themselves did not feel entirely comfortable with the consequences. So the black box model is not quite right as a description of the way people might handle inheritance in families, but nor is it completely wrong. It does have some credence at the abstract normative level in the sense that there is some evidence that people recognize the validity of the idea that inheritance should be kept separate from these wider aspects of family relationships.

The people in our study also acknowledged the relevance of this idea, in practice, to their own families, but might try to modify it and negotiate around it if it did not allow them to acknowledge the strength of their relationships with individual members. Where this happened, it was clearly important that it be handled with care, since people's moral identities could be damaged if other people misinterpreted their actions or intentions. The cases of Avril King and Tilly Trotter suggested that even if you are apparently a 'deserving case' as a potential beneficiary because you have provided support to the testator, you still must not show that you expect to inherit, and certainly you must not demand it. We think that these data help to illustrate that the different facets of family responsibilities and commitments are linked in quite complex ways, and inheritance is a part of that. The negotiations which help to produce these commitments are influenced by both moral and material factors.

Finally, what is the relevance of our argument for debates about the law concerning inheritance and intestacy? The most important point is that it is difficult to forge a straightforward link between publicly acknowledged social norms and the law (our Levels 1 and 2 above). Our survey data show that there are no simple and widely accepted social norms in this area. People have quite widely differing responses to normative questions about a person's right to inherit in a given set of circumstances, and to questions about whether there should be links between inheritance and other types of responsibility in families. In practice, people may acknowledge that genealogical ties are an important component—possibly the central component—in working out claims to inheritance in their own families. But they may also apparently reject a rigid notion that it is *simply* the genealogical tie which creates a claim. Equally there are no easily specified social norms which would tie a special claim to inherit to other types of responsibility in families. It seems that people may want to claim the freedom to negotiate about inheritance within their own families, and to be able to acknowledge special claims in certain circumstances, though not in others.

This seems to imply that the law needs to allow for maximum flexibility in inheritance practices. The law should not make assumptions about the over-riding importance of the genealogical tie in too rigid a way. Equally it should not try to build in a check-list of other responsibilities which would lead to a stronger right to claim inheritance for some people than others in the same genealogical position. We would suggest instead that the law needs to allow for both these principles to operate, in different circumstances, if it is to be in tune with prevailing social norms about inheritance. It is not easy to see how such an approach—stressing maximum flexibility—can be embodied in the law, save perhaps through a continued emphasis upon testamentary freedom, which itself implies flexibility.

Acknowledgements

We are very grateful to Hilary Conway for her assistance in the analysis of some of the qualitative data on which this chapter is based. The project was funded by ESRC 1985–9 under the title 'Family Obligations: Social Construction and Social Policy'. Award No. G00232197. Details of our sampling strategy for this part of our study can be found in Finch and Mason. 1990. We are exploring some of the same issues more systematically in our current research project entitled 'Inheritance, Property and Family Relationships'. This project is also funded by ESRC, 1989–93, Award No. R–000–23–2035. Directors: Janet Finch, Jennifer Mason, Judith Masson.

THE HARPER VIGNETTE

Family Obligations Survey 1985

N = 987

This situation is about Mary Harper, an elderly woman who has one widowed daughter, Valerie. She has quarrelled with Valerie and has cut her out of her will. So Valerie knows that she will not inherit her mother's house. Her mother is too frail to live alone any more and does not want to go into a home. The daughter, Valerie, is not sure what to do. On the one hand she has enough space for her mother but, on the other hand, they have never got on well together.

a. What should Valerie do?

Offer her mother a home	364	37%
Arrange for her mother to go into a nursing home	496	51%
Other	93	9%
Don't know/depends	25	3%

b. If Valerie *did* offer her mother a home, would it be reasonable to say that her mother must change her will, and leave her the house? Or should Valerie offer her mother a home without conditions?

Valerie should ask her mother to change the will	124	13%
Offer of home should be without any conditions	798	82%
Don't know/depends	56	5%

c. In fact Mary decides *not* to live with Valerie. She has a favourite, unmarried granddaughter in her early twenties. She has already given the granddaughter £3,000 for a deposit on a house and has left her own house to the granddaughter in her will.

Should the granddaughter offer Mary a home or not?

Yes	722	74%
No	189	19%
Don't know/depends	67	7%

d. If necessary, should the granddaughter give up her job to look after her grandmother, or not?

Yes	288	29%
No	554	57%
Don't know/depends	136	14%

e. Why should she give up her job/not give up her job?
(Note: Answers post-coded).

(i) Why granddaughter *should* give up her job
  (291 'reasons' given by 288 people)

Reciprocity (her grandmother has been good to her; she has received a lot already; she should help in return etc.)	228	78%
Other	63	22%

(ii) Why granddaughter should *not* give up her job.
  (779 'reasons' given by 554 people)

Her long term future (e.g. she might not get another job)	248	32%
She is too young (e.g. a young person should not take on these commitments; she's just starting in life)	125	16%
Independence (e.g. she has her own life to lead; she should not sacrifice herself)	117	15%
She should help in some other way (e.g. paying for home help)	76	10%
She has no reciprocal obligation (e.g. the gift doesn't matter; references to bribery, blackmail)	64	8%
It's not her responsibility	63	8%
She's only a granddaughter	18	2%
Other	68	9%

REFERENCES

Davey, M. (1988), 'Testamentary Promises', *Legal Studies*, 8/1: 92–110.
Finch, J. (1987), 'The Vignette Technique in Survey Research', *Sociology*, 21/1: 105–14.
Finch, J. and Mason, J. (1990), 'Decision-taking in the Fieldwork Process: Theoretical sampling and Collaborative Working' in R. G. Burgess (ed.), *Reflections on Field Experience* (JAI Press, London).
—— —— (1991), 'Obligations of Kinship in Britain: Is There Normative Agreement? *British Journal of Sociology*, 42/3: 345–67.
—— —— (1992), *Negotiating Family Responsibilities* (Routledge, London).
Law Commission (1989), *Distribution on Intestacy* (HMSO, London).
Wistow, G. and Henwood, M. (1991), 'Citizenship and Frail Elderly People: Changing Patterns of Provision in Europe', in N. Manning (ed.), *Social Policy Review 1990–91* (Longman, London).

PART THREE

Families and the Role of Law

7. Allocating Resources at Times of Crisis: Divorce and Separation in Poland

Andrzej Szlezak

Introduction

If we consider the position of spouses *vis-à-vis* each other after divorce, and also the position of spouses during divorce litigation, in both situations we are faced with the problem of sharing resources. After divorce, the term sharing denotes the distribution of assets acquired by the spouses during their marriage and the organization of other consequences of marriage, such as the post-divorce duty of support. During a divorce, the term sharing denotes the way of organizing relations with respect to property that still remains the common property of the litigants.

Both these situations require some comment, and it should be borne in mind that a provisional arrangement at the time of divorce litigation may influence or even predetermine the contents of the final divorce decree.

Polish family law has been tailored to the needs of the poor rather than the rich. The reasons for this are very simple. In a Communist society most people were supposed to have little wealth, and the little they possessed was supposed to be consumed rather than invested. People were supposed to provide labour, and remuneration for work was considered the only honourable, or ideologically correct source of income. In turn, the state assumed the role of an almost exclusive employer (with the exception of a large-scale private sector in agriculture), and provider of health care, schooling, pensions, etc. In such a context, the legislative activity of the state was oriented towards the promulgation of laws that corresponded with the image of society as a more or less homogeneous entity in pursuit of socially desirable, rather than individually profitable, goals. In family law such an attitude resulted in much stress being put on an egalitarian approach to the regulation of family life, and in the designation of norms directed first at the satisfaction of the consumption needs of the whole family rather than at the protection of or growth in individual wealth of some members. While such an outcome need not be a bad thing even under the new ideology in force in Poland today, some aspects seem obsolete, especially those which do not fit into the model of a market-oriented economy.

This egalitarian approach to family matters is combined in Polish law with another feature which affects divorce and post-divorce regulation of the rights and duties of the spouses. At various stages in divorce proceedings the question of guilt appears. In fact, economic considerations based on the criteria of poverty or a degree of participation in creating the common property may be blurred by reference to guilt, leading to an outcome highly eclectic in character.

Divorce

Before discussing the issue of the economic consequences of divorce, some basic introduction to the Polish divorce law seems necessary. The institution of divorce in Polish family law is a compromise between the legislator's intention to promote the stability of marriages on the one hand, and its need to provide for the dissolution of the 'dead unions' of people who no longer wish to stay together on the other. The Polish divorce law belongs to the group of no-fault divorce systems based on the 'breakdown' principle. Thus it might be termed 'divorce as remedy', that is, divorce as the means of dissolving unions which have lost their functional characteristics, and not as 'divorce as sanction', that is, divorce perceived as punishment for marital misconduct by one of the spouses. Yet such a characterization would be an over-simplification: there are still elements of sanction in the Polish divorce formulae; thus, the Polish regulation is to some extent an amalgamation of those two general concepts, even if the remedial element is unquestionably dominant. However, recent pronouncements originating in various political circles, with the tacit approval of the Roman Catholic Church, may result in attempts to redraft the Polish divorce law along different lines. Were those attempts to materialize, one might expect a considerable tightening of divorce policy, and possibly even a return to the old notions of 'divorce as sanction', with a prominent place reserved for guilt. Some signs of such tendencies can already be seen. In particular, divorce cases have recently been transferred from lower courts (District Courts) to higher courts (Provincial Courts), divorce hearings are usually being scheduled for dates several months distant from the dates of conciliatory hearings (i.e. from the obligatory opening stage of divorce litigation), and divorce fees, in the past seldom exceeding the average monthly salary of the litigants, have gone up considerably. In consequence, divorce has become more costly, more lengthy, and less accessible.

According to the law in force today, divorce may be granted only in the case of the complete and permanent breakdown of marriage, irrespective of the causes of the breakdown. Despite the breakdown, however, divorce cannot be decreed if, as a result, the best interests of the children of both spouses would suffer, or if the dissolution of the marriage would, for any other reason, be contrary to the principles of social coexistence.[1] Furthermore, despite the breakdown, divorce cannot be decreed if the petitioner was solely guilty of the breakdown, unless either the respondent consents to the divorce or the refusal of his or her consent is, in the circumstances, contrary to the principles of social coexistence. The elements of 'divorce as sanction' are, therefore, important in cases of the sole guilt of the petitioner; they also appear in the process of establishing the right to and the amount of alimony between the ex-spouses.

The notion of complete and permanent breakdown is the crucial concept in Polish divorce law. The case law, trying to fill out the general statutory formulations, is unanimous that the breakdown should manifest itself through the lack of psychological, physical, and economic ties between the spouses (Wiszniewski and Gross, 1971: 268–72). If all such ties have been severed, the requirement of completeness is usually satisfied; some exceptions, resulting from an acute housing shortage in Poland which means the otherwise separated spouses may sometimes stay together in the same apartment and therefore may still be linked economically to each other, have been allowed (Item 46, Supreme Court Guidelines, May 1955). In turn, the permanence of the breakdown consists in the extreme unlikelihood of the spouses resuming their married life in the future.

As to the obstacles to divorce, despite the explicit wording of the respective provisions, the courts have so far seldom dismissed claims on the grounds of conflict with the best interests of the children or

---

[1] 'The principles of social coexistence' is the term denoting the non-legal criteria of valuation. They perform the function of the norms of equity and are usually associated with the moral norms respected (internalized) by at least some (significant) part of society. See generally Ziembinski (1980: 472–4).

other principles of social coexistence, or on the grounds of the recrimination clause (the sole guilt of the petitioner) (Olejniczak, 1980; Stojanowska, 1977). Since the question of guilt is of vital importance for the financial consequences of divorce, some comment seems appropriate.

The notion of sole guilt has been subject to a very characteristic evolution in the case law. The decisions of the Supreme Court have gradually transformed the concept of sole guilt, i.e. guilt that could be ascribed to only one of the parties, into the concept of guilt as the sole reason for the breakdown. In consequence, 'sole guilt' could seldom be found, for it seldom happens that the breakdown is caused exclusively by the behaviour of one party, without any 'objective' contribution to the breakdown by the other party. In fact, the Supreme Court has practically abolished 'sole guilt' as an obstacle to divorce. However, I would hesitate to predict that this line of case law will be maintained in the future, especially in view of the emerging policy to make divorce more difficult. Already in 1987, in its Guidelines on Alimony Cases (*Monitor Polski*, 1988), the Supreme Court had resorted to its original view and declared that in alimony matters a spouse should be considered solely guilty *not* if his or her guilt had been the sole cause of the breakdown but if the guilt could be found only in *one* party's behaviour even if his or her guilt was not the only cause of the breakdown. Thus, the concept of 'divorce as sanction' may regain importance, placing the Polish divorce law well behind current trends elsewhere, and also well behind our own tradition of no-fault divorce, going back to the early 1950s when no-fault divorce was not even contemplated anywhere in Western Europe, with the exception of the Scandinavian countries.

Financial Consequences of Divorce

The divorce law offers the litigants a specific instrument for arranging financial relations between the parties in preparing for their hearing. The court may, upon the motion of one of the spouses, or *ex officio*, issue an order imposing on one of the spouses a duty to contribute to the satisfaction of the needs of the family for the period of the divorce litigation. Although such an order is of a provisional character and binds only for a limited period of time, the findings of the court, made in the course of establishing the earning capacity of the spouse liable for maintenance, hereafter termed the debtor, may to some extent predetermine the contents of subsequent divorce decree stipulations. It should also be noted that the means obtained through such a decree should be spent not only on the satisfaction of the needs of the claiment and the children of the spouses but also on the satisfaction of the debtor's needs, for it is intended to enforce a marital duty to contribute to the needs of the *whole* family.

Besides an order regulating the duty of support, a divorce court may also issue some other provisional orders pertaining to the arrangement of property division between the litigants. At the instance of one of the spouses, the court may regulate the way the matrimonial house (apartment) is to be shared during litigation. Furthermore, if one of the spouses decides to leave the matrimonial house, the other may be obliged to hand over to the spouse who is leaving the objects he or she may need. This order does not prejudice the question of whether such objects are part of common or separate property. It may happen that the spouse who has left the matrimonial home will have to return those objects to the other spouse later if the latter is able to prove that they belong to him or her as separate property.

The orders referred to above are meant to eliminate or to diminish the potential sources of conflict during the divorce litigation and to deal with the issues which urgently require regulation. However, it is highly doubtful whether the legislation has adopted the best way of dealing with the crisis situation. It seems that too little room is left for the parties' own initiative in matters connected with their own divorce. This remark pertains not only to the position of the spouses during the case, but also to the position of the ex-spouses after the final divorce decree has been issued.

The contents of the Polish divorce law fully justify the conclusion that while the contracting of marriage is left entirely to the discretion of the future spouses, the dissolution of their union is subjected to a degree of supervision by the state. The reasons for such an attitude are understandable and justifiable in those cases where the breakdown of marital union affects not only those who established that union, i.e. the spouses, but also those who had no part in its formation, yet fully depend on its functioning, i.e. the children who are still minors. However, in the field of property relations between the ex-spouses, i.e. interests exclusive to the spouses, the supervision exercised by the state should give way to agreements negotiated by the spouses at a pre-trial stage.

Theoretically speaking, the spouses are free to determine their property relations by means of contract, and the role of the court should then be reduced to approving or correcting, but not imposing the terms of such agreements. Again, theoretically, the court should act as sole decision-maker only if the parties themselves are unable, for various reasons, to reach any understanding. In practice, however, the spouses seldom undertake to negotiate the terms of divorce and in most instances leave such matters to the decision of the court. There has never been any express encouragement from the law inviting the spouses to seek compromise on an out-of-court basis. It seems that such stipulations might be a good solution, if only to indicate the legislator's preference for the parties to take a responsible approach to their own divorce. Furthermore, it is likely that, at least in some situations, pre-trial negotiations might help to eliminate or lessen tension between the spouses. On the other hand, the Supreme Court has stressed several times the duty of the court to seek the views of the parties and to incorporate the reasonable expectations of the litigants into the divorce decree (Pietrzykowski 1991: 295–8).

The financial consequences of divorce may be classified into two groups. Divorce may give rise to the duty of support between the ex-spouses and it marks the end of the community property system, opening the doors for the division of the matrimonial property. It should also be noted that in Polish law, post-divorce alimony and property distribution are treated separately, i.e. alimony is never considered as justifying an unequal property allocation.

Post-Divorce Alimony

Alimony claims between the divorced spouses are governed by two sets of criteria, one pertaining to moral considerations (guilt), the other to the economic situation of the claimant (poverty or considerable deterioration in his or her marital status).

There are three different configurations of guilt distribution according to the Polish divorce law. Both spouses may be declared innocent of causing the breakdown, both may be pronounced guilty (irrespective of the degree of guilt on either side), or one of them may be found solely guilty of the breakdown (Szpunar, 1981).

In the first two instances, the spouse who is in poverty may demand maintenance in accordance with his or her needs and the earning potential and resources of the other spouse. However, if the right to support is established between two innocent spouses, the debtor's liability shall be extinguished (a) upon remarriage of the other spouse receiving support, termed the creditor, or (b) after five years from the date of divorce, unless the court prolongs that period due to exceptional circumstances (Dobrzanski 1974: 373–8). In other instances including the one dealt with below, the right to alimony is unlimited in time, provided, again, that the creditor has not remarried. So far, there has been no decision by the Supreme Court as to the impact of cohabitation without marriage on alimony claims between the divorced spouses. But, in all three instances, the right to alimony may be modified following a change of circumstances, and it seems that the question of cohabitation would be considered on the grounds of the altered-circumstances clause rather on the grounds of the analogous application of the remarriage provision. The altered-circumstance clause may be invoked by either spouse: then, alimony payments may be revised upwards or downwards, or they may be terminated. But even after termination the court may reinstate the payments if changes of circumstance occur. This possibility, according to the literal wording of the statute, should be excluded in the alimony claims between innocent spouses filed after the expiration of the five-year period, for the statute provides only for the option of 'prolonging' alimony, i.e. extending in time the existing duty. However, the Supreme Court decided otherwise, allowing—in the name of equity—claims filed after the expiration of the five-year period, if exceptional circumstances justifying the prolongation were present before the lapse of the said period of time (Supreme Court decision of 2 July 1955 (OSN 1956, item 33) and 21 November 1981 (OSN 1982, item 106)).

In the third instance, where one of the spouses was found solely guilty of the breakdown, the situation is different. Here marital virtues are rewarded with a more favourable alimony grant. The innocent spouse does not have to be in poverty; instead, in order to obtain alimony, he or she has to prove that the divorce brought about a considerable deterioration in his or her material situation. Theoretically, the innocent spouse has a claim which, if enforced, might secure for him or her a living standard equal or at least comparable with the living standard of his or her ex-partner. In practice, the proof of 'considerable deterioration' should not be very difficult to produce, especially for the spouses of well-to-do partners who have never worked. However, in a society sensitive to the egalitarian ideology, any outcome leading to the unjustified economic exploitation of one spouse by the other could hardly be accepted. The Supreme Court and legal writers have often addressed the issue. The prevailing view today is that the claim for alimony filed against the solely guilty spouse does not relieve his or her partner from the duty of securing as much revenue as possible (e.g. in the form of income from his or her gainful employment, or revenues from the liquidation of marital property, with some exceptions). Only when all such sources have been utilized, may he or she demand that the other spouse should offset or diminish the remaining disparity in their living standards.

Finally, the solely guilty spouse has no claim to alimony whatsoever against the innocent spouse, irrespective of the material status of the would-be claimant. Here, the principle of punishing marital misconduct comes to light again.

Summing up, on the one hand post-divorce support is the last resort for those who are destitute and are not able (due to health, age, household burdens, or insufficient professional qualifications, or—more recently—unemployment) to secure sufficient means to satisfy their needs. On the other hand, in the case of the exclusive guilt of the defendant, alimony payments may be considered a form of indemnity for marital vices. In such a case the institution of alimony becomes an indicator of the old 'divorce as sanction' formula, where the arrangement of post-divorce rights and duties of spouses (and also the question of the admissibility of divorce) was conditional upon the conduct of the parties.

Practical application of the provisions of the duty of support may be somewhat surprising. Claims for alimony between the divorced spouses have always been very rare. For instance, a cross-national survey conducted in 1974 showed that such claims were filed in only 1.5 per cent of divorce cases.[2]

---

[2] See Stojanowska (1977: 65–8). Unfortunately, no more recent research is available. However, it seems that the conditions that might have had some impact on this figure have changed relatively little since 1974. For instance, the rate of divorce in 1975 was 1.2 per 1,000 people; in 1980, 1.1; in 1985, 1.3; in 1988, 1.3. The participation of women in the labour pool was: 1975, 47%; 1980, 46%; 1985, 46%; 1988, 45%. There have also been no attempts on the part of the Supreme Court to tighten the alimony policy over this period. (The Alimony Guidelines published by the Supreme Court in 1988 may change the proportion between alimony decreed on the 'exclusive guilt' basis and other instances of alimony, but should not lead to the overall increase in the number of claims filed by divorcees.) Besides, according to the data obtained from the Ministry of Justice, the total number of alimony suits in Poland was: in 1980, 1,498; in 1985, 1,473; and in 1989, 1,800. Even if one assumed that the

One explanation of this phenomenon may be that in a destitute society, where most income used to come from remuneration for work in the state sector, and the differences between those who earned a great deal and those who earned little were usually small, it was easy for most divorcees to offset any deterioration in their marital situation by taking gainful employment. Besides, until very recently, unemployment was unheard of in Poland, and anybody wanting a job could easily find one (although not always a job compatible with one's qualifications). It should also be remembered that before seeking alimony, any claimant was supposed to prove that he or she was unable to satisfy his or her needs from his or her own resources, and—in particular—was unable, for various reasons, to secure such means by taking gainful employment. In the absence of such proof, alimony would not be granted. In view of the above, it may no longer be surprising that alimony was sought and decreed in such a small number of cases. It remains to be seen whether the same trend will continue in the future. Rising unemployment and the emergence of more wealthy strata in Polish society may reverse this tendency.

Another explanation, derived from considerations of similarly rare claims for alimony between spouses during their marriage, is that alimony for the spouse (or ex-spouse) may often be hidden in the alimony decreed for the children (Smyczynski, 1978: 85–91). However, this is hardly convincing, for it seldom happens that alimony for children is high enough to cover their needs, let alone the needs of the custodial parent.

An additional aspect of the practical application of the provisions regulating the duty of support needs to be stressed. Although the law requires that the potential financial possibilities of the debtor should be taken into account in order to determine the amount of alimony to be decreed, the courts often confine their inquiries to the assessment of his or her actual possessions. In consequence, the sums decreed by the courts do not reflect the earning power of the defendant, and the amount of alimony is often lower than if potential earnings were taken into account. In addition, a deficient system for disclosing information about one's financial situation makes it possible for a spouse to withhold relevant information from both the court

overwhelming majority of such suits concerned the divorced spouses, the percentage of suits for alimony would still be very low, considering the fact that in those years the number of divorces was between about 40,000 and 45,000.

and the other spouse. Some of the above shortcomings may be eliminated with the introduction of a general income tax and the accompanying system of revenue control, from 1 January 1992.

Distribution of Matrimonial Property

Before discussing the financial consequences of divorce with respect to marital property, some introduction to the system of matrimonial property in force in Poland is appropriate. The shape of this system predetermines the arrangement of property relations after divorce.

Although spouses are free to arrange their property relations on a contractual basis, choosing between a system of separate property and various types of community property, the most common type of property relations arises *ex lege*. In other words, if—as appears to be the case for the overwhelming majority of couples—the spouses have failed to regulate their relations by means of a contract, a system of statutory community property comes into force (Piatowski, 1985: chs. 5–7). Statutory community property is a type of joint ownership, although modified to a considerable extent. For instance, it pertains not only to things but also to choices of action; there are no separate and definite shares ascribed to each of the spouses, and all property is considered to belong to both of them as if they were a single entity (*pro-indiviso*). The regulation of statutory community property is governed by the principle of the equality of the sexes and by the assumption that the home-maker's work in the household should be considered the equivalent of the breadwinner's financial contributions to the creation of matrimonial property. Statutory community property lasts as long as the marriage exists, although it may be terminated earlier, either by a contract between the spouses, by court order upon the request of either spouse if serious reasons such as *de facto* separation or prodigality justify such a termination, or by the operation of law—if one of the spouses is rendered incapable of acting in law.

The composition of statutory community property reflects the intention to protect the economic interests of the whole family, at the expense of the individual property of both spouses. The Family and Guardianship Code, in determining the scope of the common property and the separate property of both spouses, chose the formula which provided for a relatively wide definition of common property. Thus, the community property comprises the acquisitions of both spouses, the income from, both, and the common and separate property of each spouse. It follows that the most important sources of revenue are included in the common property, and benefit the family by enlarging the common property rather than by conserving or extending the separate one. Yet spouses who wish to include some elements of the common property in their separate property, or want to include some elements of the latter in the former, may do so by means of a contract. Similarly, the spouses may contract out of the statutory community; in such a case each spouse retains the property acquired before the marriage as well as the property acquired later. He or she is then independent in his or her management and disposal of the entire property. Such contracts are very rare in Poland. Nevertheless, sooner or later they are bound to become more popular, for the existing regulation of the composition of the community property and legal mechanisms for managing such property are a serious impediment to the efficiency and speed of economic transactions. In a state-controlled economy such considerations were of little significance; in a market-oriented economy, to which Poland aspires, this may no longer be the case.

The scope of changes brought about by divorce depends on the property system adopted by the spouses. There are few changes if they chose to regulate their relations by means of the system of separate property. In such cases, the property they acquired during their marriage remains the separate property of each of the spouses and there is no need to distribute it according to the rules of the Family and Guardianship Code. Needless to say, spouses whose relations are governed by the system of separate property may still hold joint titles to various rights acquired during (or prior to) their marriage. In such cases, their legal status is regulated by the Civil Code and the fact that they are or have been married to each other is of no significance for their legal position. In such instances they are jointly entitled to various rights just as any other pair of people would be.

However, some rights are subjected *ex lege* to the community property system, even if the system adopted by the spouses with respect to other rights is the system of separate property. Such a situation occurs in cases of some types of rights to apartments in building cooperatives and rights to municipal apartments, i.e. the two most common types of housing in Poland. The inclusion of those rights in the (obligatory) community property is the outcome of specific circumstances of an economic character. Due to the combination of various factors that are characteristic of a state-controlled economy, the market price for the right of ownership to an apartment or a house has always been several times above the official, heavily subsidized price payable for certain types of rights to apartments in building co-operatives or in municipal housing. Needless to say, waiting lists for such apartments have always been very long, since most people simply could not afford to buy an apartment or house at the market price. A right to a co-operative or municipal apartment usually represented the most valuable asset of the married couple, and as such has been included by the legislator in the (obligatory) community property. However, as far as the right to a co-operative apartment is concerned, its inclusion in the (obligatory community property takes place only if such a right was acquired by the spouses during their marriage. Otherwise such a right belongs to the separate property of the entitled spouse and is not subject to any post-divorce division. In turn, the lease of a municipal apartment is always vested in both spouses, even if one of them moved after the marriage to the apartment leased by the other partner before that date.

The fate of the common marital right to an apartment after divorce is subject to the complicated rules laid out in the Supreme Court's 'Housing Guidelines' published in 1978. Simplifying considerably, the right to such an apartment may remain with both spouses, in consequence of the transformation of a joint title into two independent titles, or may be granted to one spouse only. In the latter case, typical for co-operative apartments, such a right is usually vested in a custodial parent (most often the wife), while at the same time she is obligated to return to the other spouse half of the (subsidized) price payable for a similar type of dwelling at the time of divorce (the subsidized price increased by the rate of inflation). However, the other spouse usually retains the licence to stay in the apartment (even if he has never had any title whatsoever to that apartment, e.g. when the right to such an apartment has always belonged to the separate property of the other spouse), unless a custodial parent is able to provide the other spouse with alternative living quarters, which she is usually not able to do for economic reasons. Very often she is not even able to return to the other spouse the price decreed by the court, and, even if she were, the sum would not be high enough to enable the other spouse to rent (on a long-term lease basis), let alone buy, another dwelling outside the subsidized sector. In effect, divorcees are often condemned to living together for many years.

A similar situation occurs even if there are grounds for eviction of the divorced spouse for, according to the law in force, the eviction may not be enforced unless the evicted party has been provided (usually by the state) with alternative living-quarters. Needless to say, the state has no surplus apartments and so eviction orders are not executed. The implementation of the market economy in Poland may render some of these rules inoperative (e.g., those which forbid eviction 'on to the street', those which provide for license to stay in a formerly common apartment even if one has sufficient means to buy another dwelling, or those creating excessive protection for tenants to the disadvantage of private owners of tenement houses). So far, however, the only innovation has been a rise in the prices of co-operative apartments to market levels and a steady decline in the productivity of the building industry, all of this offering rather bleak prospects for the future.

For the couples who adopted a system of community property, divorce marks the beginning of a new arrangement of economic relations. As well as the rules pertaining to a common apartment presented above, other provisions applicable in such a situation are designed to transform the system of family-law community, with its mechanism aiming to protect the economic foundations of the family, into a system of civil-law community that is neutral from the point of view of family protection.

The system of statutory community property is terminated *ex lege* from the date of the divorce decree. All formerly indivisible rights are converted, by the operation of law, into joint-property rights (*pro rata parte*), with equal shares for each of the spouses. There is no need for the court to decide that matter separately in its decree, nor is there any need to specify the proportions of those shares. However, either spouse may, for serious enough reasons, claim to be awarded a greater share in the common property, if his or her contribution to the common property has considerably exceeded that of his or her spouse's. The care for children or home-maker's services are then regarded as equivalent to the breadwinner's contribution; the argument that one of the spouses does not pursue gainful employment (or any other profit-bearing activity) cannot be used to the disadvantage of the home-maker, as long as such a spouse has fulfilled his or her household duties properly. The determination of shares is not a purely arithmetical operation based on the assessment of market or otherwise stated value of respective services and financial contributions, but reflects the equity of the case. Similar evaluation of different types of contribution is performed also on the ground of provisions regulating the duty of marital support during the marriage. Generally speaking, 'grave reasons' should be of an economic character. It follows that fault in causing the breakdown of a marriage does not in itself result in awarding the guilty spouse a smaller share in the matrimonial property. Thus, the property distribution—unlike, to some extent, the alimony allocation—is not meant to be a way of punishing marital misconduct. Therefore, even a solely guilty spouse may be awarded a greater share in the common property if his or her otherwise innocent spouse has not contributed sufficiently to the welfare of the family, either through his or her financial means, or through adequate home-maker services.

The determination of unequal shares in the common property by the court is not possible if the spouses have concluded a contract by virtue of which they extended or reduced the scope of the common property. In such a case the spouses are bound by the stipulations of their contract.[3]

The termination of statutory community does not entail the need to divide the common property of the ex-spouses. Some rights, e.g. the right to an apartment in a co-operative, may belong only to one person or to both spouses. After divorce, such a right has to be allocated to one of the ex-spouses, and under the threat of losing this right, the divorcees may decide to remain co-owners or to remain jointly entitled to other rights. In such instances, their relations are governed by the provisions of the Civil Code. It should also be added that, in principle, the divorce court does not have to decide matters connected with property relations between the litigants (with the exception of alimony). The law provides that the court may dismiss the motion to divide marital property during the divorce trial, should such a division entail excessive delay in divorce proceedings. Most often, divorce courts confine their activities to the division of the common right to an apartment, leaving other matters to a separate trial.

A detailed presentation of civil-law rules governing the division of joint property would require a separate study. Here it is enough to say that if the parties were unable to reach any understanding as to

---

[3] Some authors postulate that the provisions on unequal distribution of shares in the statutory community property should be applied *mutatis mutandis* to the contractual community property system. See e.g. Winiarz (1987: 126).

the way their property is to be divided, the court may allocate such property to one spouse, obligating him or her to pay the other party a percentage of its value, representing the other spouse's share in the common property; the court may also order a partition of co-owned things (subject to certain conditions), or may order the sale of the property by auction. In addition, each of the spouses may demand that the other spouse should reimburse expenses paid and investment made from the common property in favour of his or her separate property, or expenses and investment laid out from the claimant's separate property in favour of the common property. Normally, such reimbursements should be made at the division of the common property; however, if the welfare of the family calls for it, the court may order an earlier repayment.

The division of matrimonial property is confined only to assets. As to debts, the Family and Guardianship Code does not provide any rules which expressly regulate their distribution after the marriage has come to an end. In the absence of such provisions, the general stipulations of the Civil Code apply. In consequence, the liability for debts incurred during marriage is vested only in that spouse who was the party to a given transaction, even if the other spouse profited, directly or indirectly, from that transaction, and irrespective of the fact that prior to divorce such debts, or at least some of them, would have been satisfied from the common property. After divorce, the debtor is obligated to meet such debts from his or her separate property and from his or her share in the formerly common property. Divorce does not significantly change the situation of the ex-spouses if they were both debtors during their marriage. Some minor changes may result from the fact that the formerly indivisible common property is now transformed into jointly owned property, with two distinct shares managed independently by each of the spouses, while before divorce all the important decisions concerning the property required the co-operation of the spouses. However, if only one of them was the debtor, and the debt was in some way connected with the common property, the other spouse leaves the marriage free of liability, even though the proceeds from the transaction may have been accrued in the common property. I do not want to suggest that there are no legal means to amend this situation. To the contrary, doctrines such as unjust enrichment, *pactum in favorem tertii*, and others, may be of some help here. I only wish to stress that if the declared approach is that of equality of the spouses, there is no

reason why the legislator should treat differently the advantages and
disadvantages of marriage, promoting equal distribution of assets but
unequal distribution of debts.

Conclusion

Finally, there comes the question of how to evaluate the Polish legal
approach to the issue of sharing resources in a crisis situation.
Generally speaking, one may agree that what the Code provides for
is indeed a system of sharing resources, and not a system of expropri-
ating property from one spouse to the other spouse, or a system leading to the home-maker's destitution. This is especially true in view of
the fact that the spouses may freely shape their property relations by
means of contract and in this way any extreme situations might satisfactorily be eliminated. Moreover, such contracts, like any other contracts, are subject to the court's examination from the point of view
of fairness and equity. It may be said, on the one hand, that the legislator has equipped the family with a sufficiently wide range of
instruments to shape flexibly the material status of divorcees. On the
other hand, however, the economy of shortage has rendered some of
the rules of sharing property inoperative. For instance, it has always
been very difficult to divide those marital assets that are or have
been in short supply in the market-place. To some extent, economic
reasons may also be held responsible for the lack of attempts to
implant into the Polish legal system the notion of 'new property' and
to divide such property at divorce. To give just one example, there
has been simply no need to assess and divide the value of a prospec-
tive professional career, for in Poland a professional career has thus
far seldom offered rewards exceeding those available for other
employees. This and other such examples will most probably disappear with the progress towards a market economy in Poland. Let us
only hope that in the process of adjusting the system of divorce law
to the changed circumstances, we will not get rid of more than is
necessary, and that we will not venture to return to the notions long
forgotten in most West European countries, especially to the notion
of fault-based divorce.

REFERENCES

Dobranski, B., and Ignatowicz, J. (eds.), *Kodeks Rodzinny i Opiekunczy. Komentarz* (The Family and Guardianship Code: A Commentary). (Warsaw).

Monitor Polski (1988), The Resolution of the Supreme Court of 16 December 1987, no. 6.

Olejniczak, A. (1980), *Materialnoprawne przesłanki udzielenia rozwodu* (Substantive-Law Premises of Granting Divorce) (Poznan).

Piatowski, J. S. (1985) (ed.), *System prawa rodzinnego i opiekunczego* (The System of Family and Guardianship Law) (Wroclaw).

Pietrzykowski, J. (1991) (ed.), *Kodeks rodzinny i opiekunczy z komentarzem* (The Family and Guardianship Code with Commentary) (Warsaw).

Smyczynski, T. (1978), *Obowiązek alimentacyjny rodziców względem dziecka a polityka socjalna państwa* (Parental Duty of Support *vis-à-vis* the Children and Social Policy of the State) (Wroclaw).

Stojanowska, W. (1977) *Problematyka rozwodów w świetle badań* (Divorce in the Light of Empirical Research) (Warsaw).

Szpunar, A. (1981), *Obowiązek alimentacyjny między małżonkami po rozwodzie* (Duty of Support between the Divorcees) Studia Cywilistyczne, vol. 31 (Warsaw).

Winiarz, J. (1987), *Prawo rodzinne* (Family Law) (Warsaw).

Wiszniewski, W. and Gross, S. (1971) in B. Dobrzanski and J. Ignatowicz (eds.), *Kodeks Rodzinny i Opiekunczy. Komentarz* (The Family and Guardianship Code: A Commentary) (Warsaw).

Ziembinski, Z. (1980) *Problemy podstawowe prawoznawstwa* (Basic Problems of Legal Sciences) (Warsaw).

8. Delegalizing Child Support

Mavis Maclean

This chapter begins by examining the background to and the development of the new British system of assessing and enforcing the financial support due from parents to children who do not live with both their parents. It argues that the scheme follows developments in America and Australia, and marks a change from previous policy towards lone parents in the UK. The parental obligation to share income with children living elsewhere is redefined as beyond dispute with respect to liability and amount, both of which become subject to clear rules administered through a semi-privatized agency. The courts are in the main excluded, with a very limited role for marginal cases and appeals on points of law. It is suggested that this marks the development of a desirable social acceptance of the support obligation, but that there is a need for caution when removing areas of dispute from the jurisdiction of the courts. The policy questions addressed were as follows:

(a) on what basis should a child support scheme be constructed?
(b) how should the financial boundaries of responsibility be drawn?
(c) how much money could be collected?
(d) how should responsibility for assessment and collection be divided between an administrative agency and the courts?

The concluding section looks to the future, identifying potential benefits as well as issues for concern which may result from the transfer of child support from the jurisdiction of the courts to the new Child Support Agency.

1. The Political Context for Action

The Child Support Act of 1991 may well be remembered as one of the last pieces of legislative action of the Thatcher administration, bearing the familiar hallmark of rapid progress from the first public-policy announcement in January 1990 to legislative enactment the following July. At the time 'the family', particularly the obligation of family members to provide each other with financial and physical support rather than looking to the state, had become a key political issue as election campaigning began.

The Conservative party which had been in power for over a decade had presented itself as 'the party of the family', resting on three main assumptions. (See Coote, 1990).

(i) That there is one true and natural family type, comprising a father who is the main breadwinner, a mother who provides care, and the children. Other family types are seen as less than perfect.

(ii) That the family is an important site of social control through the exercise of paternal authority. Families without fathers may give rise to social problems, such as juvenile crime.

(iii) That the family is seen as set against the state; it is the main defence of freedom of the individual against the threat of collectivism.

Throughout the 1980s, however, as the proportion of women entering the labour market, the numbers of one parent families, and the number of frail elderly all increased, and traditional family values, interpreted as the responsibility to care for dependent members, came under pressure, the government faced a dilemma. For a Conservative government to take action would contradict its preference for a policy of non-intervention in private family matters. But to encourage families to take responsibility for their own members, including children in one-parent households, the government was compelled to develop strategies for intervention. Emancipation from the culture of 'the nanny state' would require energetic state regulation of family obligations.

The main alternative political voice at the time, the Labour party, took a more pragmatic approach to the changes in family structures. This viewpoint had a less clear picture of the ideal family type, and was more willing both to support family groupings in a variety of forms, and also to enter the 'black box' of the family to protect the interests of vulnerable members particularly women, and children with or without both parents in residence. But the proposals to improve financial support for children in one-parent families would clearly be difficult for any party to criticize. The government had successfully identified an issue of broad popular appeal where there was a real opportunity to work towards improving the lives of children, and at the same time to make savings in public expenditure. It was an attractive proposition.

2. The International Background

(i) *United States*

This renewal of interest in child support in the UK was not an isolated event but, as was the case with other aspects of family law, followed recent developments in the United States. In the 1980s while in the UK we had discussed the problem of spousal support after divorce, inching our way towards a clean break in financial matters (see the Matrimonial and Family Proceedings Act 1984) to accompany the no fault divorce legislation of the early 1970s (Matrimonial Causes Act, 1969), in the United States the debate had shifted towards the problem of supporting children in one-parent households after divorce. Federal legislation was passed to required all states to develop guidelines for courts to use in assessing levels of child support, and the Federal Office for Child Support Enforcement was set up in 1975 to ensure the implementation of decisions made. Large sums of money were at stake. One author (Lieberman, 1986) publicly claimed that American fathers owed their children $4 billion in unpaid child support. Various methods were developed to regulate, in court, decisions which had formerly been a private matter between the parents and their lawyers, concerning the amount the absent parent should pay, whether this should take into account the income of the custodial parent, and the absent parent's new liabilities in the form of a new partner and children of that or a former relationship. These issue were given a new importance in a society where divorce had recently been seen as a decision made by two adults, who had rights to enforce in the division of the property of the marriage, and around whose wishes the children were expected to fit. In Europe levels of child support had traditionally, particularly in Austria and Germany, been based on minimum welfare standards, and related to the income of the absent parent. In the United States however various other models were developed. The most well-known in the UK was the clear though perhaps rather brutal Wisconsin standard developed by Professor Irwin Garfinkel, an expert in both economics and social work, drawing on the studies by Thomas Espenshade of the actual proportion of household income devoted to children living in two-parent households. (See Garfinkel, 1992; and

Espenshade, 1984). The Wisconsin scheme legally required parents to share their income with their children when not living with them in the same way that parents devote income to children with whom they both live. These proportions were found to be 17 per cent for one child, 25 per cent for two children, 29 per cent for three, 31 per cent for four, up to a maximum of 34 per cent for five or more children. The absent parent's (usually father's) gross income was to be attacked, without making any allowance for his personal needs and without any consideration of the income of the caring parent. Alternative schemes developed in other states, including income-pooling schemes which take the income of both parents into account, and in some states, for example Massachusetts, the Tax Department has been brought in to help with collection. But all the American assessment schemes are court based, providing guidelines for the judges to follow. In general, the judges did not appear to regard these guidelines as a limitation on their discretion but welcomed them as a useful tool in dealing with an intractable problem. Collection rates improved, but without achieving any significant improvement in the standard of living of children in one-parent families. As one Illinois judge said, 'Even if I order 50 per cent of nothing, it's still nothing' (Tjaden, Thoeness and Pearson, 1989).

(ii) The Australian Scheme

In 1985 the architect of the Wisconsin scheme, Irwin Garfinkel, was invited to visit Australia, where the government had pledged itself to tackle the problem of child poverty. Five policy objectives had been identified:

1. that non-custodial parents should share the cost of children according to their capacity to pay (an equity-based argument)
2. that there should be adequate support for children (an anti-poverty argument)
3. that there should be minimum state expenditure on collection (a public-policy argument)
4. that work disincentives should be minimized (also a public-policy argument)
5. that procedures should not invade the privacy of the individual (a human-rights argument).

These objectives were clearer and more wide-ranging than the American federal statements about the requirement to share income with children, but not to impede major decisions by the parent such as entering the labour market or repartnering.

Having agreed the objectives, the Australians then had to develop their strategy. Officials raised four questions. Who should collect the payments? Ministers decided that collection must be undertaken by the Tax Office, as only the Inland Revenue Service (IRS) had the relevant expertise to locate absent parents, and whose well-established relationships with employers would facilitate direct collection where necessary. Should the scheme only apply to welfare clients (termed pensioners in Australia)? The Ministry for Social Security argued convincingly that all cases should be included in the new scheme, in order to avoid creating a disincentive to coming off welfare. Should the scheme continue to assess child support levels in court, or seek an administrative procedure for making assessments? Ministers decided in favour of administrative assessment procedures because the court system was already seriously overburdened. Finally decisions had to be made as to how levels should be set, whether a formula could be devised, and if so whether the income of the custodial parent should be taken into account, bearing in mind that the failure to do so had led to political difficulties in Wisconsin concerning the acceptability of the scheme.

The Australian scheme developed so rapidly and with such successful consultation procedures that in the UK we have tended to underestimate the amount of opposition which developed in 1986–7, immediately after the proposals were made public. Non-custodial parents who had not previously been an organized group came together in seeking publicity for their case even to the extent of buying time on commercial television. Lawyers were adamantly opposed to administrative level setting, and concerned about the reduction of discretion in the legal system. Welfare rights groups argued that the scheme was primarily concerned with saving public expenditure on welfare payments and would do little to tackle the problem of poverty in one-parent households. Women's groups objected to the stringent requirements to identify fathers, which were to be relaxed only in cases of violence. The Child Support Scheme was clearly a radical measure, and the decision was therefore taken to implement it gradually in two stages, first collection and only later moving to administrative assessment. The non-custodial parent's maintenance obligation is set at a percentage of his taxable income according to the number of children, after exempting a portion of his income to cover his essential personal expenses equal to the amount of benefit for a single person living alone. If he has repartnered and has children of that marriage then the exemption is set at the welfare allowance for a married man with children. The percentages were based on studies of actual expenditure on children in two-parent households but with some lack of clarity as to how housing costs are taken into account. The impact is considerably modified by being deducted from taxable, not net income as in Wisconsin, by the exemptions for the payor's personal needs, and by setting an upper limit on the amount of assessable income at two and a half times average weekly earnings. Above this level the formula no longer applies, and the matter may be taken to court as before. The income of the parent with care, though taken into account by the scheme, is unlikely to have a direct effect on the absent parent's liability in more than a small minority of cases as it only comes into play when average weekly earnings are exceeded.

The Australian scheme also has two qualifying procedures known as substitution and departure, designed to maintain some of the flexibility of the previous system by which parents could bargain child support in return for a more generous property settlement, or take into account other unusual circumstances. The substitution is limited to 25 per cent of the total value of the child-support award if the caring parent is on welfare. If a caring parent is not on welfare at the time the assessment is made but subsequently becomes dependent on the state, then relief to the absent parent in respect of it may be reduced. This provision has led lawyers to advise absent parents to think very carefully about such substitution arrangements where there is any possibility of the caring parent going onto welfare in the future, and such arrangements are rarely made.

A lone-parent pensioner in Australia is required to use the system, but in other cases where there is no public interest either parent is free to enter the scheme but not obliged to do so. The court option remains as before, but in practice is rarely used, perhaps partly because legal aid is limited and less generous in Australia than the UK for such matters. Stages one and two of the scheme have been evaluated (Harrison, Snider, and Merlo, 1991) and found to be positively appreciated by lone parents who were receiving some real benefit from increased support payments. The non-custodial parents, not surprisingly, were less enthusiastic, expressing concern about the invasion of privacy associated with automatic wage withholding and collection through the Tax Office. But the expected outcry on the issue of access did not materialize on the scale expected.

The Australian Child Support Scheme, though lacking the as yet unimplemented assurance aspect of the Wisconsin scheme, is both more flexible and more sensitive in other ways. As the Australian scheme removed child support decision-making from the courts compulsorily for all welfare clients, it needed to be able to offer a degree of flexibility comparable to that formerly offered within the discretion of the courts. This need underlies the protection of the payor's personal expenses, and those of children he may subsequently father, though excluding the claims of stepchildren. The scheme also tried to avoid the political storms of protest which arose in Wisconsin as a result of not taking into account the caring parent's resources. The acceptance, though limited, of the principles of departure and substitution reduced to some extent the legitimate anxieties of the legal profession, and those concerned with access to justice. The most successful aspect of the scheme was the new use of the national tax collection machinery for enforcement. Although problems remain with the self-employed particularly among the farming community, the Inland Revenue Department had by far the best chance of assessing income and liability, and collecting the money due. The Australian system of annual tax assessment makes available accepted information about the level of the previous year's taxable income, to which the child-support formula can be applied. But despite collection rates of over 90 per cent, the projected savings to the public purse through reduced benefit payments to lone parents are not well documented, and fall far short of the expected totals.

3. The British Background

This chapter began by describing the political launch pad for the child support initiative in the UK in 1990, and showed how action here followed interest in the matter in the United States, where the rights of children to share the income of both their parents, even those living elsewhere, became a matter for federal monitoring, to be enforced in the courts. This national concern with what had formerly been individual decisions developed in the more communitarian Australian setting into a part of the national effort to reduce child poverty and welfare expenditure by regulating and enforcing the allocation of financial support by absent parents to their children largely outside the courts. In the UK the opportunity to help both children and the public purse simultaneously made the child-support issue attractive to the government. The approach taken can be seen as building on American and Australian thinking, and is in marked contrast to recent policy in the UK. The economic problems of one-parent families in the UK had, throughout the 1960s and early 1970s, been discussed in terms of improving public provision. Following the establishment of the Welfare State with universal child benefit paid weekly in cash to the mother since 1945, and the development of health and education services, children in one-parent families were seen as a special case of children for whom extra provision should be made. The social-policy debates of the 1960s were not about how to cut the cost to the state of this group, but how to deliver special help such as free school meals to them without causing embarrassment or stigma by asking for school meals' payments to be made in sealed envelopes handed to the class teacher so that no one could tell which were the empty envelopes of those unable to pay. The majority of children in this situation in the UK had lost a parent through divorce or separation, as compared with the American situation where most children with one resident parent were born to young mothers who had never lived with the father. But nevertheless the majority of British divorced and separated couples were on low incomes, and the men were likely to remarry and have second families. The British approach had been characteristically pragmatic, allowing a man to devote his income to keeping the family he currently lived with, while the first family was supported by the state through the social security system. Lone parents during the 1960s and 1970s had received reasonably generous welfare provision through Supplementary Benefit, the means tested residual welfare allowance, together with the 'passported' associated benefits including free school meals, travel, and clothing grants, and above all good access to subsidized public housing. The mother was not required to register for work until the youngest child reached 16, the school-leaving age.

The part of the system which had not worked well was the court-based maintenance system. Financial arrangements on divorce until the mid-1980s had the appearance of a hang-over from the pre-1969 fault-based divorce, incorporating an extension of the marital dispute between the parties. The greater part of the resources available for transfer between men and women after divorce were discussed under the heading of wife support rather than child support (the exception being those cases where the wife expected to remarry and therefore stood to lose a spousal element but to keep a child-support award). These spousal-support awards retained consideration of the behaviour of the parties in determining amounts right through to the 1986 Matrimonial and Family Proceedings Act. The first British research into the financial consequences of divorce, carried out in the early 1980s (Eekelaar and Maclean, 1986), had indicted that periodical payments after divorce almost always occurred only where there were or had been children of the marriage, and represented support for the caring parent or the parent who had lost the ability to earn through caring for children. Nevertheless these payments were generally thought about as due to the wife. It was common for a court to make an order for the wife and child with no distinction between the two (a reasonable practice if thinking of supporting the wife as a carer, but problematic if the mother were to remarry). Orders for children were low and rarely fully enforced. As recently as 1991, when interviewing solicitors in the study reported by Jackson (Jackson, Wasoff, *et al.*, 1993), it was clear that the solicitors first addressed the issue of housing for all parties, then, if resources permitted they would go on to look at the possibility of spousal support, and finally, if anything was left over or if the wife was likely to remarry, they would consider child support as the last element in the package of ancillary arrangements. There still seemed to be little conception of the child's independent right to support from an absent parent.

During the 1980s interest increased in children as capable individuals, with rights (see Freeman, 1984) as evidenced by the review of law relating to children culminating in the widely discussed and well-researched Children Act of 1989. At the same time research began to show that, during the battle between the interests of men and women after divorce, the interests of children were being overlooked (see Wadsworth *et al.*, 1986, and M. Richards, Ch. 17 in this volume). The issue of child support began to be discussed more widely. As the Matrimonial and Family Proceedings Act went through Parliament, a few voices (e.g. Maclean and Eekelaar, 1986) began to remark on the need to consider the interests of children at divorce. But when this legislation reached the statute book, courts were instructed when making financial arrangements to put the interests of the children first but not paramount: and these interests were not defined, nor was there any indication how they might be promoted or protected.

'Child support' remained politically invisible until the demographic changes taking place began to be documented and discussed. The proportion of lone-parent families in the population had been increasing slowly throughout the 1960s, rising from 6 per cent of all families in 1961 to 8 per cent in 1971. But with the divorce and separation epidemic of the 1970s and the increased number of children born to parents who had never lived together, the proportion had risen to 14 per cent of all families by 1987. Of these lone-parent families an increasing proportion were reliant on state benefit. In 1961 20 per cent of lone-parent families were on Supplementary Benefit, compared with 40 per cent by 1979 and 66 per cent by 1987. The proportion of lone parents in paid work was falling. Only 23 per cent of those interviewed for the recent study by Bradshaw and Millar were in full time work, 17 per cent in part-time work, and of those with a child under 5 less than one in ten worked full time and 13 per cent part time (as compared with 54 per cent of all mothers of dependent children). Social security benefits paid to lone-parent households in 1989/90 exceeded £2 billion (Bradshaw and Millar, 1990).

4. The British Initiative Develops

'In an ideal world we might progress in an orderly way from empirically grounded description, to analytic understanding and to the prescription of a strategy for change' (Rein, 1986). 'In reality analysis and prescription start from action . . . When emergencies arise, we meet them with novel administrative measures, later on we formulate a policy to justify the innovation by interpreting our legislative and administrative experiments . . . on the whole theory follows practice and serves to generalise, justify and rationalise it' (Robert Park, in Rein, 1986). The story of the Child Support Act 1991 exemplifies the above statement(s) to an extraordinary degree. In a lecture organized by the National Children's Homes in January 1990, the then Prime Minister Mrs Thatcher stressed parents' obligations to their children and indicated that the Government was 'looking at ways of strengthening the system for tracing an absent father and making the arrangements for recovering maintenance more effective' (*Independent*, 18 Jan. 1990). She was to say later in the year (*Independent*, 19 July

1990) 'Parenthood is for life'. Public expenditure was rising, and neither the courts nor the Department of Social Security seemed able to stem the tide. In the case of *Delaney* v. *Delaney* (1990 2 FLR 457) the court went so far as to put forward the availability of social security benefit to the first family as a satisfactory reason to reduce the absent parent's liability. The Central Audit Office was criticizing the Department of Social Security (DSS) for failing to pursue liable relatives effectively. The prevailing philosophy of the well-researched and widely approved Children Act was to emphasize the importance of parental rather than public responsibility for children. Action, to be followed by interpretation, might be expected. The Prime Minister set up a working group to consider lone-parent maintenance.

Rising rates of marital dissolution, falling marriage and remarriage rates, and an increased birth rate outside marriage could be interpreted in any number of ways, from the dissolution of society to increased exercise of individual freedom of choice. But the cost of this freedom could be seen to fall disproportionately on the mothers and children involved, with implications for public expenditure, thus inviting a policy response. The economic costs of child rearing have always been met from a variety of sources: parents, the wider kin network, the employer through the family wage, and the state through welfare transfers. But the balance between these sources was giving rise to concern. The state had come to accept the greater part of the costs of the majority of lone parents. Research had shown the contribution of absent parents to be small, support from the wider family network to have reduced, and the contribution from employers to be limited by the barriers to the employment of lone parents, particularly lack of child care and the low level of female earnings. In addition there are structural obstacles to making the best use of the various elements available to construct an income package arising partly from income-support rules which do not facilitate the transition from welfare dependency to part-time or full-time work. A comprehensive review of all the elements in the resource package was desirable.

A number of interest groups had different priorities. The poverty lobby was concerned with the low income over long periods experienced by children in lone-parent households (on average 5 years), with consequent adverse effects on their educational attainments and future earning capacity. Women's groups were concerned with the unequal outcomes for men and women of caring for children after divorce or separation. Men's groups, particularly those representing remarried men attempting to support two households, sought to end long-term spousal or family support. The Family-values groups sought to strengthen family ties, prevent divorce, and enhance parental responsibilities. All of these groups argued their cases forcefully in the media. But it is important to recognize that 'government' and 'Whitehall' are also complex entities with important interests operating within government departments, each with their own agenda and different spheres of influence. For example, the concern of the Treasury to control public spending is no secret, nor is the extent of its influence. The concern of the DSS to meet welfare needs but to discourage welfare dependency is also clear, and as a department with a large and increasing budget they do need to consider costs. The Lord Chancellor's Department, in the middle of a rolling review of family law, has child-centred objectives, a concern that the law should not be unnecessarily involved in family matters, and a need to control spending on legal aid.

The Prime Minister's policy statement made it clear that enforcement of parental responsibility was the government's primary objective. The issues of child poverty, equity between mothers and fathers, and legal costs were of interest, but of lesser importance. But within this primary aim a number of issues can be identified, requiring consideration to establish a reasoned framework capable of being put into effect for the assessment and collection of child support.

5. The Main Policy Issues

(i) On what basis should a child-support scheme be constructed?

What do children cost, and how should these costs be apportioned? The separate elements which can be held to constitute a child-support award include subsistence costs, actual expenditure, the costs of child care, and the opportunity costs of child rearing including earnings forgone by the caring parent. *Subsistence costs* represent the costs which must be spent on bringing up a child, related mainly to a basic diet, and adequate clothing. This is the kind of assessment used in setting levels of subsistence welfare payments such as the scale rates for children on Income Support. Such figures tend to assume that housing costs are already met. *Actual expenditure* represents the level of expenditure required to keep a child in a certain environment. Thus the average cost of a child in a middle-income household is considerably higher than the average cost of a child in a low-income household. *Costs of child care* are usually omitted from calculations of the actual costs of raising children, but are important as they increase significantly in a lone-parent household where the primary carer is likely to seek work, and where she lacks the most common source of substitute care, i.e. the other parent. *Opportunity costs of child rearing*, the major impact of a child on its parent's standards of living, arises not from direct but from indirect costs, and in particular from the mother's loss of income following her withdrawal from paid work. The average mother of two children in the UK spends three years out of paid work and a further four years in part-time work. It has been calculated that, if she has completed seven years of secondary education but has no further qualification, she loses a total £135,000 in earnings and promotion forgone over her working life, excluding her loss of pension entitlement (Joshi, 1985).

None of the formulae used in the USA and in Australia took account of all these elements. Some of those based on actual expenditure, e.g. in Australia, made some notional adjustment for increases in child care after separation. But no formula took into account the opportunity costs of child rearing. These, when dealt with at all, tended to come under the heading of property adjustment on divorce, when a house might be considered as compensation for lost earnings or pension rights. The US and Australian formulae, based on proportion of actual expenditure devoted to children in an intact family, worked well with respect to covering both subsistence needs and a share in the actual living standards of the parents. But this approach assumes that the entire income of both parents is still available to be shared with the child after one household has divided into two and thereby acquired additional basic expenses. In addition, there are problems when considering the entitlement of any second family. If a man's first set of children are entitled to share his income in a fixed ratio, why does this not apply also to any children of a subsequent relationship? If he must pay, for example, 25 per cent of his income to the children of a first marriage, this then leaves him able to devote only 25 per cent of 75 per cent of his income to a second family. Is this equitable between all the children of the same father? One American formula does attempt to deal with this problem by dividing the income-sharing process into two stages, allocating first a basic sum, called a 'primary child support obligation' for each parent, and then, if further resources are available, making a standard of living adjustment to enable the child to share in any additional resources his parents may have. This is a valuable distinction. In addition, all the formulae appeared to have difficulty in dealing with housing costs. These are referred to as one of the elements to be considered in the American guidelines and they are taken into account by the Australian formula, though it is not clear exactly how. Any discussion of the property arrangement leads into the issue of equitable arrangements between the adults and away from the specific concern with child support. The question of whether child support should be assessed without any reference to other issues, as an absolute entitlement, is a key issue, and one which can be addressed by considering a division between basic child support and additional payments to be made where resources permit.

(ii) How should the financial boundaries of responsibility be drawn?

The White Paper, Children Come First (1990), adopted the strategy of basing the child-support assessment on a basic inescapable minimum entitlement, which no absent parent or interest group could object to. The question of how to deal with any additional resources could be dealt with later, and either left within the existing system or covered by new arrangements. A 'basic child-support obligation' could be based on the levels of income agreed by Parliament in social-security legislation as the levels below which no member of society should be permitted to fall, i.e. the Income Support scale rates for means-tested benefit. Any amount assessed, however basic, would be based on the resources of both parents in accordance with the view that both parents retain responsibility for their children regardless of their own legal relationship. But any assessment would require certain devices to correct the blunt imposition of a standard deduction, first to take some account of the absent parent's expenses and, in particular, new calls on his resources. To prevent the payment of child support to a first family leading to poverty in a second family there is a need to protect the living standard of the second family. Questions arise here as to how that second family is defined, for example, does it include a new partner, married or not, new children of the relationship, children new to the liable partner? Are the resources of other members of that family to be taken into account, and to what degree?

The question of whether the child-support obligation from parent to child is finite and individual, or whether it is inextricably bound up with the overlapping responsibilities of families with members in different households remains a central concern. The solution devised, termed the 'protected income', was developed in response to concern about stepchildren and children treated as children of the family. The means of the second household were to be assessed as for income support, and its resources were to be protected from assessment for child support with the aim of maintaining that household sufficiently above income support levels to keep a sufficient incentive for the breadwinner to remain in employment. As we noted above, the traditional British approach had been to allow the man to keep his present family, and for the state to support the first. The White Paper proposal to put the basic child-support obligation to the *first* family *first* marked a significant change in our policy, and is likely to alter the balance towards first families. If the custodial parent has a high income, or repartners with someone with a high income, a policy issue arises about whether to look at the resources of the individual custodial parent, as parent, or whether to regard her, if remarried, as part of a couple whose resources should be taken into account, or whether to look at the resources of the household in which the child is living as a whole. In any welfare context, dealing with urgent and basic needs, the response is traditionally for a means-tested benefit to look at the *de facto* household. In contribution-based social insurance, legal relationships between household members, e.g. whether they are married or cohabiting, begin to affect the outcome. But in private family law individual entitlements are the primary focus. In family law when dealing with claims between individuals there is a greater scope for dealing with individuals as individuals, for example when assessing a husband's responsibility towards a former wife. Making individual decisions, most commonly about taking into account the new responsibilities of a former husband and the new assets of a remarried first wife, has been the traditional skill of the courts. But even in court-based family law it has been increasingly difficult to continue to treat post-divorce support on an individualized basis, and the court is often concerned in practice with family support rather than child or spousal support.

As we began to bring together legal and social-security approaches to child support these apparently minor questions of definition were in fact of fundamental importance to the structures being created, and it may have been difficult for the different departments involved to understand just how widespread the implications of these definitional decisions would be. These decisions reveal a great deal about our attitudes to changing family structures, first and second marriages, the relationship between parents and stepchildren, by setting firm limits on financial responsibilities and drawing the boundaries of family obligations. The issue debated in the early 1980s was whether or not the second wife's income should be taken into account when assessing the husband's alimony. The courts produced the elegant device of not assessing the second wife's resources, but taking into account their impact on the needs and resources of the husband. This issue has become of historical interest only with the growing acceptance that wives have no permanent call on their ex-partner's resources in their capacity as wives rather than mothers, but it illustrates the infinite capacity of the courts to produce subtle and complex guidance. When devising a new rule for use in an administrative context no such subtlety can be employed. The boundaries of financial responsibility need to be defined, with the result in this case that, where the need to protect a household arose, the household had to be considered. But where the issue was the allocation of extra resources, then it was preferable to focus on the individual relationship between parent and child.

(iii) How much money could be transferred?

Research had shown that many lone parents were likely to be poor—but so were the men with whom they had lived or had had children. Bradshaw and Millar reported that one third of the lone parents who did not seek further funding from the absent parent took no action because they knew he had no funds (Bradshaw and Millar, 1990). As long ago as 1980 one third of the divorced men interviewed in the Oxford study were unemployed. There was no evidence of a pot of gold waiting to be collected (Eekelaar and Maclean, 1986). Although the DSS hoped that an effective child-support scheme would produce considerable savings on welfare expenditure, similar hopes in Australia have been disappointed so far.

At what level should an effective child-support payment be pitched? The scales for Income Support rates provide a good starting-point, but these scales are immensely complex. It might have been possible simply to seek the basic welfare or Income Support allowance for the child or children in question. But as argued above such a subsistence payment is not by itself a satisfactory basis for child support. One could argue also for taking actual expenditure levels, but no UK studies were available on this matter, particularly for the costs of child care and the opportunity costs of child rearing. The Income Support scale could, however, reflect those two elements. The personal allowance for a lone parent with care of a dependent child/children was included as a minimum contribution which recognizes her(his) inability to earn or, if earning, the need to pay for substitute child care. And the Family Premium, with an addition for one-parent families, recognizes the more general 'overhead' costs of bringing up children.

The White Paper, therefore, recommended a broader construction of the child-support obligation to include the overhead and indirect costs, albeit at a minimum level, of raising children. This important decision immediately and significantly raised the sums of money involved to a level which, even with a protected household income and protected actual housing costs, the absent parent on average earnings would have serious difficulty in meeting in full. A minimum payment equal to the Income Support scale rate for a child, at that time just under £12 for one child under 11, seemed incontrovertible and collectable, and required no information other than the fact of paternity and parental absence. But the broader definition of child support in reality meant lone parent *household* support, which was the relevant unit for the Department of Social Security to approach the issue from the benefit-paying perspective. If they were to have any success in reducing the welfare bill, then they must be able to float lone-parent families off benefit and into employment. The larger the portable income in the hands of the lone parent the more likely she would be to take the step of entering the labour market. And furthermore, Income Support assessments are made and paid according to household needs and means. The basic maintenance obligation was, therefore, construed as owed by an absent parent to the lone parent *household*. The obligation was held to consist of the Income Support scale rate not only for any children, but also for the lone parent. Inclusion of the lone parent's personal allowance was held to represent her need for income if she was taking care of the children, and to recognize her extra child-care costs if she were in work. Furthermore her allowance was not related to whether or not she had repartnered, as would have been the case under any court-based award of maintenance to an ex-wife, the only category of lone parent covered by family law. This new proposal was revolutionary in its application to all lone parents, later to be termed 'parents with care', regardless of past or present marital or cohabiting status. The DSS has bitter experience of trying to establish who lives with whom, and how household finances are arranged. In this instance the incentive to discover these facts was absent. For benefit-paying purposes there is a clear incentive for the DSS to count all available resources before awarding benefit but, in this cases, the payor is not the Department. The DSS is, on the contrary, the beneficiary in cases where a lone parent is on benefit, as is the case for two out of three lone parents. So ease of administration fitted with the laudable and sophisticated aim of accepting the economic penalties of motherhood, or being the primary care-giving parent, which persist whether or not the parent subsequently repartners. This part of the obligation was to continue until the youngest child in question reached 16.

The consequence of this decision as indicated above was to greatly increase the level at which child support was to be assessed. Instead of the £15 to £25 per week most often ordered by the courts the White Paper now discussed amounts of £50 or £60 per week, which would not be universally payable in full. The obligation would need to be met by the absent parent paying a percentage of his income until the bill for his former family was met as fully as possible. After that had been done, then a further standard of living element would be sought from him. This could be achieved through the courts as before, given that under the former regime it was largely the smaller payments which had been so difficult to enforce, but was finally done by an addition to the formula. Alternatively, varying levels of payment according to income bands, and according to the number of children, could have been adopted, for example, 25 per cent for one child, 30 per cent for two, 35 per cent for three, up to a maximum of 50 per cent, the 'rate of take' at which it was thought there would no longer be an incentive to remain in work. Other jurisdictions generally relate amount paid to the number of children involved. But in the White Paper the assumption was that, if 50 per cent of assessable income (bearing in mind the procedures to protect the standard of living of the payor and his present household) could be contributed to meet the maintenance obligation without depriving an absent parent of the incentive to work, then it should be paid by *all* absent parents until their obligation to the first household had been met. After this obligation had been met in full, if additional resources were available, then these could be 'attacked' at the lower rate of 25 per cent.

Concerns were expressed from an early stage in the development of the new scheme for making child-support awards more effective about the possible 'knock-on' effects of increasing levels of child-support on the arrangements made for the family home on divorce. Our own research (see Jackson, 1991) showed that when a solicitor first sees a client seeking divorce the first decisions to be made concern the house, and where the children are to live. The absent parent 'the goose who lays the golden egg', must also be satisfactorily housed. Then attention turns to arrangements for child support, and, if resources permit, to spousal support. More often, however, the spousal element will be found within the housing deal, which can serve to compensate a wife for the lack of personal pension rights forgone as a result of having children and no history of continual employment, and also the loss of access to a share in the man's pension. But, of course, there are cases where more resources will be sought as child support rather than wife support where remarriage of the wife is imminent, or where the spousal side will be emphasized, when children are approaching 18. Any new scheme could include some mechanism for substitution or departure from any formula, as is the case in Australia, to enable individuals to make the most effective use of their resources according to their own priorities, for example, to remain in the family home albeit with a low income. It was generally expected that a new scheme would restrict such choices where there was a welfare benefit in payment, and accept the legitimacy of compulsion where a public interest was involved. But where this was not the case there seemed no reason why the individuals should not continue to make choices about the best use of their own resources.

We now have in the UK a substantial number of home owners who are in receipt of welfare payments. Home ownership has spread down the income scale, particularly with the sale of council housing in the 1970s and 1980s. High interest rates, falling property values, and increased unemployment, have resulted in a number of cases where the equity in a family home is negative, the house cannot be sold, and the owner is on benefit. In these cases the present practice is for the absent parent to walk away from the house and mortgage which simply represent a millstone around his neck, and to leave the wife and children in the home where, if she is on Income Support, the DSS will, for a time, meet the mortgage interest repayments. We were concerned that increased child-support payments could make it more difficult for a man to leave the first family in their home, and make him more likely to seek his share of even a very small equity. In addition, if the new portable child-support income helped the wife to come off Income Support and into part-time work, then she and the children would lose the security of having the mortgage interest payments met by the DSS. There are, of course public-policy concerns about making cash transfers to property owners. But in a housing market which lacks acceptable low-cost rented housing, the alternative for some of these families may be homelessness, with the extremely high costs of very low-quality bed and breakfast accommodation being met by local authorities.

The solution to this problem in the White Paper was to include the absent parent's actual housing costs in the income to be discounted when assessing the child support to be paid. In this way the man's housing needs were included in the child-support assessment process, while still maintaining the primacy of the parental obligations.

The Formula

Public discussion of the coming changes has centred on the introduction of 'the formula' for child support. This paper has indicated the path taken through the series of policy decisions to be made. The formula does no more than encapsulate these decisions and is therefore presented only briefly here.

The premiss is that all parents have an obligation to maintain their children.

The obligation to a household including a child with an absent parent is made up of the Income Support scale rate:

for the children
for the caring parent if any child is under 16
plus Family Premium
plus Long-Parent Premium (if 'she' has not repartnered)
minus Child Benefit.

This sum is to be met proportionately from the assessable income of both parents (but with the caring parent affecting the absent parent's liability rather than the lone parent being expected to make a payment).

Assessable income is income net of tax and National Insurance contributions, actual housing costs, and the Income Support Welfare scale rates for the absent parent and any biologically legitimate children in his household.

He will not be asked to bring his present household below a protected-income level, based on Income Support levels, plus a small margin to act as a work incentive.

He must pay 50p in the pound of his proportion of the basic maintenance requirement. This is calculated at 50 per cent of his assessable income divided by total assessable income, multiplied by the total needed to pay the maintenance bill. If there is additional assessable income after this has been paid, he will contribute 25p in the pound until the basic requirement for the children has been met three times over.

For example:

If the Maintenance Requirement (MR) is £50, the Assessable Income (AI) needed to meet it is £100.

If his AI is £120 and her AI is £30,

his AI for MR is $^{120}/_{150} \times 100$ of which he pays half = £40

her AI for MR is $^{30}/_{150} \times 100$ of which she is liable for half = £10.

He has additional AI of £40 of which he pays £10;

she has additional AI of £10 of which she is liable for £2.50.

Total maintenance payable by the absent parent is £50 per week.

(w) Collection: The relationship between courts and the new agency

We have now considered the structure of the new scheme, the amounts to be sought, and how they are justified, and the devices designed to maximize collection and minimize the range of decisions to be taken before an assessment can be made, particularly by excluding from the process many of the issues which take up a great deal of effort in the legal process such as the behaviour of the parties, whether they are remarried, and how the child-support amount should be set in relation to the other elements in a bargain or package including housing and spousal compensation. In short, the Child Support Agency seeks to recoup as far as possible from the absent parent the cost of the lone-parent family to the state. In the UK the Inland Revenue Department has from time to time been asked to undertake the collection of monies due to the government other than tax revenue, e.g. the collection of fines. The Department has traditionally resisted such demands, on the grounds that this could erode its efficiency as a tax-collection agency. In this particular case, to be asked to approach large numbers of people on low incomes for small sums which they might be very angry about having to pay was clearly a difficult assignment. In the end the responsibility for collection was accepted by the DSS, whose Liable Relative Officers already have a close working relationship with local tax offices.

The question of departmental responsibility for the operation of the new scheme was complex. The Lord Chancellor introduced the legislation in the House of Lords. But more and more of the day-to-day responsibilities were clearly accruing to the DSS, the department with the incentive to demonstrative that it was paying serious attention to schemes which might cut its outgoings. It is normally extremely difficult for the DSS to make savings without appearing to harm the neediest sections of the community. This was a splendid opportunity for the department to both save money and do good. It was therefore proposed in the White Paper that the new child-support arrangements should be put into effect by a new Agency, not a direct government department but a 'next steps' (i.e. semi-privatized) agency, responsible to the Secretary of State for Social Security. The nature of the assessments being planned, involving large numbers of small items of information to be processed according to strict rules lent itself well to computerization. Seven banks of main-frame computers are now ready for action. The staff of the new agency have been given some new powers of discovery, in order to investigate the means of the absent parents, or 'liable relatives' as they were traditionally called within the DSS. Some of these powers, to enter premises where it was thought such a person might be earning money and to interview people found there (at one point without even any age limit), led to these officers being described in the House of Lords as a new 'Gestapo'. But their discovery work could well be a more effective way of collecting this financial information than the present scheme whereby the solicitors for both sides argue and delay on each point. If so, this could relieve some pressure on the legal-aid fund, but only if the information becomes available to both parties.

In sum, the DSS had successfully devised a reverse benefit, in response to the pressure put on them to deal more effectively with the old intractable and underfunded liable-relative problem. Why should the hard-pressed taxpayer, perhaps with children of his own, pay the bills for men who could support their absent children directly, at least in part, particularly if by so doing some parents with care might be able to return to paid work which many of them seemed to want to do. There could be problems in collecting the large number of items of information from both sides necessary for an assessment to be made, particularly as one party might challenge the information given by the other (a new experience for the DSS), and because every case was to be regularly reviewed. Nevertheless, it is clear why the Department of Social Security, the Prime Minister, and the pressure group for one-parent families were enthusiastic.

Many of the assumptions underlying the development so far have been appropriate for dealing with welfare cases. It would have been possible to restrict the new scheme to cases where there is a welfare involvement. Such an option was discussed in Australia. It was rejected there, and for similar reasons it was rejected here, as it was not thought desirable to have one scheme for the rich and another for the poor. There is the additional problem that the welfare population is not constant. Lone parents are very likely to be on benefit at some point, particularly immediately after the birth of a baby where parents do not form a household, and at the point of separation for those who did, and it is possible that they will leave benefit either through re-entering the labour market or through repartnering. It is important therefore that any new child-support scheme places no obstacles to movement on to benefit from the clients' perspective, or off it from the government's point of view. There are practical as well as ideological reasons for a universal scheme.

But there are problems with a universal approach when defining the responsibilities for collection by the courts and the agency. It became clear, as discussion about enforcement of the new assessments progressed, that the government expected the scheme to apply to *all* lone parents and liable relatives. In the USA all child-support guidelines were introduced in court as rebuttable presumptions before becoming compulsory. As the process took place in court there was always the possibility of judicial interpretation or intervention, within the safeguards offered by due process. In Australia the formula assessment was compulsory for welfare cases and optional for others, and maintained some opportunity for private negotiation under the department and substitution clauses. In the UK the new scheme was designed to cover *all* cases of child support, and was to be administered *entirely* by the new Agency. The relationship with the courts was to be determined by the principle of parallel jurisdiction. Where the Child Support Agency had jurisdiction the court had none, and where the court had jurisdiction the Agency would have none. There was to be no overlap. The Agency was the preferred and only arena for dealing with child support, except in the clearly defined special circumstances of disabled children with special needs, stepchildren, and if private-school fees were to be negotiated. There was to be NO ACCESS to the court for child-support matters, even as part of a consent order dealing with the whole package of arrangements to be made on divorce. This was indeed a radical proposal. It has yet to be fully understood by the legal and related professions, such as accountants specializing in divorce-related financial advice. It may also be taken to give rise to issues of access to justice, in that parties with a dispute about how to arrange their financial affairs after divorce may consider themselves to be prevented from bringing this dispute before a court of law for resolution. A decision had to be made as to whether disputes arising from child-support assessments would pass to the courts or be dealt with by procedures of review and tribunal, internal to the Agency as is the case with other social-security benefits. The arguments were finely balanced, and the legislation reflects a note of caution in that disputes are to be dealt with internally but the Lord Chancellor retains the right to make orders in future to return such matters to the courts. Given the pressure on the court system and on legal-aid budgets for family matters, it is unlikely that such a course of action will be taken unless the proposed system proves to have serious defects. There are, however, some worrying aspects of the proposed tribunal system, which will be run by the Independent Tribunal Service. The Child Support Appeal Tribunals will look very like other social-security tribunals. The nature of the dispute they are dealing with, however, will be rather different. Instead of dealing with a dispute between a claimant and the Department, where the tribunal effectively offers a speedy and accessible mechanism for the 'little man' to confront the 'departmental leviathan', in the case of child support there will be two parties, who may be hostile, and where economic imbalance is the rule, with no legal aid. The DSS, with experience only of benefit disputes, may have failed to give due consideration to the different nature of child-support disputes which in divorce cases may have knock-on effects on decisions being made in court about property.

Many points of detail remain to be resolved. This is inevitable when an important matter is removed from the court system where an individualized and complex solution is produced for each case but where the burden of enforcement rests on the individual recipient, and placed in the context of a benefit system where the Department has control of the proceedings, due process is not in the frame, and administrative rules are available to cover every contingency. The DSS aims to deliver a speedy and efficient service, according to its own regulations. Justice, either in the abstract or in the concrete form of access to representation and a hearing based on full information and a decision made, may be a different matter.

6. Further Issues Arising

Was change necessary? It would be difficult to find an area of public policy which is beyond improvement, and financial support from absent parents to children living elsewhere was certainly irregular and inadequate, contributing to poverty in lone-parent households, and to pressure on the courts and the legal-aid budget. There was clearly a case for change, and I applaud the move which took the payment of a basic sum in child support out of the realm of negotiation and into the realm of a fixed duty. As such, placing the process of assessment and enforcement in the hands of an administrative agency makes sense, as does the inclusion of a substantial amount for the caring parent within the basic child support, i.e. the acceptance of the indirect as well as the direct costs of child-rearing which now fall on the parent with care. The separation between the amount of the child-support obligation, which is universal, and the payable amount, which is personal, tempered by the payor's ability to pay (including protection for the payor and his household), is neat and appropriate. But there are difficulties, some of which may have arisen from the speed with which the scheme was devised and the determination of the government to extract every last penny from liable relatives through the scheme instead of seeing it as one way of asserting the parental obligation to support, which may be met in a number of ways if the approach of making best use of the resources available is followed.

The Act is revolutionary in the way it takes an area of dispute out of the courts and places it in the hands of a next-steps agency, with its own review procedures in case of dispute, and with recourse to tribunals. It is vital that the Agency is fully answerable to Parliament through questions in the House to the Secretary of State for Social Security, and not just by placing a copy of its annual report before the House. It is vital that the Agency is properly resourced with trained staff capable of using their considerable powers for discovery and assessment efficiently, and that the tribunals are able to accept all disputed cases and deal with them speedily and effectively, particularly as there is unlikely to be any legal aid for representation. There are some built-in problems, in particular the welfare penalty for mothers who fail to identify the father without just cause (i.e. fear of violence, or abuse). It seems impossible that any reduction of benefit to households with children can avoid harming those children whose interests this Act claims to put first. We could have followed the American precedent of requiring a lone parent to co-operate with the Agency, which is not necessarily the same as giving a name. We could also have varied the 'rate of take' according to the number of children, which might have made the scheme more acceptable to the ordinary citizen. And we could have retained a procedure for 'departure and substitution', to permit complex deals about the house to be negotiated. Following Australian experience, these would rarely have been used, but their existence would have provided a safety valve, and increased the acceptability of the scheme to the legal profession.

There will be difficulties to iron out over the transitional phase, but hopefully of a short-term nature. The majority of problems of a more intractable nature are likely to spring from the relationship between the Agency and the courts. The role of law in relation to the family is often said to be in crisis: that the law is rolling back, that the family is being delegalized, or privatized. The law is clearly less concerned with telling adults how they should behave, e.g. whom they should marry, or when they may divorce. But at the same time there is increased regulation of the consequences of individual actions, particularly where public consequences follow private actions. In this context, we are moving rapidly towards administrative divorce, but we are regulating tightly the payment of child support, with draconian powers of search and discovery and with the sanction of imprisonment for those who fail to comply. This removal of an entire section of divorce arrangements from the hands of lawyers coincides with the resurgence for ideological .and economic reasons of alternative dispute resolution in divorce, that is, the development of mediation and in particular comprehensive mediation which covers financial as well as child-related matters. No wonder the legal profession is nervous and hostile to the Child Support Act. But setting aside these professional anxieties, there is a real concern about the loss of flexibility in decision-making, perhaps without very much to gain by way of clarity about the income. For although the new system has very precise rules, their application depends on the input of so many small items of information that the actual result is possibly even more difficult to predict than the decisions of deputy judges, or the solicitors who bargained in their shadow.

Winners and losers

The new scheme is likely to produce perhaps £40 per week in child support rather than £15 per week for the average family. It is entirely to be applauded that the provisions apply to all children and not only to those whose parents had at some time been married. Looked at in isolation (apart from the welfare penalty) the scheme looks splendid. But it will have to function in a world where the housing market gives rise to concern about the knock-on effects on access to accommodation, where the labour market gives little ground for optimism about the numbers of lone parents who will be able to enter paid work, and where cuts in resource allocation raise doubts about the ratio of money spent to money collected.

It is inevitable that there cannot be immediate confidence in an Act where so little appears in the primary legislation, and so much depends on the drafting of regulations, the quality of the agency staff, and the response of the judges in protecting the housing interests of lone parents. To be pessimistic, it is difficult to see how we could do much *worse* than at present for the vast majority of low-income cases. At best we could have a quick and efficient method of resolving the financial consequences of lone parenting which might encourage the development of easier ways of regulating other ancillary arrangements on divorce and even separation.

Wherever we find ourselves between these two points there is no doubt that we have taken a major step towards bringing support for children with an absent parent to the forefront of attention; child support has been redefined as a right, beyond individual negotiation. If it has been done at the expense of access to the courts for dispute resolution, the price will have been a heavy one.

REFERENCES

Bradshaw, J. and Millar, J. (1990), *Lone Parents*, Report to DSS, London, DSS.

Coote, A. (1990), *The Family Way* (London, IPPR).

Eekelaar, J. and Maclean, M. (1986), *Maintenance after Divorce* (Oxford, OUP).

Espenshade, T. (1984), *Investing in Children*, Washington, DC, Urban Institute Press.

Freeman, M. (1984) (ed.), *State, Family and the Law* (London, Tavistock).

Garfinkel, I. (1992), 'Child Support Trends in the United States', in L. Weitzman and M. Maclean (eds.), *Economic Consequences of Divorce* (Oxford, OUP).

Harrison, M., Snider, G., Merlo R. and Luciano, V. (1991), *Paying for the Children*, Melbourne.

HMSO (1990), *Children Come First*, Cm. 1263.

Jackson, E., Wasoff, F., with Maclean, M. and Dobush, R. (1993), 'Financial Support on Divorce: The Right Mixture of Rules and Discretion', *International Journal of Law and the Family*.

Joshi, H. (1985), *Motherhood and Employment*, Occasional Paper No. 34 (OPCS, London).

Lieberman, J. (1986), *Child Support in America* (London, Yale University Press).

Maclean, M. and Eekelaar, J. (1984), *Children and Divorce: The Economic Factors* (CSLS, Oxford).

Rein, M. (1986), *From Policy to Practice* (OUP, Oxford).

Tjaden, P., Thoeness, N. and Pearson, J. (1989), 'Will These Children be Adequately Supported?', *Judges Journal*, Fall, 28/4: 4–10.

Wadsworth, M. and Maclean, M. *et al.* (1986), 'Children of Divorced and Separated Parents', *Family Practice*, 7/1.

9. The Social Problem of Child Abuse in Poland: The Conflict between Privacy and Control

Robert Sobiech

It is not easy for the average citizen to understand why so many social problems which he sees in his everyday life are not met by a proper response from competent institutions. Similar astonishment arises from the fact that substantial resources are used to solve problems of minor significance, and some matters are tackled without there being any real need to intervene. People expecting effective solutions will certainly not be satisfied by assertions that converting their complaints into appropriate social policies is a complicated process, barely recognized as necessary and not easily modified from the outside. A number of sociologists think the process of defining social problems is highly selective and leaves many forms of social evil hidden from the public eye. Converting a private problem into a public issue depends, among other things, on complicated configurations of political factors, group interests, forms of social activity, and the institutional background. Studies of how social problems are created, legitimized, and solved can, therefore, provide not only practical knowledge of use in particular social-policy developments but also valuable information about the functioning of the wider social reality.

The subject of this chapter is to what degree children, the weakest family members, are protected by the law. I think we can attempt to answer this question by presenting the extent to which children's rights are encroached upon, as well as considering the public and institutional response. The problem of child abuse seems to illustrate well the question we are dealing with.

Is there a social problem of child abuse in Poland today? It is not easy to answer this. Most theoretical conceptions applied by sociologists assume that the appearance of a social problem is determined both by objective conditions and by the state of social awareness (Becker, 1966; Spector and Kutsuse, 1977). One of the most often cited definitions of a social problem is a condition which is defined by a considerable number of persons as a deviation from some norm which they cherish. Every social problem consists of an objective condition and subjective definition. The objective condition is a verifiable situation whose existence and magnitude can be checked . . . by impartial and trained observers. . . . The subjective definition is the awareness of certain individuals that the condition is a threat to certain cherished values (Fuller and Myers, 1944).

When basing assumptions on existing statistical data, which are normally one of the basic sources of information for advocates of the objective approach, it is difficult to evaluate honestly the extent of the phenomena of child abuse. Judicial statistics employ general categories, enabling assessments of limited precision. In the 1970s and 1980s, for example, the number of those convicted of having sexual intercourse with persons under 15 years of age (Article 176 of the Penal Code) did not exceed 600 cases (about 0.3 per cent of all convictions). A much higher number of convictions—about 10,000 a year (or 6 per cent of all convictions) refer to the crimes of physical and moral ill-treatment of family members (Article 184 of the Penal Code) (Statystyka Sadowa). Studies of these sorts of crime show that the most common objects of violence are women. Acts of aggression towards children took place in 25 per cent of cases (Ratajczak, 1980).

Information about the extent of the phenomenon cannot be obtained from the Health Service either. Only rarely does the professional medical literature publish statistics of physical aggression towards children or their sexual abuse. In a surgery at Jaroslaw, for example, 71 cases of battered children were recorded in the 1970s and in a surgical clinic in Lublin, the number of such cases numbered 22 in the years 1974–81 (Czyz, 1986).

The analysis of fragmentary statistical data may suggest that child abuse in Poland is a marginal phenomenon and does not deserve much publicity or social-policy interest. Such a conclusion appears to be negated by the voices of a few experts who try to describe the true reality. In the surgeons' opinion, based on their hospital experience, one in a thousand patients show features characteristic of the battered child syndrome, a rate equal to that in the USA or Western Europe (Mossakowska, 1987). A more convincing proof which confirms the dimensions of the problem is provided by the results of the few surveys carried out by psychologists. A poll by Piekarska in the mid-1980s showed that children were beaten in 82 per cent of families. Nearly 40 per cent of parents questioned admitted they gave their children 'a sound thrashing', and 44 per cent used a belt or other objects for this purpose. It is worth stressing that these studies were exclusively concerned with families enjoying high economic and social status and living in one of the best Warsaw housing estates. The widespread use of violence towards children is also attested by interviews with children who ran away from their homes, 97 per cent of whom gave as one of the dominant reasons for their decision to escape the desire to avoid severe corporal punishment applied by their parents (Piekarska, 1987). The divergence between official statistics and experts' conclusions is striking.

Researchers into social problems make clear that accumulating statistical evidence and its public presentation are one of the most effective ways to legitimize a problem. Collecting information about objective conditions is also characteristic of the institutionalization phase of a social problem, when it becomes of interest to competent agencies. Relatively small numbers of registered cases and a lack of specific categories that would register the range of child abuse make us think that this phenomenon has not yet been defined as a social problem in Poland. This thesis is confirmed by the results of public-opinion studies. Of the many social problems mentioned in surveys carried out over the past twenty years, the question of child abuse does not appear even once.

The problem is also not a significant concern for the media. They quite often expose crimes whose victims are children, but this only serves to increase the dramatic effect of the events and to show the brutality and ruthlessness of the perpetrators. Examples of child abuse in families only sporadically find their way into the press, and are usually introduced as exceptional incidents (Sobiech, 1990).

In the light of the presented data, it appears that child abuse is a 'latent' problem, or a phenomenon that contradicts values cherished in a society, but one which is not generally perceived as problematic (Merton, 1971). Assuming that, it seems easy to understand the lack of statistical data and the reason why child abuse is missing from social definitions.

We should remember, however, that one of the deficiencies occurring both in objective and in subjective conceptions of social problems is the fact that they appeal to quantitative indicators of social-system disfunctioning, or point to the existence of a significant part of public opinion that is not satisfied with the present state of affairs. There is, however, a way to identify social problems which makes it possible to avoid quantitative traps. According to the authors of this conception, a social problem is to be regarded as 'the activities of individuals or groups making assertions of grievances with respect to some putative conditions' (Spector and Kitsuse, 1977). The existence of a problem depends on the occurrence of various forms of activity, no matter how many people are involved or the value of the indicators measuring the objective conditions.

Seen this way, the question about the existence of the child-abuse problem is at the same time a question about the existence of a social movement attempting to protect children's interests.

The only example of such a movement that is known to the author is the Committee for the Protection of Children's Rights. This organization was founded in 1981, at a time when many other social initiatives aimed at demonstrating and solving latent problems came into being. The direct inspiration to establish the committee was the publicity given in one of the daily papers in Warsaw to two cases of brutal treatment of children. One of those cases was a lethal beating. Founders of the organization, representing psychologists, doctors, and lawyers, as well as other concerned citizens decided that the goal of their activities would be 'to protect the child as a being not aware of its rights and unable to fight for their execution'. That goal was to be achieved by means of disseminating knowledge about children's rights, exposing transgressions, or improving the existing law and controlling its application, intervening in, and preventing activities that could concern both families and institutions (Czyz and Szymanczak, 1986). In the beginning of the Committee's activities, the issue of child abuse was very much in focus. After some time it became overshadowed by problems such as divorce, contact of sick children with their mothers, and help for children from the poorest families. By the end of the 1970s, a mere 5 per cent of the Committee's interventions concerned cases of battered children. Since the Committee was established, it has met with several problems in establishing institutional contacts, and has been treated with indifference or more frequently aversion by the central administration (Szymanczak, 1990: 6).

From the perspective of the ten years which have passed since the Committee was established, we can say that, despite all attempts, it has failed to publicly legitimize and institutionalize the problem of child abuse. The causes of this failure seem to extend beyond the errors made by one particular social organization. The experiences of

the 1980s show that many social movements which dealt with publi-
cizing and solving other social problems, operating under similar
conditions and who made use of similar measures, did effectively persuade society as well as the authorities that certain issues were
significant. Why could problems such as drug abuse, Aids, anti-
Semitism or homelessness alarm the public, and attract the concern
of ordinary citizens, journalists, and social policy-makers, while the
issue of child abuse remains latent? It is not easy to answer this question. The small amount of literature on the problem can only facilitate a number of hypotheses suggesting possible causes.

The first probable interpretation refers to the opinions, which are
widespread in Polish society, about the causes of various forms of
social evil. According to one of the most common stances, many
social problems can be accounted for by the existence of a 'pathological margin', comprising diverse categories of deviations. In many
situations, the distinction between the 'healthy' majority and 'pathological' minorities wanting to disturb public order, is a convenient
interpretation of a complicated morality. We can, therefore, assume
that public opinion will more readily legitimize problems that are
regarded as consequences of the existence of inimical minorities. So
understood, many declared social problems contribute to moral
strengthening of the social order. A given social problem, once seen
as a transgression of moral or legal norms, shows up the border
between normality and social evil, and at the same time, legitimizes
efforts to protect the honest majority from the threats occurring.

According to another and just as common standpoint, a significant
part of the problem results from erroneous decisions made by the
Communist authorities. Problems of environmental pollution,
poverty, lack of housing, malfunction of the public sectors, delin-
quency, and alcoholism are usually mentioned in this context.

A common characteristic of both these interpretations is placing
the cause of problems on the fringes of the social structure. For a
significant part of public opinion, the wrongdoers are, on the one
hand, party functionaries with no political legitimization and, on the
other, representatives of 'the pathological margin'—criminals, drug
abusers, and social parasites. The average citizens are seen as victims
of the deviant behaviour of various 'social enemies'. The existence of
such clichés seems to play an important part in defining and legitimizing social problems. We can assume that the more frequently
social complaints are regarded as the result of external factors, the

stronger the social acceptance of threats and expectation of politicians' reactions will be. Therefore complaints about actions, seen to be the result of defects or faults within the average citizen, will stand a much smaller chance of getting public exposure and agreement for the use of remedial measures. For example, efforts to enlighten the Polish public about the threats to health caused by smoking, bad sanitary conditions, inappropriate nourishment or general lack of concern about one's health met with several difficulties. It seems that the problem of where to place responsibility for generating social evil plays a significant part in defining public preference for particular social policies.

The above interpretation seems to explain the most important reasons why the problem of child abuse has not aroused public interest. If we take into consideration the widespread use of various forms of aggression towards children indicated by survey research, giving it the rank of a social problem would mean that a vast part of the public would have to acknowledge their guilt and consequently realize the dissonance between their routine behaviour and the rights of children. With the possibility of such a development in mind it is easy to understand the lack of a wider social reaction to attempts at giving it more publicity. It is much easier to accept the version of reality propagated by the media, according to which child abuse is a phenomenon occurring only in depraved 'socially marginal' families, who are separated from the world of ordinary people. Instead of revising the way cherished values are put into practice, which cannot be avoided if the significance and extent of the problem have been accepted, the mass audience is given another argument proving the stability and invariability of the social order.

The interdependence between legitimizing a problem and the need to correct generally shared visions of the social order indicates another important cause of the lack of concern about the issue. A public admission that children's rights are being violated and that children deserve to be protected by the state or by social organizations would necessitate a change in existing social relationships within the family.

One of the most serious obstacles is the dilemma between the need to protect children's rights and traditional patterns of employing corporal punishment to execute parental authority. Use of corporal punishment is sanctioned in Poland by both customary and legal norms. In the first case, corporal punishment is seen as a guarantee of obedience—one of the basic values constituting the institution of the family. Until the beginning of the present century, the Catholic Church played a major role in maintaining this family model based on obedience and enforced by means of corporal punishment. In successive editions of popular catechisms, this form of reproaching children was recommended as one of the most effective ways to inculcate respect for the authority of parents and superiors (Pawlik, 1991). Although the propagation of such concepts seem to belong to the past, they have never been publicly denied by the Church.

Legal regulations also permit parents to exercise violence. According to Article 239 of the Penal Code, any person is subject to punishment 'who hits a man or infringes his/her corporal inviolability in any other manner'. Parents who beat their child are not subject to punishment if the beating does not endanger the child's development, is not prophylactic, or if the punisher's intentions have an educational character and the extent of the punishment does not exceed the limits necessary to achieve the educational goal.

In this situation, any definition of a new social problem would have to suggest ways of solving it. As with any other problem, social policy-makers would be faced by the necessity of choosing between two not easily reconcilable models of checking it: education or public control and repression.

The first of these would involve various forms of collective persuasion, and would need to show possible ways of achieving educational goals without resorting to corporal punishment. An example of such procedures was the 'education without beating' campaign conducted by the Committee for Protection of Children's Rights in its early days. A major fault of this strategy, which discourages its potential followers, is the need for prolonged and systematic efforts that may not bring about the expected results. In a situation where child-abuse incidents are publicly seen as a marginal problem of pathological families, and the traditional family model is backed by powerful institutions, the effectiveness of educational efforts seems extremely limited.

Heard more often are suggestions to change the penal law regulations and to control their observance. Lack of precision in legal regulations, which in many cases sanction brutality towards children, is the most common argument substantiating the need to employ the control and repression model. Advocates of this approach realize that defining an unequivocal borderline between a justified and an unjustified punishment is a highly arbitrary choice. They are also aware that the effectiveness of such a procedure is connected with putting into practice an extensive system of controlling the ways families function.

The possibility of this solution seems present to a degree in the public mind. An average citizen appears to sense that public presentation of the child-abuse problem will sooner or later lead to a situation where his own family might become an object of observation by government agencies or social activists. On the whole, these are not groundless fears. In post-war history, the sphere of family life has repeatedly been an ideological battlefield. As one of the most significant institutions of social control, it has been subject to incessant pressures from authorities wanting to limit its influence. State efforts aimed at secularizing the family or taking over its socializing functions assumed the shape of interference which hurt citizens. The reaction to attempts at behaviour control was to form a whole range of defensive devices, which in many cases meant the maximum separation from the unfriendliness of external reality. Sociologists who studied Polish society in the 1970s and 1980s often found the phenomenon of escape from official structures into privacy. The family and its extension in close friends became a place which compensated for numerous needs that, willingly or unwillingly, could not be met at official levels. Apart from fulfilling traditional tasks, in many situations it took over the functions of cultural and educational institutions and formed the basis for building political opposition. Finally, through a complicated network of interdependencies, frequently far from legal, it assured redistribution of income and services which facilitated the protection of living conditions. Although private and official realities were not wholly separated, the maximum limitation of outside control was the requisite condition under which the above mentioned functions were carried out effectively.

The experience of the three years 1989–92 shows that behavioural rules, worked out over the last four decades, have been little modified. In many situations, we still come across social resistance to changes which interfere with privacy. We can assume that attempts to protect children's rights would be thought by society to be yet another interference with the closed sphere of privacy.

It is hard to say to what degree fears of such a reaction cause the lack of interest in the problem of child abuse. If the hypothesis discussed above is correct, we are confronted by a situation where the side-effect of devices once meant to defend society against a totalitarian system would spell the lack of social agreement to the effective protection of children's rights.

REFERENCES

Becker, H. S. (1966), *Social Problems: A Modern Approach* (John Wiley, New York).

Czyz, E. (1986), 'Zjawisko maltretowania dzieci w swietle medycyny, prawa i psychologii' in E. Czyz and M. Szymanczak (1986), *SOS-Dziecko, Materiały informacyjne Komitetu Ochrony Praw Dziecka* (Warsaw)

Fuller, R. C. and Myers, R. R. (1944), 'The Natural History of a Social Problem', *American Sociological Review* 6 (June), 320.

Merton, R. K. (1971), 'Epilogue: Social Problems and Sociological Theory' in R. K. Merton, and R. Nisbet (eds.), *Contemporary Social Problems* (Harcourt Brace Jovanovich, New York).

Mossakowska, B. (1987), *Zespół maltretowanego dziecka* in E. Skrzypczak and M. Matna (eds.), *SOS Dziecko* ii. *Materiały informacyjne Komitetu Ochrony Praw Dziecka* (Warsaw).

Pawlik, W. (1991), *Bóg, Szatan, Grzech* in J. Kurczewski and W. Pawlik (eds.), *Dzieje grzechu. Obszary grzechu* (Warsaw).

Piekarska, A. (1987), *Agresja rodziców wobec dzieci. Przejawy i psychologiczne uwarunkowania* (Wydział Psychologii Uniwersytet Warszawski).

Ratajczak, A. (1980), *Przestępstwa przeciwko rodzinie, opiece i młodzieży w systemie polskiego prawa karnego* (Wydawnictwo Prawnicze, Warsaw).

Sobiech, R. (1990), *Środki masowego przekazu a problem przestępczości* (Wydział Socjologii Uniwersytet Warszawski)

Spector, M. and Kitsuse, J. I. (1977), *Constructing Social Problems* (Cummings, Menlo Park, Calif.).

Statystyka Sądowa (1979–1989), Warsaw: Ministerstwo Sprawiedliwości.

Szymanczak, M. (1990), *Dziecko maltretowane i dziecko w innych krytycznych sytuacjach życiowych (z doświadczeń Komitetu Ochrony Praw Dziecka)* (Komitet Ochrony Praw Dziecka, Warsaw).

10.   Children's Rights and Adoption

Anna Kwak

The rights of children have been taken into account to a considerable extent in Polish law. They are included in the Constitution, and detailed solutions are present in the regulations of civil law, law on family relations and guardianship, as well as in administrative, labour, and criminal law.

A child, as the most powerless individual in as family group, has always been subjected to direct parental control. According to the Family and Guardianship Code, the essence of parental authority consists not only in powers over a child, but also in duties to it. Hence, parental authority involves both rights and duties. Legal rules give both parents equal rights in this respect. The Family and Guardianship Code regulates the range of parental authority. According to the Code parents are not given unlimited power over a child and are not allowed to exercise it in discretionary manner. The basic principle in relation to the execution of parental authority provides an obligation to promote the interests of the child, and take into consideration the interests of society. Parents' duties are to provide care for the child's progress, guidance, and due preparation for work for the benefit of society.

Do the legal regulations define precisely 'the interest of the child'? Definition of the term is lacking in the regulations of the Family and Guardianship Code, despite its frequent use. In legal references, 'the interest of the child' is defined as a set of values of material and immaterial character that are necessary for the child's proper development and due preparation, according to ability, for work for the benefit of society (Stojanowska, 1988).

The law accords powers over a child to the parents, but reserves the right to interfere in their realization. The basic criterion in evaluation of the execution of parental authority is consistency between the activity of the parents and the interest of the child. In a case where reservations appear of the way parents make use of their rights towards a child or fulfil their obligations, there is ground for court intervention. These cases would include the abuse of parental authority and negligence towards the obligation, such as beating a child to force obedience, not providing for the child's needs, or not taking an interest in the child. If the interest of the child is violated, the Family and Guardianship Code gives three solutions: suspension, limitation, or deprivation of parental authority. Judicial proceedings can be taken up as a result of indictment, or private accusation by one of the parents or a third party.

What are the grounds for allowing an application of these judicial decisions and what are the consequences for the parents? Suspension of parental authority is temporary. The court revokes the sanction after the obstacle to the execution of parental authority has been removed, for example, if one or both parents are abroad, or serving a prison sentence. The decision is taken with the object of providing care for the child for the period when it lacks parental care.

Limitation of parental authority is used preventively, and applied in cases when the interest of the child is in danger, but before violation. This regulation is used in two situations. First, it is used when negligence threatens the interest of the child. The parents' inability to cope with educational difficulties because their own educational knowledge is limited, or because the child has a psychological problem, is the most frequent kind of case here. In these situations the parents are not to blame, and the limitation of parental authority is meant as a protective measure on behalf of the endangered interest of the child rather than against the parents. Secondly, limitation of parental authority is often employed while a divorce is taking place.

Deprivation of the parental authority of one or both parents is the most severe form of legal intervention in parental rights. It is used when no other means can secure the interest of the child. Deprivation of parental authority may come about as a result of the parents' behaviour, e.g. negligence or abuse. The following are included here: use of punishment which could endanger the child's health, forcing the child to perform excessive work, inciting a child to perpetrate a criminal offence, starving the child, tolerance of the child's improper mode of life, alcoholism of the parents. However, there may also be cases where the parents are without fault but have, for example, serious mental illness, with a bad prognosis which indicates that neither parent will be able to take care of the child.

As a consequence of deprivation as well as limitation of parental authority, the child may be placed in a foster family, or in a guardianship and educational institution. Judicial decision on limitation or deprivation of parental authority does not automatically exclude the possibility of contact between the child and parents. However, it may restrict, or even prohibit, personal contacts between the parents and the child, should such contacts influence the child negatively and thus imperil its interests (e.g. when they hinder the educational activities of the foster family).

The law makes provision for the possibility of restoration of parental authority when the causes for application of the measure have ceased to exist. But deprivation of parental authority may be irreversible and mean a 'loss' of the child for ever. Deprivation of parental authority makes adoption without the consent of the parents possible. In this case parental authority cannot be restored.

From what has been said hitherto, it appears that the legal rules try to protect the child in the name of the 'best interest', taking into account that the natural family is the best educational environment for the child. There is no intervention, therefore, if the family functions properly, and the parents create optimum conditions for the child's development. Intervention occurs only when some harm is done from the perspective of the 'interest of the child'. Nevertheless, the legal solutions make possible mitigation or revocation of the restrictions applied to the parents.

Knowing the principles and potential for court intervention into the execution of parental authority, it seems right to analyse whether the principle of the 'interest of the child' can be observed in practice. To what extent do divorce proceedings take into consideration the child's interest? When the family breaks up, the interests of its adult members and children may conflict. The adults lay claim to the realization of their own plans and the improvement of their own lives. On the other hand, the child has the right to have and be brought up in a family with both parents. There is no doubt that a divorce is disadvantageous to the child's interests. Studies of the phenomenon emphasize that the predivorce situation can be filled with anxiety and conflicts and so equally disadvantageous for the child's development. Hence it is not so much the divorce itself, but a delayed decision on separation and a prolonged period of insecurity in the family that puts the child in jeopardy.

In Poland during the period 1960 to 1985 the divorce rate increased threefold. In 1989, the rate of divorce was 18.5 per cent of all contracted marriages. This high level of divorce has persisted since 1985, with only slight fluctuations in individual years: 1985—18.4 per cent; 1986—19.6 per cent; 1987—19.7 per cent; 1988—

19.5 per cent; 1989—18.5 per cent as reported in *Rocznik Demograficzny* (1986: 114; 1988: 89); and *Demografia* (1990: 117). An alarming change in the divorce pattern has been the increasing proportion of couples with children who are divorcing. In the years 1960–89 this increased by 18 per cent. Between 1985 and 1989 the divorce rate for families with children increased more slowly but still systematically. Thus, the percentage of divorcing families with children amounted to 66.6 per cent in 1985; 67.4 per cent in 1986; 67.7 per cent in 1987; 68.1 per cent in 1988; 68.5 per cent in 1989. Table 1 gives family size of divorcing couples. The largest groups are the families with one child; over 30 per cent of all divorcing families containing under-age children. However, in those years there was a constant tendency towards a decrease in the rate of divorce in families with one child, and an increase in divorces in families with two or more children. In 1989 families with two children accounted for one third of all divorces.

TABLE 1. Divorces according to number of children under age of 18

		Percentage of families with				
Year	No. of divorces	1 child	2 children	3 children	4 or more children	TOTAL
1985	32,646	62.7	31.3	4.3	1.7	100
1986	34,102	60.2	32.4	5.7	1.7	100
1987	33,660	59.1	32.9	6.2	1.8	100
1988	32,813	57.7	33.7	6.8	1.8	100
1989	32,337	56.6	34.6	6.9	1.9	100

In 1989 the couples who divorced had 50,095 children under the age of 18. Distribution by age was as follows: 0–2 years—14.2 per cent; 3–6 years—29.4 per cent; 7–15 years—51.6 per cent; 16–17 years—4.8 per cent. It is evident that the disintegration of the family and formal divorce in over 50 per cent of cases took place while the child attended elementary school, and in over 25 per cent of cases during the pre-school period. Thus is can be assumed that the child participates in the process of the disintegration of the family, living in a stressed atmosphere deprived of natural contact and positive relations between the parents. The child may be a passive participant and observe the situation, but he or she may also be drawn into it and used in the conflict between the parents.

Is divorce always incompatible with the interest or minor children? Or is a continuation of an unsatisfactory marriage more threatening to the child's interest? Psychologists agree that the unhappy married life of the parents is a decisive cause of acute anxiety for the child, and in the longer term leads to some disorders in the development of the child's personality and social adjustment.

One of the main problems related to the increased divorce rate in Poland is the growing number of incomplete families and stepfamilies, that is to say, the changed conditions for bringing up children. In what way is 'the interest of the child' observed in divorce cases? The court of law is obliged to decide on parental authority in a divorce decision, regardless of the parents' requests. Thus the court has to decide on whether to continue or limit the parental authority of the divorced parents. This is based on the assumption that settling the distribution of parental authority rather than leaving the question without any solution is the lesser of two evils for the child. However, any decision taken by the court must be preceded by a thorough analysis of the situation of the family in question. Reports made by social workers (psychologists) from the family diagnosis and consultation centres, after extensive examination of the child's situation, are of considerable use here. Most often the analysis is concerned to evaluate the emotional ties linking the parents and the child, and the parents' predisposition to continuing parental care. Other items of information are also collected with regard to the child's living conditions and health, evaluation of the origins of the family conflicts, interaction between the family members including those between siblings, the elder generation, and so on. Both parents and children are subjected to psychological tests. From the age of 13 the child's preferences for one or other of the parents are given weight. The analyses are intended to assist the court in finding the best solution, from the view-point of the child, to the family situation. But the evaluation of the interest of the child and the main decision rest exclusively with the court of law.

Divorce proceedings in Poland usually end by giving the mother parental authority over a minor child. This accords with the traditional role of women in the family in Poland. The right to the execution of parental authority is taken from the mother only in exceptional cases such as proven alcoholism or prostitution. Statistical data for 1989 confirms this tendency, which has already been noted throughout the 1970s. According to 1989 data (*Demografia*, 1990), the court entrusted divorced families with the execution of authority and care of children under the age of 18 as follows:

74% to the mother
21% to both mother and father jointly
1% separately to mother and father
0.7% to foster families (mostly related families)
0.3% to specialized institutions

In principle, complete parental authority may be left by the court with both the divorced parents. However, such a solution is only possible in cases when there is considerable chance of co-operation by both divorced parents for the benefit of the child. A decision of this kind may only be made when it is known that the relations between the divorced parents and their emotional relationship with the child augur well for harmonious co-operation in bringing up the child. However, should one of the parents not accept such a solution, the court cannot impose complete parental authority for both parents.

The decision most often used in divorce cases is limitation of parental authority. It follows complete and permanent disintegration of the marriage of the child's parents, which, as a rule, precludes the normal execution of parental authority. However, the limitation of parental authority allows it to be exercised within boundaries outlined in the divorce decision. These boundaries may vary considerably, from narrow ones such as meeting the child at a definite time and place, to much wider ones, such as spending holidays with the child, making decisions in important matters, helping with lessons, and so on. The specification of obligations and rights depends to a large extent on the wishes of the parents.

The next question about the realization of the principle of the 'interest of the child' is connected with adoption. The implementation of this principle constitutes the basic assumption for adoption. Adoption presents the possibility for the creation of a new legal relationship similar to that which exists between natural parents and children, and aims to place children deprived of their natural parents in a new family. The new family ought to secure proper conditions for the development and upbringing of the child. Adoption may only be carried out for the benefit of the minor.

During the past twenty-five years, there have been changes in the regulations of the Family and Guardianship Code and regulations concerning birth, marriage and death registers, with regard to the rules for adoption. In 1964, consent in advance by the natural parents for the future adoption of the child, without identifying an adopter, the so-called *consent in blanco* became possible. This solution was implemented with regard to children held to be social orphans (i.e. the children who have one or both parents alive but not interested in taking care of them). It secures prompt settlement of the child in the adoptive family, if the parents refuse to take care of it. Amendment of the law in 1975 for blank adoption introduced the possibility of writing out a new birth certificate for the child, in which the adoptive persons are registered as the child's parents. In 1986 new birth certificates were made available for all adopted children.

At present the importance of adoption lies in the fact that it helps social orphans. A substantial number of children are placed in adoptive families from orphanages. The number of natural orphans in these institutions has been decreasing while the number of social orphans has been increasing (Kozak, 1986). Children aged up to 3–4 years, that is in their early childhood, are the ones most often adopted. The youngest children, babies up to six months, form the majority for the 'blank' adoptions. Children over 4 years of age have little chance of adoption, and the chances decrease with age. Any longer residence in an institution is harmful for the child. It is generally known how important it is for the child to live, as early as possible, in a family environment in view of the irreversible effect of the absence of individual care in babyhood. Lack of emotional contact with the mother or another person playing her role in the first period of the child's life leads to development of the 'orphan disease' and as a consequence produces disturbances in the development of the child. In view of the harmful consequences of collective upbringing, the earliest possible placement of the child in a foster environment is necessary, or better still in an adoptive family. The longer the child lives in the institutional environment, the more difficult or even impossible it becomes to reverse the symptoms of the orphan disease.

According to the Family and Guardianship Code, the legal act that forms the parental relationship between an adopter and an adoptee is the decision of the guardianship court. For adoption to acquire the force of law, the following conditions have to be fulfilled:

application and consent of both potential adopters who are married partners, approval of the parents or guardians of the child, and the consent of the child itself if he/she is over 13 years of age. A child of this age must also consent to the alteration of his first name or surname, and to the transition from incomplete to complete adoption. The right of parents to consent to adoption of the child by a specific person constitutes an element of parental authority. It is also the right of parents who do not execute parental authority, but have not been deprived of it by court of law. The law also provides that, until one month after giving birth to the child, its mother cannot give consent to adoption. So the law protects the parents, but does it secure the interest of the child in these cases? The law allows situations in which parents, showing a blatant lack of interest in the child and its development, have, at the same time, the right to execute parental authority. Thus, doing nothing for the benefit of their own child, they hinder the prospects of the child for adoption. The debate has taken place for some time now, and tends to support an increase in the competence of the court to make decisions on adoption when parents do not want to consent to it, in spite of manifest harm to the child. Permission for the mother or both parents to hand the child over for adoption immediately after is birth in a hospital would also facilitate adoption. After leaving a hospital, it is usually very difficult to get in touch with a mother, if she has left the child in the hospital, but has not given up her rights. These children cannot be made available for adoption and must be sent to orphanages.

To protect the parents against precipitous consent to giving up parental rights, a regulation could be made to give the mother the right to rescind her consent during the first month.

There is also the phenomenon of stepparent adoption. This type of adoption is not intended to create a supplementary family environment for the child. It has an orderly character, as it tends to adjust legal status to existing family bonds. It is adoption within family bounds, and a biological parent is included. Adoption in this case means an addition of a missing element to the family structure. It is difficult to determine the extent of this type of adoption against the background of adoption generally. There are no official statistics, but some cautious estimates indicate as many as 40 per cent of adoptions are of stepchildren. A considerable number of adoptions of this kind are linked to the high rate of divorce and remarriage by persons with children from earlier marriages. The number has also been extended by a group of unmarried mothers who often get married to partners other than the fathers of their children.

In practice, the law is not able to contain all the family situations in such a way that 'the interest of the child' principle can be unambiguously and unmistakably implemented. In Poland, secrecy of adoption is obligatory. This is in accord with the expectations of the persons who adopt the child, but it is in accord with 'the interest of the child'? The child often learns about the adoption from third persons and this information may be shocking and lead to behavioural disturbances, and to changed attitudes towards the persons acknowledged until then as parents. It may also give rise to an urgent need to know the 'real' parents.

Stepfamilies create a different situation. The biological parent enters a matrimonial relationship in order to fulfil his or her needs. The child, then, gets a new person as a father or mother. On the one hand, it creates for the child an opportunity to be brought up in a complete family with role models of both sexes; however, new problems arise of an emotional nature in relation to a new situation, i.e. the arrival of a new parent for the child, only one of the biological parents living with the child, and a biological parent who no longer executes a direct parental authority.

Signature of the International Convention on the Rights of the Child has obliged Poland to introduce many changes in its legal regulations. It requires adjustments to new demands of Polish legislation and practice. It relates mainly to the extension of the rights of the child in civil, family, and guardianship law. From the perspective of the Convention, the child becomes not only an object of protection, but also a subject in law. Some work on changes in the regulations for adoption law have already started, for example the age for a child's consent on adoption can be reduced from 13 to 10 years. Another change provides the possibility for adoption despite the absence of the consent of the biological parents to give up their parental rights. This would give more powers to the court of law and improve the situation of social orphans, and emphasizes the primacy of the principle of the best interests of the child in any situation of conflict.

REFERENCES

Stojanowska, W. (1988), *Władza rodzicielska* (Parental Authority) (Warsaw).
Demografia (1990) (Warsaw).
Kozak, S. (1986), *Sieroctwo społeczne* (Social Orphans) (Warsaw).

11. Implementing the Children Act 1989: The Changing Relationship between Local and Central Government

Judith Masson

Introduction

This chapter examines the impact of the Children Act on the roles of and relationship between central and local government in promoting the welfare of children through measures for child protection and provision of services. Its focus is the development and implementation of the Children Act 1989, a piece of legislation which has been described as 'the most substantial reform of child law this century' (Mackay, 1989). This Act has not been chosen because it typifies the way legislation was developed or central–local relations were negotiated in the 1980s: it does not (Jordan,1991). Far greater efforts than usual were made to achieve a consensus before, during, and after the Parliamentary process. Consequently, this Act provides a rare modern example of consensus reform through which the limitations of that approach may be examined. In addition, in an attempt to ensure that the Act was implemented, central government went beyond its previous practice of merely informing those concerned about the contents of new legislation and developed an implementation programme. This gave it new ways of influencing the operation of law and provides another model for exerting control over local action.

Background

In the UK there is no Ministry for Children. The Department of Health (DH),[1] in conjunction with the Welsh Office takes responsibility for child care at central government level. It formulates policy, prepares legislation, and issues guidance. It acquires the knowledge necessary for these tasks from its substantial research programme,

---

[1] Until 1989 a single department, the DHSS dealt with issues of health, child welfare, and social security.

consultation with individual experts and interested organizations, and its Social Services Inspectorate which inspects social services, 'supplies knowledge and experience of social services, social work and the conduct of professional business in government [and] uses methods of inspection development and negotiation to implement Departmental policies and professional standards' (SSI, 1989). Social services are delivered in England and Wales through 104 social services departments within the metropolitan borough (City), London borough, and county councils. Social services departments are required to act under general guidance from the Secretary of State.[2] The cost of services is divided between central and local government using complex formulae which are discussed below.

The relationship between central and local government has been changing throughout the 1980s and consensus has yet to be reached about the powers which should be held at local level, the type or body which should exercise that power, and the methods of control which the centre should retain. The Conservative government often portrayed local government as profligate, incompetent and, at least in metropolitan areas, largely controlled by extremists. In this way it justified reforms which restricted local authorities' influences on their committees by exerting increasing control over revenue-raising and expenditure and removing some matters (particularly relating to education) from the local sphere. Personal social services have not been immune from change but the direction of change has been rather different (Jordan, 1991). Such services, that is, helping and caring services for the old, the young, and people with disabilities have always been viewed as local services with local policies determining their scope and nature, not merely local delivery of a national service. Consequently, the option of direct control from the centre was not realistically available. Services could have been transferred to other bodies, either the National Health Service or a newly established 'care corporation' but the Griffiths Report (1988) supported enhanced powers for local authority social services departments. Under the NHS and Community Care Act 1990 local authority social services departments have acquired new responsibilities to assess the needs of the individual for services, to arrange for these to be met either by providing them directly or purchasing them from the voluntary (charitable) or 'for-profit' sectors; and to ensure the

---

[2] Local Authorities Social Services Act 1970, s. 7.

quality of all services through registration and inspection. Resources will be transferred from health authorities and the Department of Social Security to local authorities. Difficulties in making this change and ensuring that local authorities have established adequate procedures have lead to the postponement of the introduction of Community Care.

Services for children come under the Children Act 1989 not the NHS and Community Care Act 1990. There are many parallels between the two Acts but social services departments have additional powers and duties to protect children from 'significant harm'. Child protection or state intervention in family life—the phrases were used almost interchangeably in the 1980s—became the focus of considerable professional and public concern in the 1980s. The law was seen to be over complex for social workers and families to understand (DHSS 1985*h*), to fail to meet the requirements of the European Convention on Human Rights (*R* v. *UK* (1988)) and not to provide a clear standard for acceptable child care. In addition, practice appeared unsatisfactory with widely publicized cases of children being re-abused or killed while subject to local authority protection (DH, 1991*a*) and the Cleveland affair where 121 children were removed from home over a short period after only limited enquiries because of concerns about sexual abuse (Cleveland Report, 1988). Emphasis on protecting children through court proceedings meant that services which might have removed the necessity for compulsory measures had low priority. This was particularly the case in areas where there were not sufficient resources to allocate a social worker for each child whose name was entered in the local child-protection register (House of Commons Health Committee 1991). Research evidence also indicated the need for changes in practice in many areas of child care to improve the quality of services (and reduce the damage done by poor services) and increase the confidence in social services departments of those using or needing to use them (DHSS 1985*a*; DH 1991*b*).

The Children Act: An Overview

The Children Act 1989 is a substantial piece of legislation with over 100 sections, 15 schedules, and over 30 regulatory powers. It is a major reform replacing nine separate Acts concerned with child law and significantly reforming many more. It is intended to provide the legal framework for relationships between children and their carers into the next century and to put an end to repeated and conflicting changes in child-care law by providing a consistent and agreed basis for social work with families. The government wanted to establish a 'better' or a 'new' (DH, 1989*a*, *b*) balance between families and the state.

Five distinct themes can be identified in the Act. First, it brings together public and private law relating to children. By using the same terminology and a single court structure disputes between parents may be resolved by public-law (care or supervision) orders if the necessary criteria are established, and public-law cases may end in private-law (s. 8) orders and no compulsory state involvement. Some distinctions remain: children are automatically parties to public-law but not private-law proceedings; private-law proceedings may start at the lowest level in the family-proceedings court. Both these reflect historic differences rather than reasoned debate. They were controversial. The government resisted change because it wanted to limit costs by creating a system which could largely operate with existing resources.

Secondly, the Act provided a consistent framework for regulating all forms of substitute care ranging from privately run residential homes and boarding schools to private foster parents, day nurseries, and child-minders. It was thought that adequate regulation would help to develop confidence in services generally, irrespective of whether they were provided by local authorities, charitable groups, or profit-making bodies. This would facilitate a mixed economy of service provision and move away from the view that all services must be state provided. Many of the changes in this area built on and updated existing law.

Thirdly, the Act sought to regulate parenting by defining parental power in terms of 'parental responsibility'. The new language is intended to indicate that a parent's role involves not rights but obligations and that powers exist so that duties can be carried out. Non-parents may acquire parental responsibility by court orders. Parental responsibility can only be removed by adoption, reflecting the view that parenthood is for life, but its exercise may be restricted when the child is subject to a care order. John Eekelaar has commented that the notion of parental responsibility in the Act reflects the view that responsibility for children belongs to parents not the state (Eekelaar, 1991).

Fourthly, the Act defines, limits, and controls state intervention in family life by setting a single standard, 'significant harm', for intervention and a single procedure for obtaining public-law orders. There was some controversy over defining this standard and the removal of an alternative, based on the child's welfare alone, because of fears that it might prove too difficult to rescue children at risk. The government also experienced great difficulty in identifying the basis for emergency protection orders. Despite court controls such orders had been too readily obtained but raising the threshold might preclude essential orders. In the end the test was hardly changed but procedural changes were made in the court rules which had been designed to inhibit the use of emergency orders.

Fifthly, the Act provides a framework for state support of 'children in need' and their families by imposing new duties on local authorities to provide services for them. Duties were already owed to children with disabilities but the new provisions extend their scope to socially disadvantaged children including those at risk through abuse or neglect. The intention behind this part of the Act is to forestall the need for compulsory intervention by encouraging local authorities and families to work in partnership. A duty to work to keep children out of care had been introduced in 1963 but the new provisions go further. Accommodation by the local authority was just a service, not something to be prevented, which existed alongside other services, all with the purpose of safeguarding and promoting welfare. The fact that it was theoretically a matter of choice for families whether or not they accepted services and they had a right to be consulted was intended to remove the stigma attached to use of social services and to make more families willing to seek help when necessary.

Three aspects of service provision were amongst the most controversial as the Bill went through Parliament, each leading to divisions during the House of Commons' stages. The ending of parents' obligation to give notice before a child was removed from local authority accommodation after six months worried local authority organizations and directors of social services who faced loss of control over difficult parents. It was also criticised by parents' and children's organizations who thought that this might encourage compulsory action and undermine the partnership ideal. However, the government was adamant that arrangements should be entirely voluntary: the equivalent of a child staying with relatives. Some organizations were concerned that targeting services on 'children in need' would encourage local authorities to take a restrictive approach, lead to expenditure on assessment rather than service provision, and stigmatize those seeking services. An amendment was tabled to widen the scope of the local authority's duty by removing the 'in need' requirement. A division was forced but was lost. A further amendment to impose a duty on local authorities to provide financial support for all young people who had been in care was also unsuccessful despite attempts and votes in both Houses of Parliament.

Universal services have long been identified by the Labour Party as a key way of improving conditions but were rejected as wasteful and promoting a 'dependency culture' by the Thatcher government. The value of welfare benefits declined for families during the 1980s and young people aged 16 and 17 were virtually excluded from receiving benefits in their own right (FPSC, 1991). Had these amendments succeeded they would have undermined the reforms in the Social Security Act 1986 and could have substantially changed the relationship between central and local government by enabling the latter to have an income maintenance role. However, they seem to have been promoted more with the intention of getting changes in social security policy rather than of building empires in local government.

It is too early to establish the extent to which the principles in the Act are being achieved although some research has already been commissioned by the Department of Health to monitor the Act's operation. It also remains unclear how long the principles will be seen as desirable and adequate ones on which to base the obligations of parents and the state to children. Previous law in this area, notably the Children and Young Persons Act 1969 and the Children Act 1975, has failed, remaining only partially implemented or becoming unacceptable because of the lack of belief in or commitment to the ideals it contained. This failure has emphasized the need to establish a consensus as a basis for the reform of child law.

Consensus

Despite differences of view in the main political parties about the causes of disadvantage, the responsibility of the state, and the role of the family, child-care law has rarely been seen as a party political matter in the UK. The sensitivity of decisions to remove children from their parents or foster parents is such that politicians have preferred these to be viewed as professional matters and thus to avoid blame when tragedies occur. This made achieving consensus possible even at a time when the government was heavily influenced by the 'new right' and opposition parties were unwilling to accede to this shift. It also meant that it was likely to be more difficult to place this reform on the government's legislative agenda which was already packed with changes designed to create 'Thatcher's Britain'.

During the early 1980s consensus developed amongst professionals and organizations concerned with child care about a need for law reform. The Social Services Select Committee chose 'Children in Care' for the topic of its second report and proceeded to take evidence from the DHSS, local authority associations, Directors of Social Services, academics, child-care experts from voluntary organizations, and pressure groups (House of Commons, 1984). It rejected a call for a major inquiry into public care for children but recommended that the DHSS establish a Working Party on child-care law. It also identified individual areas for reform, the extent to which concern about these were shared, and gaps in knowledge about current practice. This information provided a foundation for the work of the Departmental Review on Child Care Law (DHSS, 1985*h*).

There are a number of reasons why consensus was considered sufficiently important for efforts to be made to maintain and develop it. The Select Committee noted how susceptible child-care policies had been to 'the swing of the pendulum of fashionable trends and theories' and that change had not brought solutions to the problems. Stability could only be achieved if there was agreement based on sound understanding of what was needed and how it could best be obtained. Differences in approach had also brought unacceptably wide variations in the way cases were handled in different authorities. The numbers of children in compulsory care, the placement of those children in foster or residential homes, the success of placements, and many other aspects of child care could all be seen to vary between authorities. This was not only an issue of justice for the families concerned but also wasted resources. Changing the law could not mean removing all discretion because decisions inevitably depended on assessments by social workers and had to fit the complex circumstances of individual families. Flexibility and fairness could only combine if there were agreed principles on which decisions were taken DH, 1989*h*). Establishing consensus during the law reform process was therefore an integral part of creating a framework which would ensure greater consistency in practice.

The need for collaboration and co-operation between social services, education, health, housing, and the voluntary sector in order to provide services for families and children underlined the need for a wide consensus. It also made it more difficult to achieve since these organizations had their own priorities and also a long history of failing to agree. The consequences of lack of agreement were only too clear in failures of the child protection system and led to the Department of Health, the Home Office and the Department of Education collaborating on guidance on these matters (DHSS, 1989).

The perceived failure of previous reform of child-care law with the Children Act 1975 also highlighted the need to ensure consensus. There was broad consultation on reform before the 1975 Act but some groups, notably those which might have represented parents and children did not then exist; indeed the Family Rights Group was started because of concerns that the importance of families to children's welfare was being overlooked. Implementation of parts of that Act was delayed because of lack of resources; and professionals who had supported the Act became less happy with the way it addressed problems. Even when the Act was fully in force is remained only partially implemented.

The Department of Health had a clear interest in obtaining a consensus. Unless consensus were achieved the effort expended in attempting to obtain it would seem wasted. Consensus would strengthen the case for further resources, particularly the Parliamentary time needed for a major Act. The more successful and visible child-care organizations could lobby for reform and increase the chance that legislation would be prepared. In order to generate a consensus the Department sought to create a forum for focused debate. It established an interdepartmental working party involving civil servants from the DHSS, the Home Office, the Lord Chancellor's Department and including Professor Brenda Hoggett, a Law Commissioner and child-law expert, which issued a series of discussion documents about the law and sought preliminary views. It also commissioned research. The Department also disseminated the results of earlier research to inform both current practice and future policy development (DHSS, 1985*a*). Child-care organizations expected consultation. Many had given evidence to the Select Committee and for the 1975 Act; they were thus geared up to respond. Meetings and seminars were held. The resulting review (DHSS, 1985*b*) was followed by a further consultation period and meetings; the process was repeated following the publication of the White Paper, *The Law on Child Care and Family Services* (DH 1987, Cm. 62).

Two related but somewhat less extensive reviews were also being conducted, one by the Home Office and the Lord Chancellor's Department (LCD) into family courts and the other by the Law Commission into the private law relating to children. This followed the standard Law Commission pattern and culminated in a report in 1988 (Law. Com., 1988). The report of the Cleveland Inquiry (1988) led to a further consultative document from the Lord Chancellor's Department on the Inquiry's proposal for an Office of Child Protection. There were also other consultative papers from the DHSS on fostering, day nurseries, and juvenile offenders.

Consultation served two purposes. It enabled the departments to find out what practitioners perceived the problems and their solutions to be. It also allowed them to frame the issues and direct comments to their proposals. Research provided a firmer basis than individual experience for proposals—although there remained many areas where research was lacking—and was also used to dismiss suggestions. The LCD proposals for an Office of Child Protection fell into this category. Consensus did not mean that there was complete agreement about the direction or scope of changes, rather that the conflicts between the perspectives of different groups were contained. Contradictions between the competing notions of parental rights and children's rights, *laissez-faire*, and state paternalism remained (Fox-Harding, 1991*a,b*) but were buried so that the agreed goal of law reform could be pursued. Nor did it mean that the Department of Health abandoned principles which were rejected by a wide range of practitioners and interest groups. The generality of discussion at the pre-Bill stage meant that some areas of disagreement were not identified. The tensions and potential for further conflicts meant that continued efforts had to be made to maintain consensus and that the resulting legislation might lose support because it could not satisfy the diverse expectations.

Although consultation periods sometimes appeared short, the process extended between 1984 (or 1982 if the Select Committee's deliberations are included) and the end of 1988 when the Bill was introduced. Consultation then continued while amendments to the Bill were negotiated with civil servants continuing to hold meetings with child-care organizations and those organizations meeting together to lobby jointly for selected amendments. After the Bill was passed the process continued as regulations and guidance were drafted and implementation planned. In this way, and in marked contrast to most other great reforms of the 1980s—health, education, and local authority finance—the Children Act 1989 became law.

The Parliamentary Process

Although it had been feared that the Cleveland Inquiry would delay reform, the timely publication of the report allowed the Government to consider its recommendations and prepare the Children Bill for the 1988–9 Parliamentary session. The Bill was introduced in November 1988 with an expectation that it would receive the royal assent in June 1989. The draft Bill was incomplete, lacking the expected provisions relating to day care and with only the barest outline of those relating to the court system. It is quite normal for the government to proceed in this way, introducing its own amendments to complete a Bill or replace clauses which have only been prepared as drafts. Even where the provisions appeared complete, many gave only a limited idea of what the law would be like because of heavy (and increased) reliance on secondary legislation. Details such as time limits, information to be included in applications, and fees are generally left to regulations so they can be amended without further statutes. Not all the matters included in regulations are mere detail; for example, regulations about secure accommodation details, the length of detention periods and, for some children, the grounds on which they may be made. Nor has the ease of change meant that regulations are regularly reviewed and kept up to date; the regulations relating to facilities for children in care, foster home, and residential homes has remained unamended for twenty and thirty years. Amongst other regulation-making powers the Children Bill gave the Secretary of State for Health power to 'modify or repeal . . . or add any further duty or power' to a list of local authority functions relating to children in need (cl. 15(4)). This was described as an 'astonishing and unprecedented step' and termed 'a constitutional outrage' by one of the Law Lords. The Lord Chancellor agreed to remove the word 'repeal'.

While the Bill was before Parliament, child-care organizations co-operated over the preparation and proposal of amendments. Baroness Faithful, a former Children's Officer who took a close interest in the reform, agreed to table some amendments and helped to find sponsors amongst the Lords for others. Some organizations had patrons or members who were peers; this did not, however, guarantee support for amendments. Lord Mottistone spoke against restrictions on corporal punishment to the chagrin of the National Society for the Protection of Cruelty to Children! Debates in the Lords took up much of the time over eight days but only a very few non-government amendments succeeded. The Lord Chancellor was very unwilling to make concessions. Some proposals were rejected but accepted at the Commons stage. Six matters were pressed to a vote in the Lords, but all these non-government amendments were lost. However, two amendments which sought to direct the Secretary of State to ban corporal punishment in foster homes and secure accommodation in privately run children's homes must have had considerable impact because the necessary regulations have been made. Other amendments, rejected by the Lord Chancellor without a division, also found their way into regulations.

The Bill's passage through Parliament was delayed because the government had not prepared all its amendments and it was still incomplete when it went into committee in the Commons. The time allowed for the committee stage was brief; sixteen half-day sessions were held. The committee consisted of volunteers; MPs who had a particular interest in children. At least two had close links with child-care charities, one was a former social worker, one a former local authority solicitor, and two represented constituencies in Cleveland. Again there were large numbers of government and 'opposition' amendments. A child-abuse scandal in a private boarding school led to the Department of Health proposing further duties for local authorities. Child-care organizations, the Association of Directors of Social Services, and the Local Authority Association met Department of Health officials to convince them of the need for changes but had limited success. Organizations renewed their lobbying attempts; divisions were forced on seven matters but all were unsuccessful with the Conservative majority voting against them. A few concessions were made with promises to include particular points in guidance. Differences in philosophy towards the family and social service provision rarely surfaced and the committee completed its work with self-congratulatory exchanges. Although the final stages produced dissension because of limits placed on debate by a guillotine motion, the appearance of consensus was retained. The Children Act 1989 emerged in November 1989 largely unchanged by the Parliamentary process and still containing tensions between conflicting approaches. But the delays to regulatory powers and the promises about guidance meant that the original date for implementation of April 1991 seemed optimistic.

Implementation

The Department of Health was preparing for the implementation of the Bill from the Summer of 1989. A committee, JAFIG (Joint Action for Implementation Group) consisting of civil servants from the Department, members of the social services inspectorate, representatives from local-authority associations, and others concerned was set up. Its role was to act as an advisory and co-ordinating body for the organizations who would be implementing the Act. It also provided a channel of communication for information between these groups and the Department of Health. JAFIG agreed a dissemination and training implementation strategy. In parallel with these national developments a Family and Child Care Law Training group, established through the London Boroughs' Training Committee (LBTC) and the London Boroughs' Children's Regional Planning Committee analysed the Act to identify training needs for different personnel in social services and estimates the cost of such training (LBTC, 1989).

From the earliest stage, implementation was seen in terms of training. Those who would have to work with the Act needed to know about its philosophy and provisions and have the opportunity to reflect on the implications of these for their professional practice. Although it was recognized that local authorities and other agencies would have to develop new policies and procedures, training was seen as having a role in these too (LBTC, 1989). It was recognized by both groups that the training needs were very great. Large numbers of people needed to understand the Act; this would require them to come to terms with very different approaches to their existing work. Individual trainers and commercial organizations were expected to publish material and offer training. LBTC recognized that it would be a waste of resources for local authority training officers to prepare their own materials. Instead the group could help to identify and vet suitable material nationally for use locally. The Department was concerned that a clear and consistent message should be provided about the Act. Materials prepared or commissioned by the Department of Health or the Social Services Inspectorate (SSI) were more likely to meet these requirements than independently produced works.

JAFIG's strategy had three basic principles: wherever possible training should be conducted on a multi-disciplinary, inter-agency basis; it should involve both the voluntary and private sectors as well as local authorities; and it should fully reflect issues of gender and culture. The first and third of these were major issues within child care in the 1980s; the second was linked to the changes the Government was seeking to promote in the personal social services generally. Three phases of training were identified: Phase 1, providing initial awareness of the Act; Phase 2, developing broad understanding of the provisions and their underlying philosophy; Phase 3, building on the first two with specialist training in the operation of the new law.

Very shortly after the royal assent the Department of Health published its plain man's guide to the Act, *An Introduction to the Children Act 1989* (DH 1989*a*). This had been prepared by a civil servant who worked for the Law Commission and later on the Review of Child Law. It highlighted the major changes in the law and the principles behind them but gave little hint of the potential conflicts. It provided the Department with an opportunity to 'sell' the legislation by promoting its best features—simplicity, praticality, and consistency—without the buyer seeing the Act itself (let alone the complex regulations which were still to be drafted). Whilst distributing large numbers of free copies of the *Introduction* but not the Act, the Department acknowledged that the government was not entitled to give an authoritative interpretation of any legislation.

Shortly afterwards the Department published *The Care of Children: Principles and Practice in Regulations on Guidance.* This was prepared by an advisory group led by Jane Rowe, a highly respected researcher and child-care expert under the auspices of the Social Services Inspectorate. It was intended to be a foundation for practice in implementing the Act and to be 'read and used alongside the *Introduction to the Children Act 1989* and the regulations and guidance' (DH, 1989*b*). This document explained the status of statute, regulations, and guidance: 'Regulations say *"You must/shall"*; codes say "you ought/should". When guidance explains regulations, it reaffirms the "you must" messages. However, when it goes beyond regulations in setting good practice, it conveys the message that "it is highly

desirable to . . ." or "Unless there is good reason not to, you should
. . ." rather than "You must".'

It went on to identify forty-two principles of good practice. These
were the 'colours on the social worker's painter's palette to be used
in the combinations and patterns required'. Although these principles
are unexceptionable and would probably all be readily accepted by
most social workers the method of their creation detracts from the
democratic endeavour which might have been expected by those
implementing the Act. In other professions these ethical precepts
might have been developed through debate within the professional
organization and amongst it members. Principles developed in that
way might have been more naturally incorporated into decision-making than ones sent from the Department. When Parliament was
debating child law and enacting principles such as the paramountcy
of welfare it might also have been expected to legislate more clearly
on these other principles. Although the language is different many of
the principles have images within the Act but there they have been
tempered with concerns about creating enforceable rights or providing opportunities for judicial review. For example, the principle
'Siblings should not be separated when in care or when being looked
after under voluntary arrangements unless this is part of a well
thought out plan based on each child's needs' (principle 13) becomes
'where a local authority provides accommodation for a child . . .
they shall so far as reasonably practicable and consistent with his
welfare, secure that . . . [siblings] are accommodated together' (s.
23(7)(b))—a provision added through an amendment tabled by the
National Association of Young People in Care.

Training together, the LBTC curriculum guidance was also made
available at this stage. The combined effect of the *Introduction* and
Practice guide was to provide a framework for the new child-care
practice which could be studied without reference to the Act or the
discussions that led to it. They also avoided the need for those not
used to legal materials to read legislation and thus removed one barrier to understanding the changes.

In addition to these materials the Department of Health assisted
consciousness-raising by establishing a clearing-house for the
exchange of information. This began to publish a monthly newsletter, *Implementation News* with details of courses, information about
progress in preparing consultation documents on the regulations and
guidance, occasional articles about the progress of implementation in

different agencies, and interviews with key people. The Department arranged for the Association of Directors of Social Services and the National Children's Home jointly to run strategic development seminars (road shows) for senior managers and also used the SSI to raise awareness in their discussions in the regions.

It was not only those working in the personal social services who needed to understand the Act. The Lord Chancellor's Department was well aware of the needs of judges, magistrates, and court clerks. It also began to consider training and started a newsletter. The Department of Health was less successful in establishing collaborative links and ensuring that the need for training was recognized in other departments; the Department of Education & Science (DES) only provided materials for schools late in 1991.

The second and third phases of the implementation strategy focused on the commissioning, preparation, and launch of training materials. The Open University was asked to prepare a training pack which would meet the basic training needs of a large number of workers in local authorities, courts, and voluntary agencies. The remit was for interdisciplinary training, delivered by trainers, which could also be studied alone. Materials were to be available by January 1991. Other topics and target groups for specialist training were identified but ideas in the Department of Health were rather fluid. Eventually five further projects were commissioned: two projects on Part III of the Act; one on management issues for local authority councillors and senior social services managers; the other on the new-practice issues for social workers and projects on child protection practice, on registration of day-care facilities and for health service personnel. The intention was that these materials should be available in the spring of 1991 to allow a six months intensive preparation period. By this time all the regulations and guidance were expected to be available. Material for management and especially councillors was needed earlier so that account could be taken of the demands of the Act when local authority budgets were prepared for 1991–2.

The Department had clearer ideas about the form and content of some of these training packages than others. For example it was clear that management needed to rethink issues relating to service provision but saw changes in child protection as affecting field workers not managers. However, it generally accepted the costs set by the projects and agreed with their decisions about the format of materials and their method of delivery; the amount of training magistrates could be required to attend limited the Open University Course.

The Department of Health maintained oversight of the projects; civil servants attended advisory meetings and the members of the Department, including the SSI commented on drafts. The Department held a meeting for all the people involved to present and discuss their work. Its purpose was unclear but it provided an opportunity for civil servants in the Department to stress what they saw as the key messages in the Act. These focused on changes in local authority services rather than changes in the courts system, perhaps reflecting the Department's prime concern and the need to raise the profile of principles which might be lost because of the way the Act had been drafted. For example, the view that delay in legal proceedings is damaging is more clearly put forward in s. 1(2) than the view that children are best brought up within their families because of the risks associated with substitute care in s. 17(1). The Department also wished to stress the need for integration in local authority services. This issue seemed to demand greater co-operation with other central government departments, particularly the Department of Environment whose new code of guidance on homelessness was awaited.

The Department had a clear need to ensure that the materials it was sponsoring were accurate but the concern 'to get the right message across' seemed to go beyond this. The contents of material were closely vetted with the expectation (not always met) that texts would be changed. For example, issue was taken with statements about how the law had changed ('we do not wish to highlight this provision'); the effect of the new law ('we do not accept that it has made it more difficult for local authorities to obtain control in some cases'); and about factors which bring children within the 'in need' category ('there is too much emphasis on poverty, housing needs, defects of social security etc.').

In parallel with the development of training materials the Department was preparing regulations and guidance. These provided a further opportunity to stress the messages in the Act or add new ones. The draft document on foster placement stated, 'No one has a "right" to be a foster parent. "Equal rights" and "gay rights" policies have no place in fostering services.' This statement was heavily criticised and the references 'Equal rights and gay rights' were removed from the final document (DH, 1991*b*). Elsewhere the opportunity was taken to emphasize the needs of children and families to services which are culturally sensitive, despite the very limited provisions in the Act relating to this (DH, 1991*c*). The Department also acknowledged that the term 'foster carer' was now more commonly used than 'foster parent' by professionals (DH, 1991*d*), having advised against amendments proposed by child care organizations which would have used it in the Act. Again, duties could be stressed more positively in guidance than they were in the Act. For example, local authorities are only required to publicize complaints procedures (s. 26(8)) as they consider appropriate but guidance recommends 'publicly announcing the setting up of procedures' and widely available posters and leaflets (DH, 1991*c*).

The implementation process culminated with a series of launches. Individual training packs were launched generally with a press conference attended by Mrs Virginia Bottomley, the Minister of State in the Department of Health. These events served to raise awareness of the Act even in those who were not directly targeted by the packs. The finale was a reception attended by both the Lord Chancellor and the Minister of Health on the day the Act came into force and substantial media coverage of the key changes in the Act. However, concerns about resources undermined government statements about the importance of the reform and threatened 'like Banquo's ghost to destroy the self-congratulatory fun at the Children Act Party' (INIG, 1991).

Resources

The Financial Statement attached to the Children Bill identified costs for the courts of between £0 and £7 million and a further £4 million in local authority social services costs. Just over half of this related to court proceedings and the rest to the provision of services under Part III (£1.7 million) and £0.2 million for registration and inspection of children's homes and setting up complaints procedures. In addition there would be training costs. Only limited staff increases were identified including 150 for the new services under Part III, approximately 1.5 staff members for each local authority. Had the Department made a less conservative estimate of costs it is unlikely that the government would have enabled the Bill to go forward, considering its firm control over public expenditure. The local authority associations and the Association of Directors of Social Services (ADSS) produced far higher estimates for the costs of local authority duties. These were largely ignored. This was in marked contrast to the approach to implementing the ill-fated Children Act 1975. In June 1979 Ministers endorsed a decision to establish a joint working party between government departments and the local authority associations to examine the costs of implementing the unimplemented provisions of that Act (DHSS, 1980). The working party recognized that cost was the most important constraint on implementation even though the costs associated with some provisions were very small. In consequence the local authorities were able to resist implementing that Act until they were provided with the necessary resources. No doubt the Department of Health would not have wished to be so dependent on local government for the implementation of the 1989 Act.

Local authorities have two main sources of money, the locally raised Community Charge and money provided by central government from general taxation, the Revenue Support Grant. The control exercised by central government severely limits the ability of local authorities to increase the Community Charge (or sell assets) in order to fund its own chosen level of expenditure. Rather, by setting the amount which it thinks is sufficient to provide a standard level of service, the Standard Spending Assessment (SSA) and charge-capping by the government fixes the amount each local authority can spend. Charge-capping, introduced in the early 1980s, results in loss of central government finance to local authorities who seek to spend 'excessive' amounts or increase their budgets 'excessively'. Spending may be seen as excessive if it is above the SSA amounts (DH, 1991*f*; DOE, 1991). The SSAs are also used to allocate centrally provided finance between local authorities. The SSAs are complex formulae which relate to the size of population, measurements for deprivation, and adjustments for area. They have been the subject of considerable criticism because of the failure to use up-to-date information and even specially commissioned research (House of Commons, 1991; NISW, 1992). The formulae do not ensure that the amounts available are shared equitably (George, 1991) or that departments raise sufficient money to fund their chosen level of service. Many authorities spend in excess of the amount allowed on social services although their ability to do so has been severely restricted by charge-capping. Some authorities have not been able to increase or have had to reduce social services budgets, despite increases in SSAs, to avoid charge-capping (NISW, 1992).

The House of Commons Select Committee on Health (the successor to the social services committee) has been inquiring into public expenditure on the personal social services. In relation to child care, it did not accept that shortcomings in the child-protection services were solely due to poor management and considered that the responsibility was divided between central and local government. It noted with concern the limited increases in resources for social services in London and the effect that this appeared to be having on child-protection services. It recommended that the Department of Health and the local authorities conduct a review of the relationship between needs and resources with a view to establishing the validity of the SSAs. Changing the SSAs would only change the way the available resources were distributed between authorities. The Committee also repeated an earlier recommendation that the Secretary of State should announce measures to ensure that local authorities can fulfil their statutory functions—a coded message to increase resources (House of Commons 1991).

The only references to resources in *Implementation News* relate to money for training. The central government view seemed to be that the Children Act 1989 was providing a clearer framework for good practice; local authorities could not expect extra resources for doing properly what they were already expected to do. If more money was needed for prevention this should and could be found from departments' own budgets. The suggestion that local authorities simply could not afford to provide services for all those who might be considered 'in need' was met by letter to chief executives in January 1991 (*Implementation News* 14, 1991) advising that the definition of children in need could not be restricted, and guidance which states, 'Local authorities are not expected to meet every individual need, but they are asked to identify the extent of new and then make decisions on priorities for service provision in their area . . .' (DH, 1991*e*). It was unclear what remedies a person assessed to need services which were not provided might have.[3] It seemed unlikely that the Secretary of State's default powers (s. 84) would be used against a local authority complaining that it had been denied sufficient resources.

[3] There is a possibility of judicial review quashing a decision to refuse services. In autumn 1992 an application to review a local authority decision not to provide services it had assessed a person as requiring was successful. The case has not proceeded because the authority agreed to provide the service, compensation and costs, *Community Care*, 24 Oct. 1991.

At the time the Act was implemented the Minister, Mrs Bottomley, denied suggestions that resources had not been made available and repeated that social services budgets had been increased by 23.5 per cent (*Independent*, 14 Oct. 1991). The Department of Health annual report showed increased expenditure on personal social services of 23.9 per cent between the out-turn of 1990–91 and budgets for 1991–2 but also noted a decline in expenditure on children related to the decrease of residential child care (DH, 1991*g*). These figures are misleading since they related to permitted expenditure (SSAs) which were in many cases being exceeded to provide current services. A more realistic figure is 10 per cent (NISW, 1992). The House of Commons Health Committee noted that, when allowances were made for inflation, expenditure on social services had increased 22.3 per cent in the nine years from 1979/80 to 1988/9. The average increase was only marginally above the amount allowed by the Department of Health for 'demographic and other factors'. It took no account of the higher expectations service users might have because of changes in law and the work of advocacy groups. These national figures conceal substantial variations at local level. A number of authorities faced the implementation of the Children Act 1989 with reduced social services budgets.

The SSAs used for dividing amounts for children's services were not changed between 1989 and 1991. This could be said to reflect the view that the demands of the Children Act 1989 were in line with other spending on children's services. However, the weighting of the 'children's social index' changed so that this measure of deprivation declined in importance in the calculations (Revenue Support 1990, 1991). In consequence authorities which had scored highly on the relevant factors lost support in comparison with others. Changes were made in the formulae for education. This too had the effect of reducing the effect of deprivation in the calculation of revenue support grant (RSG) relating to services for children under 5. These changes seem to ignore, and run counter to the new duties in the 1989 Act to provide services, particularly day-care for children in need.

Although child-care organizations were not able to refocus the consensus around law reform on to the level of service to be provided before the Act was implemented they are now attempting to do so. The House of Commons Health Committee has brought these issues into the open as its predecessor had done with the need for law reform. A Social Services Policy Forum has been formed including the Association of Directors of Social Services and the National Council for Voluntary Organizations. It has published a wide-ranging report in an attempt to address the issue of how to resource needs-led services such as those the Children Act 1989 has legislated for. It makes a case for increased but not unlimited resources. More importantly it argues that the gap between needs and resources should be recognized and decisions about resource levels made openly. This would seem to require a return to central–local discussions on resources, involving groups representing service users.

Conclusion

Government policies to improve services but to control local authority spending are in direct conflict. Despite a common legal framework there are huge differences in provision of children's services nationally which relate to many things including variations in resources (DH, 1991*h*). Implementation of legislation relating to children's services involves changes in attitude, reformulation of local policies, and the development of new services. In each of these areas those concerned have to start from their existing position. Without new services, provision will continue to be resource, not needs, led. Changing the law, issuing guidance, and providing training will not remove local variations and inequalities unless resources are redistributed to allow this to happen. Moreover, failure to address the issue of resources may lead to greater imbalance in service provision as hard-pressed authorities pursue the new legislative ideals less vigorously.

It is too early to determine whether the programme for implementation adopted by the Department of Health has been successful in achieving any change for children and families who need services. Theory on implementation suggests the need to develop guidelines, distribute resources, and monitor effects. These are interrelated: the process is circular not linear. The Department of Health's programme has stressed the first and to a lesser extent the third. However, lack of resources for implementation has certainly become an issue and may be exploited to excuse lack of change. Dissemination of information and training have raised the profile of the legislation and the expectations of workers and families. It seems unlikely that these will be met.

REFERENCES

Cleveland Report (1988), *Report of the Inquiry into Child Abuse in Cleveland 1987*, Cm. 412.

Department of Health (1987), *The Law in Child Care and Family Services*, Cm. 62.

—— (1989*a*), *Introduction to the Children Act 1989* (HMSO, London).

—— (1989*b*), *The Care of Children: Principles and Practice in Regulations and Guidance* (HMSO, London)

—— (1991*a*), *Child Abuse: A Study of Inquiry Reports 1980–1989* (HMSO, London).

—— (1991*b*), *Children Act 1989 Guidance and Regulations: Family Placement* (HMSO, London).

—— (1991*c*), *Children Act 1989 Guidance and Regulations: Residential Care* (HMSO, London).

—— (1991*d*), *Children Act 1989 Guidance and Regulations: Private Fostering* (HMSO, London).

—— (1991*e*), *Children Act 1989 Guidance and Regulations: Family Support* (HMSO, London).

—— (1991*f*), *Children in the Public Care* (Utting Report) (HMSO, London).

—— (1991*g*), *OPCS Annual Report 1991*, Cm. 1913.

—— (1991*h*), *Patterns and Outcomes in Child Placement* (HMSO, London).

Department of Health and Social Security (1980), *The Cost of Operating the Unimplemented Provisions of the Children Act 1975* (HMSO, London).

—— (1985*a*), *Review of Child Care Law* (HMSO, London).

—— (1985*b*), *Social Work Decisions in Child Care* (HMSO, London).

Eekelaar, J. (1991), 'Parental Responsibility: State of Nature or Nature of the State', *Journal of Social Welfare and Family Law*, 37.

Family Policy Studies Centre (1991), *Supporting our Children* (London).

Fox Harding, L. (1991*a*), *Perspectives in Child Care Policy* (Longman, London).

—— (1991*b*), 'The Children Act 1989 in Context: Four Perspectives in Child Care Law and Policy', *Journal of Social Welfare and Family Law*, 179.

George, V. (1991), 'Fair or Foul', *Community Care*, 11 July.

Griffiths Report (1988), *Community Care Agenda for Action* (HMSO, London).

House of Commons (1984), Social Services Select Committee, 'Children in Care' (1983–4 HCP 360).

—— (1991), Health Committee, Public Expenditure on Personal Social Services: Child Protection Services (1990–1 HCP 570).

In Need Implementation Group (1991), *The Children Act and Children's Needs* (London).

Jordan, B. (1991), 'Social Work, Justice and the Common Good', *Social Work and Social Welfare Year-book*, 3.

Law Commission (1988), *Review of Child Law: Custody and Guardianship* (HC 594).

London Boroughs Training Committee (1989), *Training Together.*

Mackay, Lord (1989), 'Second Reading of Children Bill', *Hansard*, HL vol. 52, col. 488.

National Institute of Social Work (1992), 'Great Expectations', Policy Forum Paper 1.

R v. *UK* (1988), 10 **EHRR** 29.

Revenue Support Grant Distribution Report (1989–90 HCP 049; 1990–1 HCP 095).

Social Services Inspectorate (1989), *Decentralization of Social Services Departments* (HMSO, London).

12. Social Work, Law-Jobs and the Forms of Modern Law: The Children Act 1989

Suzanne Gibson

A poor girl from the East End of London was invited to a charity tea at the home of a local magistrate's wife.

The little girl sat down at the table, turned to her hostess and said: 'I see you keep your house very clean. Cleanliness is next to godliness, you know.'

The lady smiled, and gave her husband a knowing look.

'Is your husband working?' asked the little girl.

'But of course', said the lady. 'What a strange question for you to ask.'

'And are you both keeping off the drink?'

'What an impertinent little girl!' cried the magistrate's wife. 'When you are out visiting you should take care to behave like a lady, my child.'

'But I do!' said the little girl. 'When the ladies visit our house they always ask these questions.'

(From *No Laughing Matter*, by S. Lukes and I. Galnoor)

This chapter is about different points of view, an attempt to reconcile different perspectives on the ways in which law and social work interact in modern times.

The Children Act has been described as the most important reform of law concerning children this century. In writing this chapter I had three concerns. As a lawyer I wanted to work out whether there was anything special about the Act *as law*. So the first section discusses the general nature of modern lawmaking. Then, I wanted to try to understand the nature of the relationship between law and social work, because a large part of the Act is concerned with just that. So the second section looks at some recent attempts to define that relationship. Finally, I wanted to try a new way of looking at things.

Modern Law

Neo-liberal values like the commitment to the rule of law have been reaffirmed in the rebirth of liberal democracy in Eastern Europe. But what does it mean to speak of the rule of law in modern times? It has been argued that modern law is quite unlike the law that, say, A. V. Dicey had in mind when he wrote *The Law of the Constitution* in the late nineteenth century; so unlike it, in fact, as to call into question the role of modern law as a foundation for democracy in the modern world. According to F. A. Hayek (Hayek, 1944, and at greater length Hayek, 1960 and 1982) a large part of modern lawmaking is really no more than the issuing of bureaucratic commands. Such 'law' relies for its power and moral validity on a misappropriation of the legitimacy of 'true' law, a body of general rules of just conduct derived from established principles of social order.[1]

What is distinctive about Hayek's analysis of law is his claim that we can distinguish two principles of lawmaking, the results of which he refers to as *nomos* and *thesis*. *Nomos* is the true law, derived from the established practices and norms of everyday life. It is, perhaps, the mythic ideal of the common law. *Thesis* is law in name alone, the instrumental imposition of means to prescribed ends. The definition largely, but not exclusively, applies to legislation. In modern law we witness, in Hayek's view, the displacement of *nomos* by *thesis*. He asserts that, as *thesis*, modern law is simply the conduit through which the contemporary bureaucratic will is channelled. In claiming the status of law for this bureaucratic managerialism, the state, by stealth, commands obedience from citizens accustomed to respecting the institutions of law proper. Whether or not we agree with Hayek's rather doom-laden and arguably reactionary conclusions, his thinking about the nature of modern law raises some interesting questions.

First, Hayek does not deny the necessity of organization or of organizational rules promulgated by governments; what he does question is government's desire 'to confer on its rules of organization the same dignity and respect which *the law* commanded'. (Hayek, 1982: i. 126). So, what *is* the power of 'law' that government wants to take its name in vain?

Secondly, in differentiating between the different types of law (rules of just conduct and bureaucratic instructions) and their associated purposes (ordering justice and executing government tasks), Hayek reminds us that under the general heading of 'law' in a common-law jurisdiction are rules performing a variety of qualitatively different roles in a variety of different guises. Perhaps we should not

---

[1] A helpful analysis of Hayek's legal theory may be found in Thomson, 1991.

need to be reminded of this simple proposition. But some of the recent diagnoses of the condition of modern law have been written at a level of abstraction which treats all of law as essentially the same thing doing essentially the same jobs. So, exactly what kinds of task are we asking law to perform?

Thirdly, Hayek emphasizes the purposive nature of modern socio-political thought and its effects upon law; he reminds us that the legislative enterprise creates a law which is instrumental and purposive, a rational system of administration directed towards the pursuit of specific ends. So, how far may we describe modern law as the expression of government will alone?

Lastly, Hayek maintains that societies evolve their own principles of order. These principles, he argues, should be the source of a society's true law or *nomos*. Because *nomos* is distilled from the evolved order of society, it will contain the twin essences of legitimacy and appositeness. This means, suggests Hayek, that *nomos*-type law will work. *Thesis*, on the other hand, is law imposed upon the evolved social order in order to achieve specific ends, ends towards which the evolved order has obviously itself not evolved. Hayek concludes therefore that *thesis*-type attempts to legislatively direct social order are neither legitimate nor apposite. This means that *thesis*-type law is unlikely to work. So, how apposite and effective is modern law?

If we were to rewrite those rather general questions in the specific context of the Children Act, we would ask the following. Why did government desire to confer upon the detailed rules of public child care the 'dignity and respect' that law commands? To perform what roles, and in what guises, does law appear in the Children Act? To what extent does the Children Act merely represent the specific purposes of government, and to what extent does it create rules of just conduct? What is the basis of the Children Act's legitimacy? Can its success be assured by its being derived from an existing social order?

I shall return to these intriguing questions at the end of this chapter. Before we proceed to contemplate them, with others which will arise along the way, it will be instructive to take some other opinions upon the general nature and condition of modern law.

Max Weber

In the course of his account of how capitalism came to Western Europe, Weber outlined a useful typology of legal thought. He was also interested in the organizational structure of law, but here I want to focus upon what he had to say about styles of decision making (cf. Bell, 1987).

Weber's scheme combined two elements: rationality and formality. Rationality, in David Trubek's words, 'means "following some criteria of decision which is applicable to all like cases' and thus measures the *generality* and *universality* of the rules employed by the system' (emphasis added) (Trubek, 1972: 729). 'Formality' means '"employing criteria of decision intrinsic to the legal system" and thus measures the degree of *systemic autonomy*' (emphasis added) (Trubek, 1972: 729). In principle then, we should be able to differentiate types of legal decision according to how general and universal are any rules which may be used, and how intrinsic to law are the methods of making and applying them.

We turn first to 'irrational' legal decisions. Legal decisions derived case-by-unique-case according to some special procedure (by divination, or reference to an oracle, for instance) exemplify the 'formally irrational' style of decision-making. The decision is made as a matter of form rather than substance, and no reference is made to any body of substantive rules or principles. Next, case-by-case decisions which are made by actually looking at the matter in hand, but where there is still no use made of any systematic body of principles, exemplify 'substantively irrational' decisions. Such decisions are made by giving due consideration to the problem's substance, but they are not rationalized by being referred to a set of known and legitimate principles. We turn now to 'rational' legal decisions. 'Substantively rational' decisions are those made without reference to special legal procedures, that is, not formally. But they are made nevertheless rationally, by reference to a body of general principles of a non-legal nature (such as psychology or a political ideology). Coming last to 'formal rationality', we arrive at what Weber identified as the hallmark of European law. Legal decisions are made by reference to the body of legal knowledge itself, according to a specialized method. Moreover, legal rules are general and universal. 'Formal rationality' is the juridical ideal which is invoked by calls for 'government according to the rule of law'.

As Weber was a German lawyer and legal historian, it is not altogether surprising that he concluded that the place where the most perfect 'logically formal rationality' was to be found was in the nineteenth century German legal system. The English common law, as Hayek approvingly observes, claims custom and community, as well as legal rulings, as its source; it is not, in Weberian terms, fully developed 'logically formal rationality'. German law existed in the form of a civil code, and was understood to be more formal, more cohesive, and more rule-bound than English law.

It is tempting for the common lawyer to associate Weber's 'logically formal rationality' with bureaucratic-style decision-making. But, as Hayek has done, Weber distinguished administration, which he saw as government's pursuit of specific, concrete objectives, from law, which he saw as the promulgation of general, universal rules. In Weber's view, where legal justice is marked by 'formal rationality', administrative justice is more akin to 'substantive rationality' (cf. Harris, 1987). 'Substantive rationality', we recall, means decisions made by reference to acknowledged principles but not deduced by formal logic from a body of legal rules. 'Substantively rational' decision-making will often, argued Weber, be pulling in two directions. One way lies the abstract formalism of legal certainty, and the other way lies the realization of substantive goals.

The particularistic mode of decision-making in many areas of contemporary family law does appear to be the very epitome of Weber's 'substantive rationality'. The Children Act's s. 1(3) checklist, with its attempt to balance substantive considerations (the desire to consider each child's welfare as a unique set of circumstances) with rational ones (the specification of general categories of concerns which should be considered in all cases) is an exemplar. In accordance with Weber's typology, therefore, there would be good reason to regard such modes of decision as closer to administration than law, regardless of the institutional setting in which the decision is made.

Roberto Unger

Unger's persuasive account of the nature of modern law emphasizes its purposive, end-oriented instrumentalism. By purposive legal reasoning, Unger means that official decisions are justified on the basis that they achieve the purposes ascribed to the rule; and by implication, that new rules themselves are justified on the basis that they can achieve certain ends. Echoing Weber, purposive legal reasoning results, Unger argues, in 'open-ended clauses and general standards [which] force courts and administrative agencies to engage in *ad hoc* balancings of interest that resist reduction to general rules' (Unger 1976: 197). This would seem to be so: the open-ended standard of 'the child's best interest' for instance, has resisted reduction to a general rule to the extent that, where the attempt has been made, we have ended up with the s. 1(3) checklist.

Does this imply that traditionally, law has not set general standards at all? This cannot be so: the doctrine of notice, say, sets a general 'prudent purchaser' standard by reference to a general rule (or at least a general doctrine, which is arguably rather different from a rule). So why is it that *some* general standards cannot apparently be reduced to general rules or stated as general doctrines? Unger answers that it is because 'the *kinds of problems* to which comprehensive standards characteristically apply . . . involve the conflict of numerous and inchoate interests against the background of a refusal to sacrifice any one of these interests completely to the others' (emphasis added) (Unger, 1976: 197). This is a fine description of the welfare checklist.

But a resistance to general rules cannot be just something to do with the *kind* of problems modern law addresses. There is in principle no constraint upon how we choose to conceptualize a problem, other than the requirement of plausibility. So our tendency to deal with modern-law problems in a purposive, technical way is not due to the intrinsic nature of the problems: rather, as Unger recognizes at other points in his own argument, it is something to do with the way that we are prepared to think about them. When all is said and done (and in law it must be said in order that it can be done), we are simply not willing to hear that a judge has narrowed his or her consideration of a child's domestic welfare down to the one or two telling facts which would allow comparison of one case with another by juridical analogy. Judges could do this, in residence disputes for instance, by making a presumption (in the technical sense), that a child is better living with its mother until it is old enough to make up its own mind; or a presumption that boys should live with their fathers and girls with their mothers; or, a presumption that the child should reside with the parent who has been, hitherto, its primary carer. But in modern times we don't want judges to think about the issues in this way. And we don't want them to, because this is the kind of problem about which we expect them to think purposively, not juridically.

What should strike us is that the 'numerous and inchoate interests' which are articulated in the purposive resolution of problems, do not lead towards numerous solutions or even confident decisions. (This mundane but important observation is one which we will return to at various points below.) The 'numerous and inchoate interests' of the checklist as applied in residence disputes, for example, cannot disguise the fact that one parent will get what they think they want, and one parent will not. Using the checklist to make the decision will not ameliorate the pain and disappointment of the parent who must inevitably lose having gone as far as litigation in the conviction that he or she must have a good case. Nor, I think, can the use of the checklist bring us confidence that the child's best interests, for years into an uncertain future, will be better served by being with one parent rather than the other. Ironically, those cases which are not sufficiently clear cut for the application of presumptive juridical reasoning are likely to be just those cases where the application of the welfare checklist also produces an ambivalent outcome.

So we have to ask ourselves this question: why does purposive thinking come to be applied to some problems but not others? Michel Foucault may have the answer.

Michel Foucault

A social theorist, Foucault has given a partial and somewhat cryptic account of the changes to be witnessed in law's engagement with modernity. Foucault depicts modern Western societies as societies dominated by the rationalistic, end-oriented human sciences, and by the obsessive categorization and administration of the body politic which the human sciences have made possible. His views on law are largely to be gleaned from his treatment of it in his history of sexuality and in his earlier work on punishment and prison reform (Foucault 1979*a*).

Foucault asserted that during its classical phase law 'display[ed] itself in murderous splendour . . . to draw the line that separates the enemies of the sovereign from his obedient subjects'. But in modern society, where populations are regulated in accordance with social standards derived from the knowledge-base of human science, law's role becomes that of effecting 'distributions around the norm'. But, 'I do not mean to say that law fades into the background, or that the institutions of justice tend to disappear, but rather that the law operates more and more as a norm, and that the judicial institution is increasingly incorporated into a continuum of apparatuses (medical, administrative, and so on) whose functions are for the most part regulatory' (Foucault, 1977*b*: 144). Elsewhere, Foucault has written that the activity of judging is now conducted more by the 'judges of normality' than by the judges of law: by the teacher, the doctor, the social worker.[2]

For Foucault, then, modern law itself has become concerned with the enforcement of norms and judgment; the traditional activity of law has been adopted as the *modus operandi* of welfare professionals. Some commentators have taken Foucault to mean broadly that 'the function of classical law' has been extended 'from proscription to prescription' (Harris and Webb, 1987: 68). I think that by caricaturing the two types Foucault rather exaggerated the extent to which modern law departs from law in its classical form. Be that as it may, I think he also identified a crucial element in modern-law thinking: governmentality. Foucault's concept of governmentality will serve us as a description of the modern-law *zeitgeist*. It is a general and abstract concept (Foucault 1979*b*). But it can be useful to us because it is more specific than Weber's description of the shift towards technical rationality, and it has greater explanatory power than Unger's argument that law is increasingly oriented towards purposive reasoning and society towards welfare corporatism.

Governmentality is an attitude made possible by the rise of the human sciences. Foucault implies that 'societies like our own are characterized by a particular way of *thinking* about the kinds of problems that can and should be addressed by various authorities. They operate within a kind of political *a priori* that allows the tasks of such authorities to be seen in terms of the calculated supervision, administration and maximisation of the forces of each and all' (Miller and Rose, 1990: 2; Foucault, 1979*b*). Governmentality is not an attitude exclusive to government, but one which infiltrates specific groups such as welfare professionals, and (I think) communities more generally.

The answer to the question of why purposive thinking comes to be applied to some problems but not others, is governmentality. It is governmentality which filters the problems that may plausibly be handed over for juridical resolution from those which must be dealt with instrumentally and purposively. The latter are the problems which have been identified by specialists of various sorts thinking and acting governmentally. Governmental types of problem inspire governmental types of resolution: checklists, or the exercise of discretion,

---

[2] But Foucault fails to acknowledge the extent to which welfare professionals may refuse to exercise their social-control function, or the extent to which an organizational ethos of optimism may lead them either to suspend their judgment or refrain from enforcing it (Dingwall, *et al.*, 1983; Smith, *et al*, 1988).

or reports from welfare specialists, and so on. I think that it was this perhaps that Foucault alluded to, when he referred to law's role in effecting 'distributions around the norm'.

Although I find Foucault's thinking about governmentality quite compelling, I confess I find some of the more hyperbolic conclusions which have been drawn from his work rather less so. I now move on to discuss Nigel Parton's Foucauldian perspective on contemporary child law in the light of this discussion of the form of modern law.

Child Protection: Social Regulation and Legalism

Nigel Parton writes that child protection is now perceived as 'a socio-legal issue where social workers continue to be central, but where the agencies of the law (courts, police and lawyers) play a crucial role in helping to constitute what the problem is and what should be done about it. In the process, the nature of social work is itself refashioned' (Parton, 1991: 214). What is the nature of the relationship between law and social work?

Social regulation

To understand Parton's argument we must cast another cursory glance at the views of Michel Foucault, whose work has exerted a strong influence on Parton's and others' analyses of contemporary social policy.

The historical argument. Foucault argued that the emergence of the human sciences had had a profound impact upon our understanding of what goes on in the human social world. As a result, they had a profound impact upon the way in which we manage our social affairs. Foucault argued, as we have seen, that where sovereign authority and the law were once the primary means by which the 'powers that be' governed, the new knowledge of the human sciences gave the tools and the impetus to new forms of regulation.

In *Discipline and Punish*, for example, Foucault (1977a) argued that the way in which punishment was justified had changed. Whether corporal punishment or incarceration, punishment had been more or less straightforwardly retributive until the 'science' of penology emerged. Then, the purpose of incarceration became reform, and its nature the disciplined regimentation of the prisoner's daily life. Such discipline was supposed to rehabilitate the prisoner's wayward soul, and prepare him for a useful role upon his return to civil society.

The socio-political argument. What was important about the emergence of the human sciences was the power they gave to the 'powers that be' to control the population with ever increasing subtlety. First various standards of 'normal' behaviour could be identified and defined in the course of 'scientific' investigation; then this 'normality' could be enforced in ways ostensibly more progressive and humane than had been seen in the past. In *Madness and Civilization*, for instance, Foucault (1977*b*) argued that the emergence of the science of psychiatry led to the insane being regarded not as people who were in some way morally offensive, but as people who were sick. Granted, they were still to be confined, but the confinement was now justified as treatment whilst in quarantine. (An earlier age had bluntly regarded the disorderly insane as the same sort of problem as criminals or beggars, and simply locked them all up together.)

The human sciences are intensely concerned with the human subjectivity of the individual: with what she thinks and feels, eats and drinks, what she hopes and fears, with her daily routines, her nightly dreams. The rise of the human sciences meant that all the ordinary everyday stuff of mundane individual lives came under increasingly broad and deep scrutiny. The upshot of the countless surveys, physical examinations, psychiatric speculations, and rehabilitative ruminations, Foucault suggests, is that the 'powers that be' can lay claim to the subjectivity of the citizen and will seek minutely to regulate her thoughts and actions. Most of us assume that the liberal welfare state is a good thing. We might examine all the evidence and still be right to conclude that, on balance, it is. But Foucault argues that its organization both necessitates and makes possible the deployment of that power which can be grabbed along with knowledge.

In *Governing the Family*, Nigel Parton has argued that we can best understand modern social work and the contemporary politics of child protection by embracing Foucault's approach to analysing modern society. Social work has integrated various elements of the human sciences to form its own distinctive 'psy-complex' knowledge base: a little psychology and psychiatry, a bit of modern medicine, some sociology, parts of criminology. Social work is then, a body of knowledge which enables its practitioners to engage in surveillance and discipline of the population; it is the exercise of a distinct form of discursive power. Accordingly, social workers' knowledge will determine whom they regard as the client population; it will enable social workers to judge the behaviour of those in whom they have an interest; and, ultimately, it will determine the types of treatment to be administered to the client population (but cf. Sibeon, 1989–90).[3] Foucault does not try to explain the *causes* of social action. He does not try to claim that knowledge rather than, say, poverty, makes us do a thing. Instead he tries to account for the 'conditions of possibility' of social action. He tries to understand what knowledge makes it possible for us to think of doing the things we do. So, it is through 'psy-complex' procedures of gathering and presenting information 'that the "object" of the family, child care and child abuse are presented in a particular form and hence made amenable to intervention and regulation', writes Parton (1991: 10).

The emphasis on the significance of, in this case, 'psy' knowledge in structuring social relations is exactly what has made Foucault such a popular theorist; it matters, we academics argue, what happens in the corridors of knowledge, because these lead into the corridors of power. There is an important point made here, and yet I cannot help thinking that the importance of the point that knowledge affects our actions in the world has obscured an equally important one; that sometimes, the knowledge we have can make little difference to what we do, because the range of possible actions open to us is limited. Then, the conditions which make a discourse possible become almost an irrelevance. The mad, to adopt Foucault's analysis and an earlier example, may have come to be confined for subtle psychiatric reasons; but they are still confined.

Once Parton's 'object family' comes into view, we might be forgiven for wondering what difference, in the end, the possession of the 'psy' knowledge makes. The proliferation of 'psy' knowledges indicates neither that they will be diligently or accurately applied in practice, nor that they will be matched by a proliferation of solutions open to social workers. Dingwall *et al.* (Dingwall, Eekelaar, and Murray, 1983) have strongly suggested that the outcome of case conferences owes more to the rhetorical strategies deployed by the participants than they do to the content of the 'psy' knowledges paraded therein. Moreover, the types of new provision in the Children Act owe little to the theoretical sophistication of the 'psy' knowledges, although their presence there does owe much to social research. 'Psy'

---

[3] There is not the space here to embark upon a full discussion of Parton's Foucauldian thesis, but there is considerable evidence to suggest that the relationship he assumes between knowledge and practice is over-simplified and reductive. Sibeon (1989–90) provides a helpful survey and overview of current debates around this topic.

knowledge may have resulted in more intervention, over larger areas of human failing, but there is little indication that in the field of child care it has provided much more diverse scope for practical action. There are limits to what can be done; should the sexually abused child be left in the home or not? (cf. Gordon, 1989 and Ferguson, 1990). Hence there are limits to the effects of knowledge: where a decision is to be made whether to grant an Emergency Protection Order any subtle nuances of 'psy' knowledge will be confronted by the blunt binarism of 'order or no order' (see also Moore 1984: 416ff.).

It is at this point, I think, that we find the reason why recent legal and social theorists have advanced two distinctly different visions of the relationship between law and welfare expertise. On the one hand it has been argued, as we have seen, that law is both saturated with, and displaced by, 'psy' knowledge. On the other hand, it has cogently been argued that law and legal institutions are deeply resistant to welfare expertise and even hostile to welfare experts. Michael King and Christine Piper have argued,

The problem for child welfare science is that within the legal arena the information will almost invariably be constructed according to the demands of the legal discourse . . . The law's demand for decisiveness and finality, for winners and losers, for rights and wrongs to be identified and exposed to the public gaze in order to further its normative objectives tend to force legal judgements out of the mouths of child welfare representatives . . . The broad range of factors, genetic, financial, educational, environmental and relational, which science would recognize as capable of affecting the welfare of a child are narrowed by law to a small range of issues which fall directly under the control of the judge, the social workers or the adult parties to the litigation process . . . Thus the scientific discourse of child welfare in all its richness and complexity is reconstructed as concepts which 'make sense' within law (King and Piper, 1990: 43).

At Foucault's theoretical extreme, we learn that law has more or less given way to the new knowledges of modernity. At King and Piper's, we learn of 'law's inability to incorporate external discourses except by reconstructing them' (King and Piper, 1990: 43). A sensible if bland middle course has been steered by Paul Hirst, who argued that 'without a publicly assigned position and legally defined exclusiveness in the performance of their role, the key institutions and agents of the "disciplinary" region could not function" prisons, psychiatry, medicine, social work and so on' (Hirst cited in Parton,

1991: 17). What weakens each of these accounts is their sweeping treatment either of the operation of law, or of the operation of non-legal knowledges. What we really need are answers to two questions. What law-jobs is law doing? And what 'psy' jobs are 'psy' knowledges doing? I shall focus on the first of those.

Legalism

We have seen that there are opposing views on whether law has absorbed 'psy' knowledges nearly to the point of its own negation, or rather resisted and reshaped them to the extent that they have themselves become almost unrecognizable. There is another apparent contradiction in arguments around child protection: it seems simultaneously to have become both more legalistic and more structured by expert knowledge. Parton has suggested that an attitude of legalism began to emerge in child care around the late 1970s, and that at the heart of the Children Act lies the question of the nature of the relationship between legalism and the 'psy' knowledges. What is legalism?

[I]t is important to differentiate between the law per se and legalism which refers to a particular set of assumptions regarding the best way that society should be organised. It is a particular discourse which, according to Judith Shklar, refers to the ethical attitude that holds moral conduct to be a matter of rule following and moral relationships to consist of duties and rights determined by rules. (Parton 1991: 193)

Legalism, then, is not so much a description of legal activity as a description of a certain moral and political outlook. As Shklar herself defines it, it is an attitude which is expressed at one end of a continuum as an ethical stance, and expressed at the other by all the institutions of law. The attitude that is 'legalism' is a celebration of such things as: '[o]rder and formality', '[t]he dislike of vague generalities, the preference for case-by-case treatment of all social issues, the structuring of all possible human relations into the form of claims and counter-claims under established rules, and the belief that the rules are "there"—these combine to make up legalism as a social outlook' (Shklar, 1964: 10).

At the risk of being diagnosed as legalistic I am bound to say that given such a fuzzy definition as 'the dislike of vague generalities' it is difficult to bring into focus any analytic utility in the term 'legalism' for Parton. I think this becomes obvious when Shklar states that

Weber's notion of 'rationality', 'meant exactly what has here been called legalism. The predisposition to discover, construct, and follow rules was, in his view, the distinguishing mark of European culture.' Such rationality, we have already observed, is thought to be an integral component of human-science thinking and, arguably therefore, modern social work.

But perhaps *pace* Shklar's own comparison, her concept of 'legalism' is not really the same as Weber's 'rationality' at all. '[T]he structuring of all possible human relations into the form of claims and counter-claims under established rules' or expecting 'moral relationships to consist of duties and rights determined by rules', are far more specific definitions of the ethos of legalism than is the comparison with Weber. The problem then is to reconcile the more specific definition of legalism with what we know of the spirit of the modern world. We have already seen that much modern law is not so legalistic, embracing as it does discretions and open-ended standards and concepts like *'Gillick* competence'.[4] And most of us know that familial relationships, social or moral, are not conceptualized in legalistic terms. (see Finch, 1989).

On the other hand, we also know that the Children Act has been accompanied by an astonishing outpouring of detailed rules, promulgated under its various provisions, in the form of regulations (DH, 1988). Such rules, however, are the hallmark of bureaucracy in rather the same way as are discretions and open-ended standards. I am inclined to think that the spirit of the age would be far better described as 'municipalism' than 'legalism'. Municipalism better captures the concern with petty by-laws, the authority of minor officers, and administrative detail.

Although Parton cited Shklar's definition of legalism, I think he may have had something else in mind, and that something was the type of job that law was being brought in to social work to do.

In the child care field, [legalism] is focused upon the relationships between professionals, particularly local authority social workers, and their clients, parents, and children. It involves the superimposition of legal duties and rights upon the therapeutic and preventative responsibilities, essentially for

---

[4] A minor is deemed competent to give consent to medical treatment where a physician judges that he or she is sufficiently mature to understand the nature of the decision. *Gillick* v. *West Norfolk and Wisbech Area Health Authority and the DHSS* [1986] A.C. 112. But note the definitions of the scope of *'Gillick* competence' in *Re R* [1991] 3 WLR 592 and *Re J* [1992] Fam. Law 318.

the protection of clients. Within an emphasis upon 'legalism', the rule of law as judged by the court takes priority at the expense of other considerations, including that which may be deemed, by the professionals concerned, as optimally therapeutic or 'in the best interests of the child'. (Parton, 1991: 194)

Parton is not making quite the same point here as that made by King and Piper in the passage quoted earlier. King and Piper refer to the different jobs law must do and their effect on legal process. Because we demand decisiveness and finality, the settlement of conflicting claims, and the vindication of rights and wrongs, they suggest, law cannot be expected to trade in ambiguities, or equivocation, or subtleties. Parton, too, alludes to the different jobs law does, but, committed to the constricting notion of legalism, he notices less of law's activity than he might. Shklar's tunnel vision has narrowed his own.

I do not entirely mean to rubbish the notion of legalism (although I do a bit). It is just that the concept of legalism is really of little use at this stage in our argument, because it is concerned with a very amorphous outlook rather than the concrete matter of what we want to do and how we get things done, in law or elsewhere. We have already, more precisely, identified the *ethos* of modern law in Foucault's governmentality. What we need to know next is what, in general terms, law is being asked to do, and why. If we were able successfully to generalize along these lines we would gain some further insight into the nature of both law and social work.

Law-Jobs

What we would find useful is a general term referring to a complex of legal objectives, rather than attitudes or an outlook. Following Karl Llewellyn (1940) I am going to use the idea of 'law-jobs' to serve this purpose, although I am going to diverge in the second part of this section from Llewellyn's own ideas. The comments which follow should be read in the light of what I have written so far. Where I refer, therefore, to the performance of law-jobs by formal law, I generally mean law in its modern form.

Karl Llewellyn's Law-Jobs

'The law-jobs are in their bare bones fundamental, they are eternal' wrote Llewellyn, in his enigmatic way. 'Perhaps they can all be

summed up in a single formulation: such arrangement and adjustment of people's behaviour that the society (or the group) remains a
society (or a group) and gets enough energy unleashed and co-ordinated to keep on with its job as a society (or a group).' A little later
he continues, 'the law-jobs hold, as basic functions, for *every* human
group, from a group of two persons on up . . . law-jobs and law-
ways, I repeat, go to the essence of *any* group'. Law-jobs are essential
to the functioning of human groups; and 'society' is, in effect, a
group of groups, each of which must perform its law-jobs. This second point is very important, as it enables us to abandon the common
view of legal activity as a triangular hierarchy of commands.[5]

The specific nature of Llewellyn's law-jobs, which I will describe
first and then discuss in the context of provisions in the Children
Act, will illuminate, if not, perhaps, surprise us greatly. At various
points Llewellyn expanded his list, and the following is not exhaus-
tive.

1. *The disposition of trouble-cases.* This involves what Llewellyn calls
'garage-repair work' on general social order. It is the day to day settlement of grievances and disputes.

2. *The preventive channelling and the reorientation of conduct and expectations
so as to avoid trouble.* This is 'law-stuff' effectively used to channel
people's conduct, and their attitudes towards one another. It is for-
ward-looking and preventative, and of real importance in areas of life
where there may be inherent conflicts of interest. It is also of importance in areas where life and work must be co-ordinated, because
hitches in organized action can product conflict simply because they
are disruptive of the collective effort.

3. *The allocation of authority and the arrangement of procedures which legitimize action as being authoritative.* This Llewellyn calls 'the job of *arranging
the say and its saying.* There occur doubts as to what to do, in drought
or war, or petty crisis; there occur disputes as to what to do, and as
to whose say is to go.' Crises are generally unexpected and unset-
tling. But if we settle in advance whose say is to go, what procedures
must be gone through in order to make key decisions legitimate, and
what the limits are on any person's authority, we can at least anticipate that when the crisis arises we will have procedures to manage it.

This law-job will not necessarily, however, be seen as exclusively

---

[5] In this respect Llewellyn's functionalism led him down a path not altogether dis-
similar to the one Foucault trod in conceptualizing power. Both men wanted to avoid
the image of purely hierarchical social control.

or even mainly concerned with crisis management. The need to make provision for 'the say and its saying' means that moderately stable 'constitutional' principles will come into being. Llewellyn comments that this law-job 'differs from ordinary channelling of conduct in looking to allocation rather of powers than of rights, to indication of the person and the procedure rather than the substance'.

4. *The net organization of the group or society as a whole so as to provide direction and incentive.* In his description of this law-job, we read Llewellyn at his most florid and elusive. He wished to emphasize 'the *positive*, the constructive, side of the 'legal': the net organization around something, toward something: the Whither of the net Totality'. The job includes 'that co-ordination, direction, and incentive-unleashing which . . . "the legal" *can* vitally effect'. I think that what Llewellyn was trying to describe was some sense of commitment to the law, a belief maybe in its beauty and rigour and what it expresses about the ideals of a society: how it can draw people together, perhaps to defend it as part of a heritage or to assert its superiority over other laws and legal systems and societies.

5. *Juristic method.* Llewellyn thinks that this is the inevitable outcome of the performance of the other law-jobs. We will consider whether or not this is so below.

We could sort our way through the entire Children Act allocating this or that provision to the category of this or that law-job. But we won't. Instead, I will take two different approaches to doing the first law-job (dealing with the 'trouble case') and consider precisely why they differ. This will entail some consideration of the second and third law-jobs. I will not comment on the fourth law-job beyond recalling here the fanfare of mingled optimism and self-congratulation when the Act came into effect in October 1991.

The thinking behind the Act reflects how some law-jobs—as Llewellyn emphasizes—must be performed both by institutional law and by non-legal social groups. Consider orders made under s. 8 of the Children Act. These enable the courts to settle the mundane and predictable problem of estranged parents' disagreements over a child's upbringing and the child's contact with the parents. The principle of non-intervention in s. 1(5) of the Act, however, specifies that a court shall not make the order 'unless it considers that doing so would be better for the child than making no order at all'. Judges are to exercise restraint in their issuing of orders, even perhaps when a dispute is so bitter that it has gone as far as litigation. This restraint should have the effect of both encouraging settlement of the case in hand and of discouraging future potential litigants. The responsibility for settlement of this sort of dispute has thus been placed initially in the hands of the parties to the case (parents) and any conciliators or mediators who may be working with them. It has been said that by the principle of non-intervention the frontiers of the state have been rolled back, and/or that private ordering is now the preferred method of resolving intra-family disputes. In law-job terms the non-intervention principle clearly delegates minor dispute resolution jobs to non-legal groups. But the principle as it is laid down in law also assists in preventively channelling behaviour, by indicating in advance that parents are expected to put their own differences aside when making decisions about their children.

At this stage one is inclined to think, so what? (Or at least the author did.) Well, conceptualizing ss. 1(5) and 8 as law-jobs in this way may not tell us a great deal about the sections themselves, but it does enable us to make what might turn out to be a fruitful comparison. The interesting question, as ever, is why apparently similar law-jobs (garage repair work on the 'trouble case') are done in quite different ways. We will begin to see why when we examine the resolution of the 'trouble case' in the context of public-authority activities.

The 'garage repair work' law-job is handled in, amongst other places, s. 26 of the Children Act. S. 26 requires local authorities to review the cases of children in their care and give due consideration to any complaints which may arise. The Representations Procedure (Children) Regulations 1991 (promulgated under the Act) establish a quasi-judicial complaints procedure which requires, for example, that one of the members of the panel hearing the complaint should be an independent person. In contrast with the effect of delegation of the 'trouble case' law-job in the private sphere, where the outcome is private ordering, here the local authority is compelled to deal with the 'trouble case' of a complaint in a formal manner.

At one level this is simply because the power of public authorities must be constrained in an appropriate manner, and it would be reckless to argue otherwise. But the formality also arises because not one, but two, law-jobs will actually be done here: in the interests of the parties concerned, the resolution of the immediate 'trouble case' (the complaint) which may be of limited general interest; *and*, in the interests of authority, the 'channelling of behaviour' to avoid a secondary 'trouble case' (the unpredictable effects of an unheeded complaint) which may be of far greater general interest. From this perspective, the fact that one dispute concerns a private family and the other a public body is of less significance than the fact that the 'channelling' law-job, mainly because it is preventative, requires the exercise of authority. That authority may be provided by a tribunal, a panel, a court or, in a different context, some sort of leader. What is important is that we know who has authority, that is to say, whose say is to go. In order to constitute the authority required for 'preventive channelling', the third law-job, 'arranging the say', must have been done beforehand. The Representations Procedure (Children) Regulations do just this for the complaints to which they apply.

'Channelling' will occur in the private sphere where disputes have to be more or less formally heard by the courts because they cannot be resolved by the parties concerned. The judgments made public in such cases, those reached with the assistance of due process and marked by its authority, are then available to 'channel' the behaviour of future and potential disputants. As we have seen, channelling may also occur when a judge refuses to intervene: importantly, though, the refusal to intervene and the message that the parties must act responsibly for themselves, also comes from an authoritative source. Channelling does not happen in purely private settlement of 'trouble cases'.

Much of what has been said above about the multiple locations at which law-jobs are done, and the close association between 'preventive channelling' and the whose-say-is-to-go aspect of 'arranging the say' is demonstrated in one paragraph of the Department of Health's guide to *Protecting Children*. We are told

Child protection work inevitably involves the use of authority. The positive use of power and authority can be a helpful tool in the therapeutic process . . . Using authority and control does not necessarily involve initiating legal action to obtain control through a court order, but it does involve explaining to parents what the social worker's *statutory duties and powers* are and their relevance to the particular child's and family's situation. (DoH, 1988: 11) (emphasis added)

The point of this excursion into the Children Act on the back of Llewellyn's law-jobs is to emphasize how some broad notion like legalism does not begin to express the variety of tasks that are undertaken in the Act, or why it was felt they needed to be done. There is some scope, though, for defining the law-jobs in a different way, and that is what I shall do next.

My Way of Looking at Law Jobs

Lawrence Friedman once commented that the place where we would uncover the essential features of modern law was not law itself, but the demands which people made of it. 'The important point' he said, 'is not that modern law *is* rational (in the sense of consciously choosing appropriate means to achieve given ends) but that people *think* it is, or more importantly, that it ought to be, and they expect it to behave accordingly.' (Friedman 1969, 29) The reader who has laboured over my earlier points will understand that I do not wholly agree with Friedman on the topic of law's rationality, but I do agree with the general spirit of his argument. Would we gain greater insight by asking what jobs we *expect* law to do, rather than by asking what jobs law *does?*

Among the most telling documents from which we may elicit 'our' expectations of law are the reports of formal child-abuse inquiries. 'Our' is in inverted commas because many of these reports have been written by lawyers who chaired quasi-judicial style inquiries. They may therefore reveal more about what lawyers expect of law than what people in general expect of it. But having entered that caveat we might also bear in mind that the formal inquiries are called for by politicians and media as much as by lawyers, and the reports are generally welcomed, raked over with much relish (especially if they are critical of public servants), and finally used to quench our rather feeble consciences. What the reports may achieve, therefore, is the dissemination of legal expectations which, once they have been disseminated, do become a part of the general cultural stock. Turning the pages of these inquiry reports (useful synopses of which were published by the Department of Health in 1982 and 1991), six clear expectations emerge.

Control. Law is expected to provide control in two ways: by regulating social-work organization and decision-making, and by providing the means whereby social workers have authority to act against the wishes of parents. The call for an investigation is often the first psychological step in the process of reasserting control when things seem to have gone unexpectedly wrong. In the end, law (in the form of statutory requirements) is upheld as the mechanism by which control *should* have been exercised, and calls are made for new law to avoid any repetition of past failure. When the calls for law are accompanied in the same report by a recognition that the failure to comply with the already existing laws was the consequence of lack of resources or poor management, we are entitled to wonder quite what yet more law is supposed to achieve.

There is a general, and highly questionable assumption that the provision of practice guidelines in the form of law is more effective than the provision of the same guidelines in the form of strong management. It may be that this is a point at which legislation deceives us: 'government talking to itself' (the provision of guidelines for government agencies) has become confused with 'the majesty of law which commands obedience'. Law does of course have a role to play in securing appropriate behaviours, but the 'call for law' is as likely to result in more lapses from the new legal norm as it is in a greater level of compliance. (See Judith Masson's chapter in this book, which identifies inadequate resourcing as one of the most likely sources of compliance problems.)

Authority: Constitutes the second angle on the issue of control. Loss of control over the abused child's circumstances has often been precipitated either by an unwillingness to use the authority already vested in the social worker, (DoH, 1991*a*: 5) or by a lacuna in legal authority (such as the absence of any right to require a child to be brought for medical examination, now rectified in s. 43 of the Children Act). More and better law is expected to provide a sound basis from which authoritative action will emerge. In Cleveland of course, the problem of control emerged not from a failure to exercise authority, but from the injudicious and excessive use of it. The question is, however, the same. How can law be used to bring crises under control?

Certainty. To bring order out of chaos, we feel we need to find out exactly what actually happened. Although there is much to suggest that law is not very good at helping us to do this, there is widespread belief that the adversarial process does make this possible, and an expectation that it ought to do so. It might be supposed that in an inquiry, proceedings would, by definition, be more inquisitorial than adversarial, but non-legal commentators, at least, have tended to identify the inquiries as adversarial in nature (DoH, 1991*a*: 110). The question of evidence is posed time and again. Many inquiries emphasize the inadequacy of records, to the extent that it must have been impossible for workers involved in the case to know what was going on and was now impossible for the inquiry, in retrospect, to know what had really happened (DoH, 1991*a*: 99). The Tyra Henry report, amongst others, identified preparation, specifically for legal proceedings, as a valuable opportunity to assess all the available evidence.

Accountability. In quasi-judicial form the inquiries do what we implicitly expect of law, that it should compel an account to be given as well as call the guilty to account.

Consistency. This expectation has to be teased out from the inquiry reports, but it is, nevertheless, there as a concern. In the context of inter-agency working it is expressed as the problem of different points of view from different professionals about the same situation. This echoes a point we discussed earlier, that is, the confrontation between the binarism of (legal) decision-making and 'psy' complexity. In other places it manifests itself as a struggle between the inquiry's application of its own *ad hoc* standards of judgment, and an attempt to define overarching standards of professional practice (DoH, 1991*a*: 111). Aristotelian justice demands that like situations be treated alike: administrative justice, as exemplified by the welfare checklist, demands consistency, then clarity and systematicity. The checklist is 'a means of providing greater consistency and clarity in the law and was welcomed as a major step towards a more systematic approach to decisions concerning children' (Law. Com., 1988: para. 3.18).

Legitimacy. The expectation that law will somehow confer legitimacy on certain courses of action is an amalgam of other expectations, primarily of authority and of accountability, and to a lesser extent, of consistency.

All these things, then, are what we look to law to do for us. Again, we *could* work our way through the Children Act finding these expectation principles put into effect, and again, here we won't. Rather, I will conclude by returning to the questions which I posed at the beginning of this chapter.

Conclusion

Why did government desire to confer upon the detailed rules of public child care the 'dignity and respect' that law commands? I hope it will have become clear in the preceding law-jobs section that 'dignity and respect' is both too narrow a description and too vague. Many law-jobs are concrete tasks that can be done either by legislation or the common law. The 'call for law' by a community trying to respond to a child-abuse crisis, and the provision of law by the powers that be, involve expectations of law more complex and intriguing than that it be dignified and worthy of respect.

To perform what roles, and in what guises, does law appear in the Children Act? This question has already in part been answered in all of the preceding discussion. What I have not yet defined as a legal guise are the efforts to ensure that the Children Act is properly used, through the medium of the published *Guidance and Regulations.* The most informative passage in any of these volumes appears on p. 2 of the introductory booklet *Principles and Practice in Regulations and Guidance,* headed 'The status of regulations and guidance'. We know the status of legislation and regulations: it is the ambiguous status of guidance and codes of practice which is interesting. 'Though [guidance documents] are not in themselves law in the way that regulations are law, guidance documents are likely to be quoted or used in court proceedings . . . they could provide the basis for a legal challenge of an authority's action or inaction'. Then again, '[c]odes of practice fall between regulations and guidance notes. They may be "statutory" . . . but they are not law in the way that regulations are law . . . courts expect detailed justification for not following codes of practice, but some flexibility to suit the needs of a particular case is allowed and expected.' (DoH, 1989).

The process of inserting new law into the fabric of daily life is fascinating and a proper discussion of it is beyond the scope of this paper. We might ruminate, however, on how guidance and codes of practice extend the reach of law, making detailed its imperative and making plain what are its implications.

To what extent does the Children Act merely represent the specific purposes of government, and to what extent does it create rules of just conduct? It should be apparent from this chapter that many members of the community desire law (even modern bureaucratic law) for the fulfilment of various purposes. Governmentality is not the prerogative of government alone. There are very few general rules of just conduct in the Children Act. Those which we do find are, for reasons which I hope are moderately clear, primarily concerned with private law.

What is the basis of the Children Act's legitimacy? Can its success be assured by its being derived from an existing social order? This question of legitimacy arises, the reader will recall, out of Hayek's conviction that *nomos* ('true' law) is law derived from the principles of social order which have evolved in the community. Can it be said of the Children Act that it fulfils this requirement? The problem, of course, is to identify which community and whose values the Act represents. Having said that, there is a remarkable degree of consensus surrounding the Act's provisions. It has been widely remarked that the Act is the final outcome of a great deal of consultation and research. From the point of view of the social work and social-research community therefore, the legitimacy of the Act rests upon foundation stones which they have not just carried but quarried.

The political legitimization of the Act was perhaps rather less sound. It would be not entirely unfair, I think, to say that the Act was approved in the wake of Cleveland on the basis of two misunderstandings: that social workers' interference in family life was excessive, and that the Act would impose strict limits on whatever powers of interference they possessed. In fact, Cleveland aside, the evidence suggests that social workers have interfered in family life very much less than they might have done. There is also a certain amount of anecdotal evidence to suggest that some of the problems for which the Act was loudly hailed as a long-awaited solution had anyhow already been solved in practice.

If anything in the Children Act represents the political moment of its inception it is the double face of parental responsibility. In one direction it looks to parental rights, so that parents are protected from welfare interference. In the other direction it looks to parental duties, exhorting parents to think, not of rights but of obligations to children and the community. The Department of Health published two pamphlets when the Act came into force: in one, a general guide for parents, it is written under the heading 'parental responsibility' that the 'Children Act says parents have a number of important responsibilities—and at the same time a number of key rights' (DoH, 1991*b*: 5); in the other, which discusses the powers of local authorities, it is written under the heading 'parental responsibility' that an 'important theme of the Act is that parents have a number of key rights—and at the same time a number of important responsibilities' (DoH, 1991*c*: 7).

Where law and social work meet, so too meet the indeterminacy of legal reasoning and the logic of political ideology.

REFERENCES

Bell, J. (1987), 'The Judge as Bureaucrat' in J. Eekelaar and J. Bell (eds.), *Oxford Essays in Jurisprudence: Third Series* (Oxford University Press, Oxford).

Department of Health (1988), *Protecting Children: A Guide for Social Workers Undertaking a Comprehensive Assessment* (HMSO, London).

—— (1989), *Principles and Practice in Regulations and Guidance* (HMSO, London).

—— (1991*a*), *Child Abuse: A Study of Inquiry Reports 1980–89* (HMSO, London).

—— (1991*b*), *The Children Act and the Courts: A Guide for Parents* (HMSO, London).

—— (1991*c*), *The Children Act and Local Authorities: A Guide for Parents* (HMSO, London).

Dingwall, R., Eekelaar, J., and Murray, T. (1983), *The Protection of Children: State Intervention and Family Life* (Basil Blackwell, Oxford).

Ferguson, H. (1990), 'Rethinking Child Protection Practices: A Case for History' in The Violence Against Children Study Group (eds.), *Taking Child Abuse Seriously* (Unwin Hyman, London).

Finch, J. (1989), *Family Obligations and Social Change* (Polity, Cambridge).

Foucault, M. (1977*a*), *Discipline and Punish: The Birth of the Prison* (Allen Lane, London)

—— (1977*b*), *Madness and Civilization: A History of Insanity in the Age of Reason* (Allen Lane, London).

—— (1979*a*), *The History of Sexuality*, i. (Allen Lane, London).

—— (1979*b*), 'On governmentality' I&C 6: 5–22.

Friedman, L. M. (1969), 'On Legal Development', 24 *Rutgers Law Review*, 11–64.

Gordon, L. (1989), *Heroes of Their Own Lives: The Politics and History of Family Violence Boston 1880–1960* (Virago, London).

Harris, J. W. (1987), 'Legal Doctrine and Interests in Land' in J. Eekelaar and J. Bell (eds), *Oxford Essays in Jurisprudence: Third Series* (Oxford University Press, Oxford).

Harris, R. and Webb, D. (1987), *Welfare, Power, and Juvenile Justice: The Social Control of Delinquent Youth* (Tavistock, London).

Hayek, F. A. (1944), *The Road to Serfdom* (Routledge, London).

—— (1960), *Law, Legislation and Liberty* (3 vols., Routledge, London, reprinted 1982).

King, M. and Piper, C. (1990), *How the Law Thinks about Children* (Gower, Aldershot).

Law Commission (1988), *Family Law:Review of Child Law Guardianship and Custody* Law. Com. 172 (HMSO, London).

Llewellyn, K. (1940), 'The Normative, the Legal, and the Law-Jobs', 49 *Yale Law Journal*, 1355–400.

Miller, P., and Rose, N. (1990), 'Governing Economic Life', *Economy and Society*, 19: ,1–31.

Moore, M. S. (1984), *Law and Psychiatry: Rethinking the Relationship* (Cambridge University Press, Cambridge).

Parton, N. (1991), *Governing the Family: Child Care, Child Protection, and the State* (Macmillan, London).

Shklar, J. (1964), *Legalism* (Harvard University Press, Cambridge, Mass., reprinted 1986).

Sibeon, R. (1989–90), 'Comments on the Structure and Forms of Social Work Knowledge', *Social Work and Social Sciences Review* 1(1): 29–44.

Smith, C., Lane, M., and Walsh, T. (1988), *Child Care and the Courts* (BASW, Macmillan, London).

Thomson, A. (1991), 'Taking the Right Seriously: The Case of F. A. Hayek' in P. Fitzpatrick (ed.), *Dangerous Supplements: Resistance and Renewal in Jurisprudence* (Pluto Press, London).

Trubek, D. (1972), 'Max Weber on Law and the Rise of Capitalism', *Wisconsin Law Review*, 3: 720–53.

Unger, R. M. (1976), *Law in Modern Society* (Free Press, New York).

13. Does the Law Protect Polish Women?

Małgorzata Fuszara

After World War II, two models of family life met in Poland which both influenced the situation of women. They were largely opposed to one another, and the situation of Polish women may be considered unique for the very reason that it was shaped by these two incompatible models. The first is the official model based on equality of the sexes and mass employment of women. The creation of 'equal opportunities' found expression above all in mass access to education and mass employment of women. The other model was based on the tradition and rules of family life accepted and promoted by the Catholic Church. It is a model of divided roles, one that assumes the woman's leading role in the upbringing of children, and treats her performance of duties for the benefit of her home and family as self-evident. This latter traditional model of family was somewhat paradoxically strengthened by some aspects of political life, and also to some extent by the law. The legal provisions tried to propagate the official model: it was impossible, though, to negate completely the existence of the other based on tradition and daily functioning in social life, particularly in the private sphere of family life.

The official model with its assumption of 'gender equality' resulted in a number of specific legal solutions. Thus, equality of all citizens, men and women alike, was made a constitutional principle. According to the Constitution, what serves as a guarantee of the woman's equal rights is the right to work and 'equal pay for equal work', the right to leisure, social security, education, dignity, and distinctions, and also the right to hold public office. These guarantees are based on the principle of 'equality' or 'identity' of men's and women's rights. Other guarantees in the Constitution are peculiar to women, and are based on recognition of the woman's special needs in her role as mother. Here we have the right to mother and child care, protection for pregnant women, paid maternity leave, and so on. The Constitution also declares the aim of strengthening women's position in society, 'particularly mothers and employed women' (Article 78 of the Constitution).

The woman as employee and housewife

The main way forward to equal rights, open to women in post-war Poland, was employment. The post-war ideal, as promoted by official propaganda, was to train women for jobs hitherto reserved for men. Not only was work accessible to everybody; everyone—men and women alike—was expected to work. It is important to bear in mind that women's unlimited access to employment was not just an attempt to implement the ideal of equality but also—and perhaps predominantly—an economic necessity. Quite obviously, with the country practically ruined during the war, reconstruction seemed possible only if both men and women went to work. Admittedly, these particular grounds for the mass employment of women were never openly quoted; it is self-evident, however that the requirements of reconstruction were among the reasons for women's mass employment.

Professional equality was usually interpreted to support the model of a 'woman like a man'. The simplest expression of such models in propaganda were the notorious images of female tractor drivers shown in posters. Yet the differences between the situation of women and men in the labour market were ever-present, and it proved necessary to take them into account in legal provisions. For example, there was legislation which—although not in so many words—introduced the *duty* to work. One has to bear in mind that in the countries where attempts were made to introduce Communism, work was not only accessible and guaranteed for all; it was also the duty of all citizens. International agreements prevented the authorities from openly imposing a duty to work or to perform forced labour; all those countries, however, had statutes concerned with the so-called social parasites or spongers, that is, persons staying out of school and employment. Such persons were obliged to produce evidence of their legitimate sources of maintenance, and to report to competent agencies, since they were believed to be living at the expense of others. When this kind of legislation was introduced in Poland, interesting debates took place concerning women's work. Basing on the assumed equality of all citizens irrespective of gender, the legislators drafted a statute that was to apply to women as well. They could not ignore, however, the existence of the traditional model of family life in which the woman keeps house for the benefit of her family. Women were eventually excluded from the scope of the act, which was made to apply to men only. Behind this exclusion was a conviction which could not possibly be negated: that the women who are not employed nevertheless work at home for their families, that their work is socially useful, and that for this reason they cannot be included in the category of 'social parasites'. Thus, the work performed by women at home for their families was indirectly recognized to be unpaid professional work, although such a far-reaching conclusion as that was not propounded at the time.

The situation of women may be entirely different in countries where work is an individual *right* and the best way of gaining a living or increasing wealth, as compared to those countries where it is largely a *duty* aimed at increasing the wealth of the community. In the former countries, women struggle for the right to work. In the latter, they are given that right automatically; but some treat it as a social opportunity and a chance for self-fulfilment, others as nothing but a burdensome duty. In the countries that aimed at introducing Communism, unemployment was not only eradicated and work opportunities created for all (often by means of setting up fictitious jobs), but attempts were also made to create a climate of moral condemnation for those who did not work. Work performed at home for the benefit of the family was a specific excuse which made it possible not to include the housewife in the category of social parasites. Thus, in those countries, securing work opportunities was not the only guarantee for women's rights. Sometimes the reverse was the case: what did serve as a guarantee was the consent to a situation where the woman did not take a job and thus avoided the proliferation of her duties.

The other model that influenced the situation of Polish women was that of the traditional family which assumed prolonged care of children provided primarily by women. This model is rooted both in the Polish national tradition and in the teachings of the Catholic Church, which promotes the traditional stable family with the roles strictly divided between its separate members. As a matter of fact, the law often promotes this very model, and although attempts at creating neutral norms which would apply to men and women alike can be found in legal regulations, the impact of those norms differs between men and women. Polish families are highly 'child-centrist', a result both of tradition, legal regulation, and judicial practice, and sometimes also, somewhat paradoxically, the country's economic and socio-political situation. An example from the sphere of legal regulation is the parents' duty to provide for their student-child until he or she reaches the age of 25. The economic and social situation is conducive to the children's prolonged dependence on and bonds with their parents and includes, among other things, the housing shortage and the resulting long period in which children live in their parents' flat, as well as low wages which make adult children continuously dependent on the parents' financial assistance. The low wages also lead to parents assisting their adult children and grandchildren for a very long time indeed, such assistance being rendered in a variety of forms, financial or otherwise (baby-sitting, and, until recently, shopping, which involved a lot of queuing for basic goods). Interestingly, and also somewhat paradoxically, this traditional model was sustained by the socio-political situation under Communist rule. As can be found in many sociological studies, the value that the Poles treasured most was a happy family life. In the days of Communist rule, the family was perceived as one of the very few environments where one was to some extent independent, in one's own environment where one could be oneself. It was then practically the only sphere of freedom and an aim worth striving for. Participation in broader social structures was not only blocked but many also rejected it, because the price one had to pay for such participation was a political loss of face resulting from compromise with authority. A ban was also put on any activity where one's name and person were used by the authorities as a 'facade' and for legitimization. It soon became clear that this non-involvement in public activities was by no means tantamount to a lack of interest in public life or a consent to Communist rule. What it meant was a refusal to participate in that particular form of public life. This enhanced withdrawal from public life; consequently, respondents in all studies declared their interest in nothing but family life. Such findings were also obtained on the eve of 'Solidarity', that is, just before the Poles' mass involvement in public life. It appeared that, as soon as change became at all possible and public life acquired a new sense, the people started engaging themselves in that sphere on a mass scale. But as long as no change had been possible, the Poles took no part in public life, which automatically made them concentrate on family and upheld the traditional model in this sphere.

The traditional model of the family involves the woman's performance of many household chores on behalf of her children and the family as a whole. This often conflicts with the woman's professional work and requires the development of special regulations for the woman so that she does not lose her rights as employee and means of subsistence while she takes care of her family, the children in particular. Polish law contains a number of such regulations, some of which can be found in all legislations, other not as widespread. The commonly granted rights include maternity benefits, protection of pregnant women at the workplace, leave to take care of sick children or other family members, and the right to two days free a year, which is granted to mothers of children aged up to 14, without the need to notify the employer as to the reason for taking a day out of work. Another regulation, which is not common in the legislations of other countries, is the right to leave to take care of a small child and the so-called 'educational benefit' due to persons who take that leave. It has to be mentioned here that, although it is the mother who enjoys this right first and foremost, it can also be granted to the father. That, however, is only possible if the mother does not take the leave and gives her consent to its being granted to the father, or if the father directly cares for the child (if the mother is dead, or ill, or has been deprived of parental authority, or her authority limited). The leave is granted for up to three years. It is unpaid in principle: in many cases, though, employees are entitled to the educational benefit. The benefit was intended as the way of making it possible of persons of limited means and for single mothers to exercise their right to care personally for their small children. On its introduction, it enabled the mothers who wanted to devote their energies to bringing up their children to stay at home. According to the legal regulation, the educational benefit represented up to 100 per cent of the lowest wages in Poland in the case of persons whose families had the lowest per capita income; 75 per cent if the income per capita was somewhat higher; and 50 per cent in the case of persons who were still somewhat more better off. Single mothers were paid the benefit, increased by 100 per cent, and also an extra amount—the benefit, however, was not to exceed her former wages at work.

Several years after it was introduced, the benefit could equal the mother's former earnings at work (this was particularly the case for single mothers), and thus made it indeed possible for her to stay at home and care for her child. The benefit was paid for not longer than 1.5 years; today that period is up to two years. It is not paid at all to persons where the per capita income of the family exceeds a particular sum.

With time, however, the educational benefit started to lose its importance as a possible source of maintenance for the mother and child in the situation where the mother wants to stay at home and give her energies to the child. This trend progressed with the worsening of the economic crisis in Poland. Although the mechanism for granting benefits did not change for several years, the actual amounts granted as benefits remained the same over a long period and, with rising inflation, resulted in a situation where the benefit was no longer enough to live on. An example here is the difference between wages and the amounts of benefits over a number of years. Average wages in Poland had risen in 1989 by about 300 per cent as compared to 1988, while the average educational benefit was raised by only 30 per cent. For many years, benefits were specified amounts, and so was the family income per capita which qualified a person to be granted a benefit. Those amounts were not changed in the period of 1981–7 despite the rise in the average wages in that period by about 150 per cent. In this way, the benefit was no longer due to a large group of mothers' instead, it was due to the most indigent only, and was too low to live on. This can also be noted if we compare average benefit to average wages in Poland. In 1982, benefit amounted to 23 per cent of the average wage, and in 1985 14 per cent of the average wage. In 1987, the amounts of both benefits and the family income per capita required for eligibility for a benefit were raised twice. In this way, the group of persons qualifying for a benefit was broadened somewhat, and the benefits themselves were raised. In 1987, the average benefit grew slightly higher and amounted to 21 per cent of the average wages. In 1989, the principles for calculating the amount of benefits were changed. At present, the amount due is 25 per cent of the average wage in the socialized economy, and 40 per cent in the case of an employed single mother. The benefit is due if the average per capita income of the family does not exceed 25 per cent of the average wages in the socialized economy. It has to be stressed, though, that in 1989, which was a year of soaring inflation and a considerable increase in wages, the average benefit amounted to 6 per cent of the average wage. The new principle for calculating benefits could have improved these proportions to some extent; but the actual amount of benefits is still too low to serve as the sole source of maintenance. It should be mentioned, however, that an employee who receives the benefit is still allowed to work, but only half-time.

The legal regulations discussed above illustrate well the problems with which the legislature has to cope in trying to reconcile two trends: the growing importance of paid work for women and the woman's traditional role in the upbringing and care of children. On the one hand, those regulations show that, in some cases, the legal situation of men versus women cannot possibly be defined as identical, as this would be tantamount to a negation of the work performed by the woman at home on behalf of her family as socially useful and often indispensable. As it is, it has been indirectly recognized that household chores are a form of work even if unpaid. Moreover, the regulations discussed demonstrate that, with all the trend towards equal legal treatment for men and women, the woman's specific role nevertheless has to be taken into account. That role relates to the woman's position within the family and the duties she performs on behalf of that family. Her traditional role in the upbringing of children involves the need to grant her specific preferences, for example, the leave to take care of small children, which is granted to the mother unreservedly but to the father only with the mother's consent.

All the ways of regulating the situation of women by law discussed so far are concerned with statutory regulation. They were connected first of all with the woman's paid work and the relationship between that work and the care of children. What has to be discussed now is the law's direct intervention in family life and judicial activities affecting that sphere. I will focus mainly on the ways in which the court secures women's interests in this sphere and defines their rights and duties. The court's activities will be compared with public opinions.

The mother, the father, and parental authority

Polish law contains no rules which would favour either of the parents as the one who should be obliged to care for the child after divorce. Thus, according to the law, both the mother and the father can exercise care and parental authority over the child. In practice, in the vast majority of cases, direct care of the child is granted to the mother. There are, however, two different forms of that grant. Usually, parental authority is granted to both parents, but the child is to live with its mother, who thus exercises direct care over the child. The other form is a grant of parental authority to the mother, and to the father the right to intervene in the child's upbringing and to participate in important decisions concerning the child. The fact has to be stressed that the frequent grants of care to the mothers do not result from any preference given to them by the courts; instead, it is in accordance with the wish of the parties themselves. It is the parties in a divorce case who usually move that the mother should care for the child. Spectacular struggles for the child sometimes reported in the press do happen, but are very rare; I have not come upon a single such situation in my research. On the other hand, what I did come upon were fathers who moved to be granted the care of the child early on in the divorce proceedings, but who resigned that claim very soon. Such motions seem to have been a specific argument to bargain for the optimum position in the proceedings rather than a genuine intention to care for the child. This is also manifested by the fact that in the cases where the father does exercise care, it is only formally so, while the child's actual guardian is the grandmother (father's mother). In two cases where the care of the child was granted to the father, that decision was also in accordance to the wish of both parties.

The grant of direct care over the child to the mother is not a specifically Polish practice: it is regularly found in many other countries as well. The Polish legislation may differ from others in that it does not contain, and never has contained, a regulation which would actually favour the mother in this respect. According to the legal regulations, both parents have the same chances of becoming legal guardians of their child. In practice, though, in accordance with the traditional model of the family and the wish of both parties, care is granted to the mother in the vast majority of cases.

As has been mentioned above, parental authority is often formally granted to both parents in Poland. This gives rise to many problems also found in other countries which guarantee the father's right to decide vital matters about the child and to have contact. As shown by studies, this is tantamount in various countries to a duty imposed on the child to have contact with a parent who takes practically no part in its upbringing. It means that that parent has secured rights to the child even if he fails to fulfil any duties whatever towards the child. It turned out in Poland that often the parents who gave their consent to or even moved for a decision granting parental authority to both parents did not realize the consequences of such a decision; that is, the fact that in a variety of vital matters, each would have to get the other one's consent. In some situations, the residence of that other parent was unknown, or he took no interest whatever in the child. In extreme cases, he might need money for drink and demand to be paid for giving his consent. Thus the settlement which seemed most equitable regarding the rights of both parents and the continuation of bonds between them, may prove unfavourable not only for the parent who exercises direct care over the child, but also for the child itself.

Another aspect of the problem of parental authority and the care of children is also worth discussing. I touched upon it in a questionnaire study carried out in 1989 in Warsaw. Generally, my respondents were against rigid rules granting the child to the mother or the father in the case of divorce, and for an individual response to each case (70 per cent of respondents). None of the respondents supported a rule which would grant parental authority to the father only. About one fifth were for a rule granting authority to the mother (19 per cent). Other answers suggested taking into account the child's age, gender, and preferences.

Not only the answers chosen but also the respondents' reasons for a definite choice are interesting. Most of those who were for individual settlement in each case stated that the actual grant of parental authority should depend upon the child's needs as defined by specialists or the parents; upon which of the parents is willing to care for the child; and according to a few respondents only, upon the ex-spouses' guilt in the divorce or their material situation. The most concise was the answer given by those respondents who said a child was not an object and therefore no rules of settlement of this issue should ever be adopted.

The most interesting opinions, however, were expressed by those who supported the adoption of the rule that authority over the child should be granted to the mother. Interestingly, this answer was chosen by a nearly equal number of men and women, and the differences in the frequency with which representatives of the two sexes actually chose it proved entirely insignificant. Analysis of the reasons shows, however, most interesting differences in the opinions of men and women.

The reasons given by men who thought that authority over the child should as a rule be granted to the mother always contained an element of comparison between men and women as guardians of the child. As a result of that comparison, the woman was found a better guardian. All the statements by men contained adjectives such as 'better', e.g., 'The mother provides a better care', or 'The mother has a more protective attitude'. Another important trait is the stress on the woman's competence and talent in this sphere and their better preparation for motherhood. Only one of the men stated that the mother gave the child more emotional warmth, thus stressing the mother and child emotional union. The remaining men cited the mother's competence, preparation, and abilities as arguments for the care over the child being granted to her as a rule.

Other arguments were presented by the women who believed that parental authority should be granted to the mother as a rule. These women usually stressed the ties between mother and child as the grounds for parental authority being granted to the mother and not to the father. Such grounds were formulated in a number of different ways, e.g., 'the bond between mother and child is indissoluble', 'the mother is instinctively devoted to her child', 'the mother won't ever give her child up', etc. Other grounds cited were those characteristics of the mother such as devotion to her child, self-sacrifice, solicitude, understanding.

It can thus be said that, in general, respondents accepted the solutions contained in the legal regulations and were against a rigid rule specifying which of the parents should be granted parental authority in the case of divorce, and supported individual settlement of each case. Quite a large group, however, were in favour of the authority being granted to the mother automatically (19 per cent). They found it just that rights to the child should be guaranteed to the mother first and foremost, but also, that it is mainly the mother who should be burdened with the duties related to the upbringing of children. The proportion of men and women in this group were practically identical, but representatives of the two sexes gave different grounds for their specific choices. All the men compared the mother and the father as guardians of the child, and concluded that the mother's greater competence, better preparation and talents in this sphere inclined them to grant care of the child to her and not to the father. Finding it right to grant parental authority to the mother, they based their conclusion on an analysis of the mother– father–child relationship. Women considered primarily the mother–child relation and took its indissolubility as the basis for stating that it would be right to introduce a rule that parental authority should be granted to the mother. They quoted the mother's competence less frequently and mentioned more frequently the emotional ties which in their opinion argue for care to be granted to the mother.

Arguments for parental authority to go to the mother as a regular procedure can be found in today's literature, though rarely. Such claims stress first the specific nature of the relationship between the mother and the child that came into being in her womb. Relationships of this kind have no counterpart elsewhere and cannot be compared with any other relationships between people. Everyday practice may be based on this premiss: the parents usually move for direct care of the child to be granted to the mother and the courts decide accordingly; of course, the woman's above-mentioned greater competence is of some importance here also. It should be stressed, though, that acceptance of the equal rights of both parents in the theoretical sphere and in the sphere of general legal regulation is not necessarily tantamount to the conviction that both parents can care for their child equally well. The granting of equal rights to both parents does not negate the specific mother–child relationship: all it does is to guarantee individualized settlement in each case with no pre-assumed preferences based solely on gender. The regulation which has been in force in Poland for many years assumes equality of the parents, and the parallel practice of granting the care of the children almost exclusively to the mothers seems to confirm this thesis.

The mother, the father, and the child's maintenance

One of the basic problems that arises in the case of divorce is that of providing for the child. According to the Polish Family and Guardianship Code, the judicial grant of divorce also contains the decision as to parental authority and the amounts each ex-spouse is obliged to spend on the child's maintenance and upbringing (Article 58 of the Code). The Code does not specify the principles for calculating those services; it only contains a most general statement that the exact amounts should depend on the needs of the person entitled to the service, and on the earning capacity and wealth of the one obliged to render it.

Like many other norms, these are also formulated in neutral terms which do not refer specifically only to the mother or the father. In practice, however, with direct care being most often granted to the mother, the decisions about divorce specify the amount of maintenance due to the child from the father and payable to the mother. The situation is, of course, the opposite in the few cases when parental authority is granted to the father.

The most frequent situation with which we deal in cases of maintenance is that of bargaining about the amount. When demanding
maintenance of a given amount or moving for an increase, the parent
who exercises direct care over the child usually points to growing
child-care expenses, inflation, or her or his limited possibilities for
earning extra money because of caring for the child. The parent
obliged to pay the maintenance—the father as a rule—agrees to pay
a much smaller sum and argues, in turn, that a higher amount of
maintenance would impoverish his new family, that he earns less than
before, and so on. In divorce cases, the parties usually reach agreement as to the amount of maintenance. They seem to aim above all
at getting divorced, and therefore remove all the obstacles which
might make that more difficult to attain or the judicial proceedings
longer. Alternatively, in cases about maintenance or increase of maintenance, it is much more difficult to reach any agreement. The court
then determines an amount that is intermediate between what the
parent who exercises care demands and what the other one who is
obliged to pay maintenance actually agrees to pay.

There are also the relatively rare cases where an ex-spouse is
granted alimony after divorce. According to Polish law, the ex-spouse
may be granted alimony if he or she has not been found to be the
guilty party and is in distress. This happens where one of the spouses
was found exclusively guilty in the divorce proceedings, and that
divorce results in deterioration of the innocent spouse's material situation (Article 60 of the Family and Guardianship Code). But these
provisions are seldom applied in practice. Alimony is usually granted
to the ex-wives who had never been employed but have cared for the
children, and thus could not acquire pension rights and who, by the
time of the divorce, are past retirement age; they cannot take a job
and are consequently left without a source of maintenance. In such
situations, the court imposes the duty to pay alimony on the ex-husband. This is a typical consequence of the vague status of the housework performed by the woman: such work is not treated as equal to
employment and as such does not guarantee pension rights. In the
case of divorce, the woman is left without means of subsistence and
finds herself in the position of suppliant in relation to her ex-
husband, who for many years took advantage of her work for the
family. Yet no debates on changing this situation have even begun in
Poland so far.

It is worth mentioning that there has been, among the cases examined, one where the wife was found exclusively guilty of the disintegration of marital life and was obliged to pay alimony to her ex-husband, whose material situation deteriorated greatly after divorce.

The legal regulation of alimony, maintenance, and judicial decisions in such cases are but a fragment of a broader problem of providing for one's children or an ex-spouse in distress. A whole variety of problems still remain related to the enforcement of alimony or maintenance. Those services are executed compulsorily, and persistent evasion of the duty to pay them is an offence (Article 186 of the Penal Code) for which the statutory penalty is deprivation of liberty for a period of three months to three years. In some cases, though, the alimony or maintenance order proves impossible to execute for a variety of reasons (i.e. a complete lack of earnings or possessions on the part of the person obliged to pay, or his going into hiding or abroad). The alimony–maintenance institution fund was set up in 1985 to help people in distress in such cases. Payments are made from the fund 'for children and other persons in distress due to impossibility of executing alimony or maintenance'. The fund is composed of grants-in-aid from the state budget and of dues collected from persons obliged to pay alimony or maintenance. Benefits from the fund are paid to those who have been granted maintenance or alimony (by a judgment, judicial decision, or agreement in court) but implementation has proved ineffective. Payment is only due if the per capita income of those persons does not exceed a specified amount. A maximum sum of payment from the fund is also set. Although the fund is no doubt a most important institution for the most indigent persons who cannot obtain their due maintenance or alimony, its actual importance and the assistance it renders depends above all on the amounts paid, and the predetermined amount of qualifying income. As in the case of educational benefits, the importance of the fund was greater before the economic crisis manifested itself. The mechanism of the fund's operation remained unchanged but, due to the shortage of funds, the institution has now lost a great deal of its actual importance. It should also be mentioned that in this case, the legal regulation is formulated in neutral terms, as it concerns 'children and persons who find themselves in financial difficulties'. In practice, however, the fund provides relief for families where the mother cares for her children and finds it impossible to obtain even the minimum of financial assistance from the father.

Women and divorce

In Poland the clash between two models—the flexible model of the family contained in the law on the one hand, and the traditional model propagated by the Catholic Church which assumes the indissolubility of marriage—gives the question of society's attitude towards divorce added importance. Generally speaking, Polish society accepts divorce (as few as 10 per cent declaring themselves absolutely opposed). Over 25 per cent support unrestricted divorce. But the largest group of respondents support divorce only on certain grounds. The most frequently mentioned reasons for granting divorce were: alcoholism or cruel treatment of family members, and also persistent adultery and situations where divorce would be in the best interests of the children, or they would not be harmed by it.

The detailed questions in my study were answered in a way that showed women to be more frequently opposed to divorce than men. They were less likely to support unrestricted access to divorce, or divorce to be granted to a properly behaving couple if a child of the marriage explicitly opposes the divorce. Fewer women accepted divorce where there was a conflict between a man's original and new informal family, i.e. another woman expecting his child. The women supported the permanence of the original family—even if both parents wanted a divorce but the child was against it, and also in the situation of conflict between the first and the new family. Can we say, therefore, that a limitation on the right to divorce would be in accordance with women's preferences as revealed in public-opinion surveys? I believe this question has to be answered with caution. It should be stressed here that amongst petitioners for divorce, women constitute the majority. The woman usually moves for divorce when she is the victim of her husband: as a result of his alcoholism or cruelty. Women are much more likely to seek divorce for reasons which might be called traumatic, that is, when they can no longer endure the situation and are bearing all the consequences of the husband's irresponsibility or alcoholism; furthermore, the children from the marriage also have to endure those consequences and find themselves in the situation of victims. Thus, were the right to divorce limited, this would have a great effect on the women as the way out of their victimization would thus be barred or rendered more difficult. The reasons why women seek divorce are those most frequently mentioned by my respondents when asked about the situations in which they found divorce admissible. My questionnaire did not contain extreme situations, as I found them too obvious. Had a description of such a situation been included in the questionnaire, it might even have reduced the proportion of opponents of divorce (10 per cent in my study); as we all know, a general declaration does not always agree with the solution proposed in an extreme case.

Characteristically, men seek divorce in different situations and for different reasons. Most want the former marriage dissolved when they have already engaged themselves in a new relationship which they now intend to legalize. It is precisely in this kind of situation that the women who postulate protection of the original family declare themselves against divorce. The interpretation of this finding must not be over-simplified. It would be wrong to treat it as just a trend towards protection of the woman's interest: after all, there is another woman entangled in the new relationship. Yet women more frequently declare themselves in favour of protecting the former marriage, which is the earlier contract.

Once again, we must keep in mind that Polish law does not contain any list of reasons which would justify or render impossible the granting of a divorce. The Family and Guardianship code only provides that a divorce petition can be brought in the situation of irretrievable breakdown of the marriage. Thus in each case, the court has to decide whether that breakdown has taken place and can be called permanent and irretrievable. The court's role is, therefore, most important both in the dissolution of marriage and concerning the decision about the guilt of one or both of the spouses. On a unanimous request from both parties, the court desists from deciding about guilt; this happens in most cases. Sometimes, however, the spouses prove unable to reach agreement even on this, and the court has to decide about guilt. That decision is of great legal importance in some cases and has further legal consequences: in principle, a spouse who is exclusively guilty of the breakdown can only be granted divorce with the consent of the innocent spouse (unless the latter's refusal to give his/her consent is against the principles of social coexistence in the given circumstances—Article 56 of the Family and Guardianship Code). The court files, in cases where guilt was decided upon, provide extensive information not only about the marriage and marital conflicts but also about a variety of other problems. There is valuable information about society's conception of the husband's and wife's duties in the marriage. What is more, the files of these cases also provide information about the judges' ideas as to those duties. This is of great importance, as the judges' conception of a good husband and good wife—that is, about the guilt and innocence of the man and the woman—determine the actual settlement of matters of great import for the parties: the granting of the divorce, decision as to guilt, and the resulting further consequences. I will begin with the divorcing spouses' conceptions of the other spouse's duties. What they blame each other for during the proceedings enables us to draw conclusions about their conception of a marriage partner's duties.

Generally speaking, the model of husband and wife that emerges from the files of divorce cases is highly traditional, with the great burden of household duties falling on the woman. We have the impression that all the duties aimed at preserving the union are imposed on her. To explain this statement, let us consider the postulated duties of husband and wife which may be deduced from these files.

The husband's duties are defined negatively as a rule and mark the sphere of acts which he should not commit. Thus, the husband should not drink excessively, or beat his wife and children, or argue using coarse language or—although this aspect is not stressed as explicitly—be unfaithful to his wife. The husband has only two positive duties: to supply the means for his own subsistence, and to provide in part for the home and children; and to live together with his family. Failure to provide for the family and leaving the common flat is sometimes quoted as the husband's neglect of his duties; yet, as will be shown further on, it is not always tantamount to a breakdown of the union.

The wife's duties are defined in an entirely different way. They are positive and concern the things the wife should do. Thus, she should cook, wash clothes, tidy the flat. What is often mentioned as an accusation meant to demonstrate the wife's, at least *shared*, guilt for the breakdown of the marriage is the fact that she neither cooks nor washes clothes nor tidies up the house. Moreover, as can be concluded from the court files, the wife is also obliged to satisfy the husband's emotional needs—that is, to make him feel loved and appreciated. In extreme cases, even the husband's unfaithfulness is interpreted as the result of the wife's emotional disengagement in the marriage.

It follows from the analysis of court files in divorce cases that the husband's duties resolve themselves into the abstention from doing ill. There is nothing in the files to show that men have any positive duties whatsoever which would lead to the building of the union. Instead, they should simply abstain from destroying it.

Obviously, the women are also obliged to abstain from doing ill. This requirement is so self-evident that it does not need to be mentioned in divorce proceedings. In individual cases, the initial pleas sometimes accuse the wife of excessive drinking or unfaithfulness. But beside the 'minimum' abstention from doing ill, the wife also has a whole variety of positive duties. Thus she is obliged to perform a number of works and to render a number of services for the benefit of the family, the husband included. She is obliged to display affection to her husband; in this latter sphere, however, there is evidence to show that the husband also has that duty in relation to his wife. However, not a single case could be found in my study where the fact that the husband failed to help at home would be considered a neglect of duties. In one case, a husband who took leave to take care of a small child still expected his employed wife to do all the work at home and to attend to his personal needs, while he himself used the leave to indulge in drinking.

As long as the spouses live together, marital bonds can only be broken by the woman, who may refuse to work or render services for the benefit of the union. An example here is a case where the husband said, 'My wife moved all her belongings to the bigger room and said she would no longer have sex with me, cook my meals, or wash my clothes' (case RW–55). This situation is somewhat similar to divorce in the Zuni tribe as described by Ruth Benedict in her *Patterns of Culture*. A Zuni woman who wants a divorce puts the husband's belongings outside the family lodgings, upon which the husband moves to his parent's hut. There is yet another feature that makes divorces among the Zuni and in Poland rather similar: in the case of the breakdown of the union, it is usually the husband who leaves, and the former family union continues without him. The only way for the husband to break the bonds, or rather, to withdraw from the union, is to leave the common house. Even if he neglects his elementary duties—by drinking, arguing, and not providing for the family—the union, cared for by the wife, continues. A lack of any services whatsoever on the part of the husband does not necessarily lead to breakdown of the union. If the woman, however, ceases to render services for the benefit of the husband, the woman 'gives notice of the termination' of the union, or simply ruptures it, or removes the husband from the union, which continues, composed of herself and the children.

Of course, the husband's and wife's duties, thus defined, are not specified explicitly anywhere. They follow from statements, accusations, and questions asked in court, and sometimes even from the grounds of judicial decisions. This traditional division of duties within the family is professed not only by the parties but also, which is much more dangerous for the women, by the court. Admittedly, none of the statutory regulations provide differing definitions of the husband's and wife's duties; nor do they burden the wife with more duties than the husband. Yet law does not only consist of the statutory regulation but also, to a great extent, of enforcement. Consequently, it depends solely on the judge to decide whether to find the breakdown of the marriage irretrievable and permanent, and which of the partners is guilty. In asking questions, judges show that they themselves consider the traditional model of family still valid. Sometimes this opinion is revealed in the grounds given for decisions. One such statement declares that the wife 'contributed to the disintegration of matrimonial ties in that she neglected her duties as a wife: she neither cooked, nor tidied the flat, nor washed and ironed clothes'. This model may be astounding; it is especially so, considering that the judges in the court I examined were women. If these female judges accepted the above model of husband and wife, the line of defence taken by the wives should hardly be surprising: when accused of failure to wash clothes or cook, the wives never stated that they could see no reason why they should do so or that they had different views on the division of duties in marriage; instead, they defended themselves by trying to demonstrate that they actually did perform all the required tasks.

Some consolation can be found in the fact that such cases are scarce and concern the most litigious of divorces only. Yet even those scarce incidents require changes to bar the possibility of disadvantageous legal consequences being borne by a person for the sole reasons that she has less traditional views on the division of duties within the family, and that she refuses to perform more work than the other spouse. But changing judges' attitudes seems a much more difficult task than changing statutory law.

Conclusion

The post-war legal regulations in Poland introduced equality for men and women in many spheres. For a long time now, the law has been using neutral formulations which make it applicable to both men and women alike. This has often created conditions for the development of the 'woman-like-man' model. This is particularly evident in the sphere of professional work, where the neutral legal regulations were accompanied by slogans on equal rights and the social rise of women, who could now be trained in hitherto typically male jobs.

Similar trends to formulate law in neutral terms can also be seen in the regulations concerning the family. None of these regulations concern women only, although some are more concerned with them than with men. As in all other legislations, the exceptions are provisions related to the rights of women employees during pregnancy and after childbirth: maternity leave, job protection, and the right to easier work. Some other rights related to the care of the child predominantly concern women but can also be enjoyed by the child's father with the consent of the mother, such as leave to take care of a small child and educational benefits, which make it possible for the parent to care for the child.

Most provisions that concern the family are formulated in absolutely neutral terms which refer to men and women alike; but their actual application to men is entirely different from their application to women. This group of provisions includes first and foremost those regulating the questions of parental authority and maintenance. Furthermore, judicial practice expresses predominantly traditional views on the family and the division of roles within it. Legal regulations and judicial practice may serve here as an example of the clash between contrasting family models in post-war Poland.

Another related conflict is that between mass employment for women and the child-centrism of Polish families, which imposes a large number of duties on the woman; the devotion of a great deal of time and attention; and sometimes the resignation of her own ambitions or interests. An attempt was made to solve this problem by means of a network of cheap (state-subsidized) kindergartens and crèches. Yet resort to this kind of care was treated as appropriate only in extreme circumstances, and to be avoided for as long as possible; hence, the attempts to secure benefits, maintenance, and employee rights for women who wanted to rear their small children in person. This, in turn, strengthened the traditional model of the family which assumes that the mother should care for the child. This traditional model is preserved and continued both through the granting of care over the child after divorce to the mother as a rule, and through the economic and housing conditions in Poland which result in the children's prolonged dependence on their parents.

Another question still remains for consideration: that of the guaranteeing and implementation of women's rights in Poland in the future under the changed social and economic conditions. Due to the economic crisis, many forms of state assistance to the family and to women introduced previously became all but illusory. The propagation of the idea of complete economic freedom sometimes led to questioning of the need to express the equality of the sexes and women's rights in legal acts. Shortages of funds resulted in the closing down of crèches and kindergartens, and the lack of state subsidization made those that remain too expensive for some. Thus the situation of women grows explicitly worse. One should bear in mind, though, that even if Polish women never had to struggle for the amount of equality they enjoy today, they have become so used to it by now that they are not going to accept a changed situation in this respect. At the same time, even if many women treat employment as an economic necessity and not their own free choice, employment is nevertheless increasingly seen as the symbol of woman's independence, the way of fulfilling her ambitions and allowing her to participate in a sphere of social life of special importance in the countries that tried to introduce Communism. Thus, the situation of many women is unlikely to change any more, even if the underlying economic necessity should cease to exist.

In the so-called Communist countries, the state played a large part in solving many problems considered to be private, and in assisting members of society. Whenever 'natural' sources of relief or care (such as the family) failed, attempts were made to substitute for them from state funds or by state agencies. Today, the state has largely withdrawn from this activity. Fortunately, it has not, so far, reduced the assistance rendered to weaker family members such as children or women. Even if state assistance is rather insignificant today, due to the country's indigence and shortage of funds, the mechanisms are nevertheless preserved which make it possible to grant such assistance. This is why it can be hoped that its importance will grow again in the future, making it possible to prevent a drastic reduction in the circumstances of divorced women and their children. Because of that assistance, the women who choose to care for their small children, as well as those who decide on professional work, will be able to do just that, and the position of the woman, who is today a vulnerable family member, will be strengthened.

14. Women, Family and Property: British Songs of Innocence and Experience

Anne Bottomley

'it would seem the most natural thing in the world for any wife'

(per Lord Bridge *Lloyds Bank* v. *Rosset*)

Although it already seems history, in the sense of a distant past, it is worth recalling that in the 1970s and 1980s, when the women's movement in the UK attempted to encapsulate the struggle in a series of 'demands'; the fifth demand was for 'women's financial and legal independence'. This gave rise to a specific campaign group (The 5th Demand Group) and also gave a focus to a series of strategies developed by other women's groups, including the women's legal collective 'Rights of Women'.[1] A major concern for feminists within these campaigns was (and is) to argue that, whilst we must recognize the structural inequalities that women suffer from, any legal strategies developed as an attempt to mitigate this must not reproduce models of dependency. This is particularly problematic when a legal system is based on the free-market model of equal individuals freely entering into legal relations. Family law is a difficult area in philosophical terms for both liberal theorists and feminists—are there any compelling reasons for arguing for models of legal relations which explicitly address gender relations? If so, what conceptual frames can legal discourse offer?

In nineteenth-century England the debates surrounding the claim for married women to be able to hold separate property (most importantly at the time a claim to be able to hold income as their own), and not to have it fall under the control of their husbands, illustrated with stark clarity the tension between property relations based on marriage status and a model based on individual rights. Although each step in the process of reform was seen by contemporaries as deeply controversial, in retrospect the reformers had history on their side in the sense that their demands were couched within

---

[1] For an example of the work of ROW see the Family Law Sub-Group chapter in Brophy and Smart (1985).

the prevailing, and increasingly strong, philosophy of liberal individualism and the demand for juridical equality.[2] The reforms do have to be understood in the broader frame of the demand for legal capacity and enfranchisement; they also need to be seen (and this is very visible when one reads the debates surrounding the Acts) in terms of contemporary concerns about gender roles and the labour market. Within the debates one is presented with an attempt to bring about a reform which gives married women rights, without undermining marriage and gender roles in relation to paid and unpaid work. Indeed some reformers argued that by allowing women to keep their own income, marriage would be reinforced by forcing men to work to provide for a family rather than relying on their wives. The impact of these dimensions on the specificity of family property relations was, and is, problematic for us. How do we reconcile, in contemporary feminist terms, a wish for financial independence (beyond simple formal equality) with the reality of familial property relations, both in terms of ownership of assets as well as income?

Issues raised at the time of the reforms well illustrate this problem. The 1868 Select Committee took evidence from jurisdictions in the United States on the impact of introducing separate property. A series of questions dealt with the issue of whether, if a wife could hold separate property during marriage, she should also be able to claim maintenance at the end of a marriage (at the time this would have meant a marriage brought to an end on grounds of fault and which restricted maintenance to an innocent and chaste wife). The Select Committee were assured that the two were not incompatible. However the issue was clear. If a wife had the right to earn and to acquire in her own name, how was this to be reconciled with the marital claim to be supported: by an, albeit limited, claim against the wealth of the husband? The problem is further illustrated in the rejoinder written by Fitzjames Stephen to John Stuart Mill. Mill is well known and still read by contemporary feminists for a fine example of a nineteenth-century argument made for married women's rights, and quite rightly so. Less well known is Fitzjames Stephen's rejoinder, a classic of the Victorian genre in which the 'weaker sex' are to be loved and protected for their vulnerability. If it is read at all today it is read as an example of ridiculously outmoded views, but there is one key line in Stephens when, although he links protection

---

[2] For detail on the process of reform see Holcombe (1983).

with submission, he goes on to alert us to the dangers of one of the most obvious alternative legal models: 'Submission and protection are correlative. Withdraw the one and the other is lost, and force will assert itself a hundred times more harshly through the law of contract than it ever did through the law of status' (Stephen 1873).

However much we may dislike the linkage he makes, Stephen does sound a note of realism when he warns that most wives will not be equal in economic terms and an important note of caution, missing in Mill, when he argues against the harshness of a regime of equality before the law which is not merely gender neutral but also gender blind.

The reforms introduced in 1882, which give married women the right to hold and control their own property and income, do so under the fiction that for these purposes they are *feme sole* (unmarried).[3] No changes were made to the law allowing women to claim maintenance at the end of marriage. The Select Committee had taken some evidence on community of property regimes in certain American states but had concluded that they were essentially un-English and preferred a model of separate property as one already used by those with sufficient wealth to utilize the law of trusts.[4] A major (but unspoken) advantage in taking this approach was that not only did it provide a less radical mode of reform (and follow the model actually called for by most of the campaigners, one which fitted with the model of liberal individualism) but it also kept intact the principle of freedom of testation. A married woman remained in a situation where she was given no claims to her husband's income or estate either during marriage or on death or divorce; what she now had was simply the right to acquire property herself, plus the continuation of a claim to be maintained during marriage and a claim to maintenance after divorce.[5] She started to emerge as an

---

[3] Married Women's Property Act 1882, Section 1.

[4] Put simply this was the process by which a family could 'settle' property for a daughter's use which would provide income not under the control of her husband. It obviously required sufficient capital to establish the trust; the model then was that of a male member of the family who would be deemed to be the 'owner' in law but was actually recognized as merely holding the property 'on trust' for someone else (the beneficiary). This model of a trustee holding for the benefit of others is still extremely important in English family property law; whether constructed formally or as developed by the courts in recognition of a *de facto* situation which fails the formal rules for construction of trusts but allows for the recognition and enforcement of informal trusts.

[5] Since 1975 claims have been allowed against an estate on death but they are only for income and are based on a combination of status and actual economic dependency. The basic principle of freedom of testation remains.

individual within the market (and familial) economy, and law, a first major step towards full juridical and civic personality.

Since that time family law has been caught within the problematic of a recognition of the economic vulnerability of married women, and the correlative of whether their husband's property should be seen in more familial terms, and the wish to treat them as individuals. In classical liberal philosophy this tension can only be resolved by arguing through the language of 'vulnerability' and 'protection' (see e.g. O'Donovan, 1984); in more modern terms it is the issue of 'dependency'. This problem has as much resonance today as it did when it was debated between Mill (Mill 1929) and Stephen. For modern feminists the debate is posed in these terms—how do we find ways of recognizing women's structural inequality within marriage without reinforcing it? It has been the unhappy role of feminists in this country in recent years to have to continually argue that what might seem a more progressive philosophy of treating women as equals is too often blind to actual inequality. Noticeably the debate is still formulated in terms of claims made by individuals against other individuals; it is still very difficult to talk in, for instance, familial terms. The general tone of most English textbooks on family law is that the law has now, on the whole, found an adequate balance in dealing with these issues. On the one hand we are offered individual choice (a model of private ordering in which the couple can decide for themselves), and on the other we have court intervention on divorce, based on a flexible, discretionary model in which the court, in following statutory guide-lines, may make such property adjustments and awards which seem, to the court, to be suitable for the particular circumstances.[6]

It seems to me that this is far too simplistic a reading of what remains a very difficult issue, not only in the construction of formal law but also in the development of other patterns of dispute settlement at the end of a relationship. Is there an argument for taking into account gender specificity?

I want to address one aspect of this issue not in terms of those areas where women are most overtly vulnerable (e.g. domestic violence), or in terms of when women are most visibly economically vulnerable (on separation and divorce) but rather by arguing that we should look more closely at what brings couples together initially:

---

[6] Under the Matrimonial Causes Act 1973, as amended 1984.

their expectations of domestic–sexual relations. In doing this I am implicitly making three points. First that it is the way in which relationships are set up that must hold important clues to the confusion and bitterness that marks their breakdown. Secondly that whilst marriage holds a certain emotional, social, and legal significance, there is nothing which fundamentally distinguishes it, in terms of the issues I want to raise, from cohabitation other than the factor of legal status. Finally, that although the birth and care of children are the most significant factors in women's economic vulnerability, their very entry into a domestic–sexual relationship is the beginning of the narrative of differing expectations which lie at the base of potential conflict between men and women. What I am arguing here, crudely, is that by looking at the frame of living together (married or unmarried), rather than at the frame of separation, we can begin to excavate possible patterns of gendered behaviour and see them as normal and therefore to be addressed; rather than continue to address dysfunctional patterns of failure and separation as if, at the core of ongoing relationships, there lie no problematic issues which might prefigure patterns of conflict and separation. My concern here is to begin to consider our expectations, and our construction of the experiences of our domestic lives, and to question to what extent gender difference is visible: different enough and visible enough to the point where we cannot afford to be blind to it. Having said this I must emphasize that I am talking in terms of motifs and narratives rather than arguing that this is the case for all couples on all occasions. I do not hold to a simplistic structural argument that power relations are simply about men holding power to the detriment of women, for me, we have to face both the depth of division between men and women (e.g. Olivier, 1989) as well as the specificity of power relations within differing familial settings.[7]

Within this frame a case-study of the access women have to property ownership within the context of domestic relations, with particular reference to home ownership, is instructive.

In June 1991 Teresa Gorman (Conservative MP) introduced a

---

[7] The model I am developing certainly draws from psychoanalytical material; I prefer a reading of this material which is not determinist or absolutist and which, while recognizing dominant narratives and structures in interpersonal relations, does not finally hold our possibilities solely within these frames. A major step in not being caught within these structural limitations is simply to recognize them. This does not seem to me to be a new form of determinism but rather a new possibility of overcoming by facing the extent to which our lives are fractured by gender difference.

parliamentary bill arguing for the introduction of cohabitation contracts for cohabitants. This bill had no chance of success, but the
arguments she used in favour of it are particularly pertinent to our
discussions. Her major concern was with access to property rights for
cohabiting women. In her speech she talked of women entering into
relationships 'starry-eyed' and with no thought of the economic consequences should the relationship end. She pointed out that few couples thought of, let alone talked about, such issues and that for
women in particular this could have devastating consequences. When
no formal arrangement to share property had been made; what
claims might a woman have, especially a woman who had taken on
domestic responsibilities to the detriment of her own earning capacity
in the expectation that provision would be found within the relationship?

This has to be placed within the context of a number of political
and legal factors:

1. The emphasis in this country on private ownership of housing-
   stock and the cut-back in public housing.
2. Despite the recession in the housing market the price of accommodation is still very high in proportion to income; purchasing
   houses with a mortgage often requires a contribution from a
   second wage earner.
3. English property law allows two forms of claim to ownership:
   (a) through legal title (being the registered owner); (b) through a
   claim that, despite lack of title, an interest in the property exists
   due to financial contributions made, or as a result of an understanding of shared ownership on the basis of which the
   claimant has acted to their detriment. Such claims are made in
   equity and utilize the law of trusts; cases are heard in the
   Chancery Division.
4. Family law in England is still based on the doctrine of separate
   property established in 1882. Marriage *per se* makes no difference to claims of ownership; however it does convey rights of
   occupation and allows for claims to be made against the estate
   on divorce. Since 1973, following a successful petition for
   divorce, or judicial separation, a petitioner may ask for financial
   provision to be made; this includes capital sums and the transfer of property. Such claims are heard under the jurisdiction of
   the Family Division; the courts have not only a wide range of

powers but also a great deal of discretion. The major point here is that despite the discretion of the court to transfer property; the starting point is with property rights rather than a regime of rights based on marriage status. A woman is put into the position of asking for property to be transferred to her at the discretion of the court.[8]

This leaves a woman with three routes of access to property in the domestic scenario:

1. Through common law; have the partners put the property in joint names?
2. Through equity; can she make a claim through financial contributions or based on an estoppel argument?
3. Through family law (if married, or, more narrowly through claims via children, if unmarried, since 1989); can she make a case for the courts to exercise their discretion?

A persuasive argument was made by Ruth Deech (1984), that women would not be able to achieve full juridical equality if they continued to try to achieve property claims through arguments based on marriage status; she argued that no property claim should arise except through the rules of law and equity. In as far as property could, or should, be held as a family asset this could be achieved through simply making the decision to hold it jointly, in law or equity. The problem with this argument goes to the core of this paper as well as Teresa Gorman's bill: unless the partners are *ad idem* and make a formal agreement, what evidence do we have of the bargaining position women might hold, either at the inception of the relationship or, as seen retrospectively, when the relationship has come to an end? How successful are women likely to be in utilizing either models of contracts or of trusts when there is no formal agreement and the courts are asked to decide on the basis of evidence brought before them whether such an agreement can be implied?[9]

---

[8] See n. 6.

[9] Because of the history of the use of trusts in this country, the focus has been on trusts rather than contracts. In some jurisdictions the contractual model is more favoured; particularly when matrimonial property is held under a community regime rather than as separate property. In such situations a contractual model is used to bring the partners, by analogy, into a status model and therefore achieve rights to ownership of the familial assets. The contractual form is limited, in my opinion, as it is predicated on an exchange relationship.

Songs of Innocence

Imagine that we are at the start of a relationship: there is a great deal of mutual dreaming about what the couple will do together but evidence found in property cases suggests that rarely is there concrete discussion about the practicalities of economic relations, especially should the couple separate.

The first issue is simply how silence is interpreted; but equally important is the different ways in which the genders seem to construe what is spoken. What I am going to argue here is controversial; my argument is that whilst we have recognized access to economic resources as a problem for women, what has rarely been recognized is the equally important issue of access to language, both in the use of silence and the use of speech. Evidence given in one recent case arising under the equitable jurisdiction is not, in my opinion, unusual and illustrates my point:

> As soon as we heard he was likely to get the money. We looked round, looked for a suitable home for us and children. I always understood we were going to share whatever we had, big or little. We always discussed it as being ours. The only discussion was in very general terms. We needed a house; we would go out and look for one we could own as a couple for a family. When we found (the house), he said he was glad he would be able to provide a proper home, a place where we could be secure. I understood it would be jointly ours. He'd always indicated it would be a joint venture. Everything we did in the past had been jointly done. If you live with someone, you don't 'dissect'. It was the accepted thing . . .' (Mrs Rosset giving evidence; quoted in Court of Appeal decision *Lloyds Bank* v. *Rosset* (1988))

This was accepted in the court of first instance and the Court of Appeal, as evidence of an agreement to share on the basis of which Mrs Rosset acted to her detriment and therefore acquired an interest in the property. I would argue that other factors in the case inclined the courts towards a preference to accept Mrs Rosset's evidence rather than that of her husband (it was accepted that he had explicitly lied on at least one occasion); however in the House of Lords a more orthodox judge was able to utilize the tools of specificity and explicitness to find against Mrs Rosset. He wanted explicit evidence that there was an agreement about ownership.

I pause to observe that neither a common intention by spouses that a house is to be renovated as a 'joint venture' nor a common intention that the house is to be shared by parents and children as the family home throws any light on their intentions with respect to the beneficial ownership of the property. (per Lord Bridge, *Lloyds Bank* v. *Rosset*, 1990)

Lord Bridge did not recognize that such a requirement of evidence of an agreement specifically on the point of ownership could pose a problem:

Spouses living in amity will not normally think it necessary to formulate or define their respective interests in property in any precise way. The expectations of parties to every happy marriage is that they will share the practical benefits of occupying the matrimonial home whoever owns it. But this is something quite distinct from sharing the beneficial interest . . . These considerations give rise to special difficulties for judges who are called on to resolve a dispute between spouses who have parted and are at arm's length as to what was their common intention or understanding . . . when they were still living as a united family and acquiring a matrimonial home in the expectation of living in it together indefinitely.

Here the problem is presented as primarily one of time; but I would suggest that we need also to consider the problem of specificity. It seems to me that this is not only a requirement of a certain jurisprudential approach but also a mode of reasoning and language use which is more conducive to men than women. This may in part be due to material factors and differences in socio-economic strengths and roles, but evidence drawn from psychoanalytical material would suggest that this division derives from the construction of gender identity; in other words it is far more deeply embedded than a simple analysis of economic difference and consequent relative power relations would reveal (see Olivier, 1989; Grosz, 1989).

I have suggested two particular uses of language that need to be thought about; the use of silence, and how that might be interpreted, and the use of specificity, as a clear focus to the discussions. There is some evidence from the case material to suggest that women too often read silence as positive assent and lack of specificity as covering a number of issues with equal firmness rather than evading the particular issue. There is also evidence of the great difficulty some women experience in raising issues about property; as well as their difficulty in persuading their partners to confront the issue through discussions. Take, for example, the case of *Coombes* v. *Smith* heard in 1986. This is a case of first instance (and therefore at the most can only be persuasive precedent) but much referred to in the textbooks as evidence of a narrower definition of law (not to the benefit of the party making the claim) than had previously seemed to be the case in the higher courts. The judge accepted that 'the plaintiff was manifestly a completely honest witness'; unfortunately, throughout the case there is clear evidence of a disparity between what was being said and what was being heard:

> some time during 1980 or 1981 the plaintiff asked the defendant what security she or (her daughter) would have if something happened to him. The defendant replied, 'Don't worry, I have told you I'll always look after you' or words to that effect. The plaintiff said in evidence, 'I didn't ask that sort of question in the early days. I thought things would be OK. I let things drift along, then as time went on I started to ask him.

Later: 'the plaintiff once again raised the question of putting the property in joint names, but the defendant refused saying, "Don't dictate to me."'

It is quite clear from the case that the woman did, over the course of the relationship, begin to try to discuss her position in relation to the property but 'silence' operated in a number of ways. First, by their mutual silence on the issue, secondly by the man's later refusal to deal with the issue (except in the most general terms), thirdly by his literal silencing of the issue, and finally by her retreat in the hope that the situation would eventually be resolved. Each aspect worked crucially against her once the case came to law.

She was hopelessly optimistic to the point that she hard statements with an interpretation which was based on an attempt to find the reassurance she came to need after the honeymoon period was over. The man never actually moved in with her; despite repeated assurances that he would leave his wife to do so. In 1984 he:

> confessed to the plaintiff that he had left his wife and moved in with another woman some seven months previously. But he still professed an intention to move in with the plaintiff. He told her he couldn't let her waste ten years of her life, saying, 'leave me a couple of days to sort it out and you will have a lodger,' referring, as the plaintiff understood it, to himself. However, consistently with what had happened before, the defendant did not move in.

One could easily be forgiven for thinking that by this time the woman should have known better and withdrawn from a hopeless situation. Unfortunately economic as well as emotional dependency was now in play; she had a child and only a part-time low-paid job.

She had no assets of her own. She continued to rely on his assurances and to seek what evidence she could to confirm that his promises would eventually be performed; but as the man's lawyer argued: 'where a man and a woman live together, they always expect or hope that the relationship will be a permanent one . . . what they say at this point cannot be relied upon when the relationship breaks down.'

Again we return to specificity:

a belief that the defendant would always provide her with a roof over her head is, to my mind, something quite different from a belief that she has a right to remain there against his wishes. Moreover, all the statements relied upon by the plaintiff were made by the defendant while the relationship with the plaintiff was continuing. There is no evidence before me of any discussion at all between the plaintiff and the defendant as to what would happen in the event of the relationship breaking down and of the defendant choosing to live with another woman.

All these points, in relation to both cases, are concerned with the need to find an agreement or an assurance upon which the plaintiff acted. Both cases, to me, exemplify the problems for women in having to move into a frame of language-use which is more conducive to men than to women. This is essentially different from, although clearly closely related to, expectations based on the socio-economic construction of gender roles. We need continually to distinguish these aspects as well as play them through in relation to each other.

Songs of Experience

In the House of Lords Lord Bridge stated that there were two ways to establish beneficial interest:

[first] The finding of an agreement or arrangement to share . . . based on evidence of express discussions between the partners, however imperfectly remembered. . . . Once a finding to this effect is made it will only be necessary for the partner asserting the claim to a beneficial interest . . . to show that he or she has acted to his or her detriment . . . [secondly, when] the court must rely entirely on the conduct of the parties both as the basis from which to infer a common intention to share the property beneficially and as the conduct to be relied on to give rise to a constructive trust

This second head is concerned with conduct which contributes towards the purchase of the property or towards a substantial improvement which increases its value. In one of the most controversial aspects of the judgment Lord Bridge defined contributions which were acceptable extremely narrowly:

direct contributions to the purchase price by the partner who is not the legal owner, whether initially or by payment of mortgage instalments, will readily justify the inference necessary to the creation of a constructive trust. But, as I read the authorities, it is extremely doubtful whether anything less will do.

This is the economic problem that we were much more used to analysing rather than the use of language between partners. Mrs Rosset was typical of a housewife with children' she had no paid job and no capital and was, therefore, unable to make financial contributions even if she had wished to. Instead she contributed time and labour to finding the house, helping with aspects of the purchase and then being involved in the restoration and decoration work, including undertaking some of the labour herself. In the words of Nicholls J. in the Court of Appeal she was 'busying herself about the property day after day'. Not only did Lord Bridge in the House of Lords regard such efforts as 'so trifling as almost to be *de minimus*' in terms of the overall value of the house but more importantly he drew a line between activity undertaken in her role *qua* wife and activity undertaken which would have been evidence she undertook such work on the basis that she did so believing herself to be an owner:

it would seem the most natural thing in the world for any wife, in the absence of her husband . . . to spend all the time she could spare and to employ any skills she might have . . . to accelerate the progress of the work quite irrespective of any expectation she might have of enjoying a beneficial interest in the property

What is required is not only labour which can be valued but labour which can be dissociated from any wifely role and in which it can be proved that the woman specifically directed this activity towards ownership rather than use. We are drawn back to forms of specific thinking which seems to be at variance not only with women's socio-economic activities but with the very way in which they think them. As Nourse LJ said in the earlier case of *Grant* v. *Edwards*:

There remains this difficult question: what is the quality of conduct required . . . [from which to infer the common intention that the parties should share ownership]? . . . It would be possible to take the view that the mere moving

into the house by the woman amounted to an acting upon common intention . . . [but] the law is not so cynical as to infer that a woman will only go
to live with a man to whom she is not married if she understands that she is
to have an interest in their home. So what sort of conduct is required? In
my judgment it must be conduct on which the woman could not have been
expected to embark unless she was to have an interest in the house. If she
was not to have such an interest, she could reasonably be expected to go and
live with her lover, but not for example, to wield a 14 lb. sledge-hammer

Women then are suffering at two levels of analysis: in terms of the
value given to different types of labour and in terms of arguments
about specificity—specific agreements about specific activities or
specific goals. In my experience, and supported by emerging research
work, this is not the way in which women experience their world and
organize their activities. If women, in our present socio-economic
and cultural circumstances, are vulnerable at both these levels then
what strategies should we begin to develop that deal with the paradox of, on the one hand wanting to mitigate the consequences of disparity within the relationship and, on the other, avoiding the models
of status, dependency, or protection? Are we really caught between
the dichotomy of private ordering and public intervention?

For Teresa Gorman the free-market model of two individuals
negotiating contractual terms is the route forward. For myself both
the contractual model *per se* and the reality of unequal bargaining
power makes this a somewhat illusory benefit. It does offer the
benefits of heightened awareness and a recognition of the need to
address the issue early in a relationship; but it ignores the problems
of the use of language which I believe must now be fundamental to
our analysis. There could be a simple virtue in offering to women a
frame which requires explicit negotiations and specific goals.
However, it is quite possible that unless the tension between the difference patterns of thinking between men and women are recognized
women will continue to find such a model alienating rather than
enabling. Finding a way to recognize ambiguity, paradox, and contingency may be far more valuable. Does this necessarily require a
model of intervention or could it be contained within a more flexible
mode of bargaining and mediation which would allow competing
versions to be explored rather than require the privileging of one
account?

The present model of separate property in marriage seems to me
to be a problem in that it places the woman in a position where she

has to throw herself on the mercy of the courts. Meanwhile the attitude taken in Chancery can only be to the benefit of men or women who both knew the law and have covered themselves in being able to provide the evidence required of them.

At root, my argument is that we need to face not the specific issues of property but the deep structural differences between men and women. This goes beyond questions of access to the labour market and responsibilities for child care, and becomes the need to tackle the enormity of the gulf between us in terms of our experiences of the world, the way we understand and articulate them, and the different expectations and needs we bring to relationships.

This may seem to become involved with a structuralism so deep that we are threatened with being overcome by it, but I would argue that through facing the enormity of this we can begin to build true equality. The use of legal strategies can then be rethought, not to accentuate difference in the privilege given to one version of the world, or to attempt to build communication based on superficial similarity, rather we must now begin to ask the most difficult questions . . . 'it would seem to be the most natural thing in the world' . . .

REFERENCES

Coombes v. *Smith* (1986) (1986) 1 WLR 808.
Grant v. *Edwards* (1989), 2 All ER 426.
Lloyds Bank v. *Rosset* (1988) 3 All ER 915; (1990) 1 All ER 1111.
Brophy, J. and Smart, C. (1985), *Women in Law* (RKP, London).
Deech, R. (1984), *Matrimonial Property and Divorce; A Century of Progress?* in M. D. A. Freeman (ed.), *State, Law and the Family* (Tavistock, London).
Grosz, E. (1989), *Sexual Subversions* (Allen and Unwin, Sidney).
Holcombe, L. (1983), *Wives and Property* (UTP, Toronto).
Mill, J. S. (1929), *On the Subjection of Women* (Dent, London).
O'Donovan, K. (1984), 'Protection and Paternalism' in M. D. A. Freeman (ed.), 1984.
Olivier, C. (1989), *Jocasta's Children* (Routledge, London).
Stephen, F. (1873), *Liberty, Equality and Fraternity* (London).

PART FOUR

Family Law and Social Policy

15. Family Benefits and Social Policy in Poland

Beata Łaciak

For over forty years, broadly conceived social policy was an important element in the Communist system. In Poland, social achievements such as free health services and education or security of employment were often stressed by politicians in their pronouncements. From the end of World War II the range of different social benefits steadily grew. Even though many of these benefits existed in name only and had no practical consequences, the people learned to treat some as obvious entitlements, and to expect the state to provide such benefits. Free access to a variety of goods is guaranteed to citizens by the Constitution of 1952, Chapter 8, Articles 68–78. The actual implementation of those guarantees left much to be desired, and free access to the benefits was not a reality in many cases; yet they became embedded in social consciousness. Both the state and employers provided the people with access to free or cheap child-care centres, different forms of relaxation and entertainment, long-term loans and credits. A large part of the benefits rendered by the state and state-owned firms were benefits for the family, which, following the last census of 1988, covered 88.5 per cent of the population of Poland. The largest group, as many as 60.7 per cent of all Polish families, are families with children under 24 provided for by their parents. (National Census, 1991). For this reason, benefits for children will be discussed in detail in this account of state policies towards the family since World War II.

The post-war history of state social policy with respect to the family can be divided into stages according to the range and forms of benefits. Stage one was the period from the end of World War II to the mid-1950s; stage two lasted till the early 1970s; the 1970s and 1980s were two different stages; and the last stage includes the three years that followed the changes of 1989. The policy changes marked by these stages are linked to the political transformations in Poland. Until 1989, however, they all had common political foundations, various Soviet solutions were often involved, and different benefits were a form of compensation for low wages. The first period after the end of World War II until the mid-1950s was one of large scale mass social actions, and the introduction of benefits that were to become regular elements in state social policy. The late 1950s and the 1960s were a period of stagnation, the benefits already introduced were in force, and no serious changes were made. The 1970s brought increased social benefits and a trend towards greater equality. That trend developed further in the 1980s when the range of pronatalist benefits in particular was extended. Special facilities were provided for young married couples with small children, for large families, and for single parents. From 1989, the range of state social benefits and the numbers of recipients have been gradually reduced with changes in the conceptualization of social policy.

The origin of a great number of social benefits for the family in Poland dates back to the first few years after World War II. Initially, benefits in kind prevailed, for example the fight against malnutrition through the organization of 'milk kitchens' for children and breast-feeding mothers, and free distribution of milk to children under 14, pregnant women from the seventh month, and mothers of babies under 12 months of age. A similar benefit was the distribution of baby-linen for the newborn, introduced in 1948. Entitlement to most of the benefits for the family came through National Insurance, start-ing from 1948. The insured families of employees received baby-linen free of charge. In 1949 the line was distributed to all children born that year in Poland and was free not only for the insured families of employees but also for those of rural workers and small farmers. Early in the 1950s an upper limit for family income was introduced, and only families with income below that limit received baby-linen free of charge. It was soon to become unimportant, as the income limit was not adjusted after 1955 which in practice, with inflation, resulted in a gradual reduction in the number of families entitled to free baby-linen. By 1975 the linen was distributed to as few as 1.4 per cent of babies born that year.

Until the mid-1950s social assistance to the family took the form of mass provision, such as free meals in factory canteens and schools. To quote a publication of that period 'Owing to collective organiza-tion of social action . . . needs can be satisfied at a lower cost and with great rationality' (Kąkol, 1950). The universality of benefits which followed from the assumptions of the system was in fact some-what limited as many benefits for the family depended on a special insurance granted to some groups of the population, i.e. hired workers (and their families), particularly those distinguished by their services to the cause of building the foundations of socialism in Poland, or those in particularly difficult material circumstances. (Kakol, 1950: 13). Benefits were reduced markedly in the late 1950s to cover only the poorest families.

The socialist 'welfare state'

The early postwar years were also the time when financial benefits and other facilities for the family were introduced. A family benefit has been paid for each child since 1940. Initially, it depended on the number of children, and the amount paid for each child was smaller if the family had only one child, somewhat higher for two children, and higher still if there were three or more children. In 1953 increases in the benefit rate stopped at the level of four children, and was constant for families with more than four children. Since 1970 the family benefit has been divided into two categories depending on the monthly income per family member. The 1960s brought no changes apart from the regular rises in the amount of benefit which generally had little impact on its real value. Significant adjustment only took place in 1972 when it was decided that family benefit would be paid to the families of employees for each child under 16, and for a child who continued education after that age until that child reached the age of 25.

In the first year after the introduction of family insurance, that is in 1948, employees were also entitled to a family benefit for a jobless wife. But in 1949 this entitlement was already limited to jobless wives who cared for at least one child aged under 8, who were over 50, or were disabled.Employed women could receive an additional family benefit for a jobless husband provided the husband was over 65 or was disabled.

Maternity and 'education' leave for women was also an important element of state pro-family policy. Maternity leave for mothers of newborn babies was introduced in 1946; initially, the leave was for 8 weeks, and later for 12 weeks, during which period the woman was paid a childbirth allowance equal to the amount of her full wage. Serious facilities for the women who cared for small children were introduced in the 1970s, and in 1972 maternity leave was extended to 16 weeks in the case of the first child and to 18 weeks for every subsequent birth or multiple birth. Two years later this special case of multiple pregnancy received separate treatment and women who gave birth to more than one child after one pregnancy were entitled to a leave of 26 weeks. In 1972 women who cared for small children were granted the right to a three-year education leave; previously (from 1968 on), the duration of that leave had been one year only. The extension of leave was not the only facility for mothers of small children. The regulation of leave to care for a sick child was also changed. The right to this kind of leave had originally been introduced in 1954. According to that regulation, employed mothers and single fathers were entitled to leave to take care of a sick child under 14, and were paid a benefit for that period which could not exceed 30 days a year. In the case of manual workers, the benefit amounted to only 70 per cent of wages. A number of important changes were introduced in 1972. The total of the days on leave went up by 60 a year, and the leave could be taken to care not only for a sick child under 14 but also a healthy child under 8, (if, for example, the crèche, kindergarten, or school was closed). In addition, the rights of manual and white-collar workers were made equal with respect to the amount of benefit paid during leave to take care of a child; all workers were now entitled to 100 per cent of their wages. For the first time ever the father was also granted the right to take leave, provided both the parents were employed. This right, however, was restricted, and the father could only take leave if the mother was away from home or could not take care of the child herself (due, for example, to illness or childbirth). Starting from 1971, all employed mothers and single fathers of children aged under 14 were granted the right to two paid days off work a year. In 1976, a single payment for childbirth allowance was introduced, which amounted to three times the family benefit. Financial assistance to parents of newborn babies had been initiated in the 1950s, but it was rendered by trade unions to the families of union members only until the 1970s when it was extended to all families of employees. As can be seen, social policy towards the family in Poland in the 1970s aimed at equality and population growth. At that time the families of individual farmers were included for the first time in the group entitled to various benefits for the family; the actual payment of benefits for the family. The actual payment of these benefits, however, was scheduled to start from 1980.

The Pro-Family Policy of the 1980s

Judging from the variety of benefits for the family, the 1980s in Poland seem to have been a period of particularly pro-family and pronatalist policy. This results from satisfaction of the demands of 'Solidarity', from the state's policy of conciliation towards the Church, and also from the country's economic situation, particularly the hidden unemployment, and considerable market shortages. The growing benefits were a form of compensation granted to the people. The pecuniary benefits for women on education leave were part of the struggle against hidden unemployment, and also an element in the pro-family policy of the state. Introduced in 1981, they were originally paid for eighteen months, and later for a maximum of three years. Depending on the monthly income per family member, the benefit amounted to 100, 75 or 50 per cent of the lowest basic salary in the state-controlled economy. Single mothers received double the amount. In addition, a person who adopted a child or acted as a court-appointed guardian was also entitled to education leave and the benefit if the child was under one year of age when taken over by that person. Moreover, education leaves were made accessible, for the first time, to the fathers; the parents were to decide which of them would care for the child and resign his or her job for that period. Special entitlements were granted to the parents of handicapped children: since 1982, such parents can take education leave to care for a child under 10.

In 1983 a nursing allowance was introduced for a family member in need of regular or special care. This group included, among others, family members aged over 75; disabled children under 16, or under 25 if still at school; and disabled spouses. Also in the 1980s family benefits were extended to the families of individual farmers, who began to be paid childbirth allowance in July 1980; in 1983 the wives of individual farmers were granted the right to maternity allowance for eight weeks after one child was born, and for twelve weeks for twins. From 1985 the period of payment to this group of the maternity allowance was extended by two weeks every year until it equalled that of the other professional groups. In 1986 there was another important form of social benefits for the family: credits for young married couples to ease their entry into adult life. Starting in 1974 a single credit was given for the purchase of consumer durables to furnish an apartment. Originally, those entitled to the credit were

young couples, both aged under 30, but later one could be aged up
to 40. Finally, the age limits were settled at 30 and 35 in 1982. That
same year the access to credits was limited to those married couples
who had just got their first apartment. The period of repayment dif-
fered in different years; in some cases, the firm employing a spouse
could assist him or her in that repayment. A young family whose
income did not exceed a particular limit (3,000 zlotys at that time)
had to repay only 25 per cent of the credit, the remaining 75 per
cent being remitted. In the 1980s, a young couple who were given
the credit additionally acquired a special entitlement to buy the
durables to furnish their apartment, as such goods were practically
unobtainable in Polish shops. Young families could also rely on the
state and their work places to assist them financially with loans and
credits to joint a housing co-operative. This type of crediting was
more generous to young married couples, large families, and single
parents.

As follows from the above examples, the 1980s abounded in a
variety of benefits for the family; many of which, however, were
actually forms of financial assistance to the most destitute families
whose number increased with the escalating economic crisis. Thus
the introduction of the new benefits was only apparently a symptom
of the authorities' concern about the people. In fact, such benefits
were temporary measures to cope with the economic crisis without
any radical solutions or plans for the future. An important new element of state policy towards the family in the 1980s, however, was
the focus on single mothers and attempts at improving their situation. This is important since, as has been mentioned above, a large
proportion of one-parent families live below the poverty line. By
1989 they constituted 15.4 per cent of all families in Poland (13.7 per
cent are families with the mother only, and 1.7 per cent are composed of the father and his children).

The political and economic transformation initiated in Poland in
1989 resulted among other things in great changes in the sphere of
social policy. Quite often the new situation compels a definite change
in that policy, as is the case, for example, with the need to take into
account unemployment which had been hidden before. The range of
some benefits was limited. For example, the principles of payment of
the education allowance were changed. In 1989 the amount of that
allowance paid to complete families was settled at 25 per cent of the
past year's average wages in the socialized economy, and at 40 per

cent of those wages in the case of one-parent families. Admittedly, a favourable change was introduced the next year—three-monthly updating of the amount of the benefit. At the same time, however, the entitlement to a full benefit was limited to those families where the monthly income per family member does not exceed 25 per cent of the average monthly wages in the socialized economy. If the amount in excess is not higher than the amount of the benefit, a portion of the benefit is paid; otherwise, the family lose their right to the benefit. As can be supposed, it was this very decision that made the number of persons on education leaves go down markedly: in 1985, for example, there were 839.8 thousand such persons in Poland, in 1986 there were 802.6 thousand, and in 1991 as few as 517.9 thousand (Statistical Yearbook, 1992).

The New Era

It is not only on the macro scale, that is in state social policy, that the range of social benefits is limited. In the new conditions, many firms are also renouncing various benefits they previously granted to their staff, such as a partial refund of the costs of accommodation in workers' hostels, of factory canteens, crèches or kindergartens. Usually, the firms are forced to take this step by their economic difficulties. These economic reasons and growing unemployment are also leading to a situation where families cannot avail themselves of their valid social rights. More and more often, for example, working mothers refrain from taking not only the education leave but even, for fear of losing their job, days off to take care of a sick child.

Today state policy towards the family is shaped by a number of central authorities, the most important of which are the Cabinet (the Ministry of Labour and Social Matters in particular), parliamentary commissions, and also the Office of the Plenipotentiary for Women and the Family. The latter institution is a novelty in Poland. The Plenipotentiary was first appointed in April 1991 and was to perform his functions through the Office which is part of the Bureau of the Cabinet. The range of the Plenipotentiary's activities originally planned was extensive and included, among other functions, 'appraisal, participation in the elaboration . . . and preparation of draft programs aims at improvement of the material, social and cultural conditions of the women, children, young people and families . . . analysis and appraisal of the social situation and living conditions of women, children, young people and families, including one-parent, and large families and also those in danger of becoming socially pathological or otherwise handicapped'. (Resolution of Council of Ministers, 53 (1991), April 12). Thus the Office of the Plenipotentiary was originally designed as a second centre alongside the Ministry of Labour and Social Matters independently to develop social policy towards the family. Its independence, however, proved rather short-lived as the first Plenipotentiary was dismissed in February 1992, and the Office was subordinated to the Ministry of Labour and Social Matters, and its work is now headed by an under-secretary of state of that Ministry. It is probably for this reason that the Office has so far failed to come up with any interesting ideas, and sees both its own role and state policy towards the family mainly in terms of the pro-tection of society against poverty through securing the minimum social benefits for the families in the most difficult circumstances. Obviously, this is a very serious problem indeed. As the data from the Main Statistical Office indicates, the earnings of a considerable proportion of Polish households are below the poverty line. The largest group among them are one-parent and large families. In 1990 three-quarters of the single-mother families and over a half of fami-lies with at least four children were living below the poverty line (Panek, 1992). Thus the standpoint of the Ministry of Labour and Social Matters seems quite justifiable: that in the present conditions and with the existing state of the budget, the Ministry should concen-trate on single parents, and families with at least three children. The government programme provides for preservation of the present principle of maternity and education benefits and for a reform of the family benefits. The government also planned to submit, by the end of November 1992, alternative proposals concerning that reform for consultation with the trade unions. Four different proposals can be distinguished. One provides for no changes in the present principles, and for an equal benefit for every child in the family; the remaining three proposals assume differentiation of benefits depending on the number of children, the income per family member, or both factors jointly (the family income and the number of children). Expressing her private opinion on the suggested solutions, Mrs Joanna Starega Piasek, Under-Secretary of State in the Ministry of Labour and Social Matters, decidedly rejected the former system of family benefits as ineffective and a serious burden on the state budget. The present level of family benefit for wealthy families is so low as to matter not at all as part of the total family incomes. For the most destitute families, however, although the benefit is a vital part of their income, it is still too small to assist the family budget. According to the Under-secretary of State, the best solution is one where both the family income, the number of children financially dependent on the family, and the family's general situation (one-parent or complete, with or without disability or old-age pension recipients among the family members) are taken into account. What is most important in this connection is the decentralization of decisions on the form and extent of social assistance in general, not just of family benefits. The Ministry aims at a situation where it would set out the general principles of social policy and the policy would then be implemented by local authorities. In this model, the local authorities would take over the responsibility for implementation, in their respective territories, of policies for education, health, and social policy. According to the Under-Secretary of State, in at least half of all cases, such duties of the local governments are performed well enough. Decentralization of this type is a novelty in Poland. The main feature of the forty years after World War II having been centralistic policy in all spheres of social life. The Ministry of Labour and Social Matters is convinced that decentralization of social benefits will permit a more equitable and efficient distribution of resources and better social control over that distribution.

There is a new trend in state social policy, aiming to limit the regular welfare benefits and reducing the number of families who permanently receive such assistance. This is why the government programme repeatedly stresses the fact that different forms of state assistance are meant for families which 'cannot reach the necessary material standards for objective reasons (such as disability, chronic illness, or unemployment). (Program Rządowy, 1991). This policy is often criticized, with the present inflation and growing unemployment, because state withdrawal or limitation of payment of social benefits will lead to a marked lowering of living standards for most families, not just the poor. Political opposition and some circles of opinion-makers (scholars and publicists) accuse succeeding Cabinets with 'Solidarity' origins of a failure to formulate and implement a social policy which would protect the people against the social consequences of economic reform. The philanthropic model of welfare is also criticized which consists of pecuniary and non-pecuniary transfers to the poorest families. This, according to the critics, forces a part of society to 'hold out their hands for help all their lives long' (Tymowski, 1991). Dissatisfaction with state policy towards the family is expressed in the media, during mass protests, and also at meetings of scholars and politicians. One such meeting was the X National Family Council organized in October 1991 by the Polish Christian Democratic Forum, the 'PAX' Association, and the 'Assistance to the Family' Foundation. The participants called the situation of Polish families disastrous, and sharply criticized government policy mainly for the 'absence of a program of social policy' which has resulted in 'degradation of the family . . . disastrous devastation of the social infrastructure, and drastic differences between earnings and consumption in the period of political transformation' (Pernal, 1991). The present Cabinet and its critics put forward opposing conceptions of social policy. The policy of the Ministry of Labour and Social Matters can be called liberal. It is criticized from the left and the critics assume that social policy must necessarily be populist, and 'building anew social reality, but should however take into account that certain aspirations have been roused in the postwar period that cannot possibly be abandoned altogether (Tymowski, 1991: 7). The Ministry has a different opinion on this point: it argues that the state must necessarily abolish some benefits because of the economic situation, but also because, as the Under-Secretary of State in the Ministry of Labour and Social Matters stated, 'once, we were all recipients of welfare. Today, the taxes a citizen pays entitle him to certain social benefits; but he should first look after himself' (personal communication). This is why the government programme states that social policy towards the family 'will create the basis for individual enterprise, free choice, action, and responsibility of the family' (Program Rządowy, 1991). An example of such action is the Ordinance of the Minister of Labour and Social Matters concerning the grant of an allowance for economic emancipation. This type of allowance can be given to a family member to cover the cost of starting up independent economic activity, to pay the interest on credit for economic activity, and also to pay for training in a profession or qualifying for a new job if such a step offers the chance of improvement of his family's material position. The allowance is paid in full or in part; in some cases it is non-repayable provided the income per family member does not exceed the minimum old-age pension. The actual amount of the benefit cannot exceed thirty times the minimum old-age pension. This latter reservation gives rise to doubts about whether this benefit is really an efficient form of social assistance which would help a family to become independent financially.

It is also difficult to define today the future effectiveness of state housing policy, which also assumes that the state will assist families in their independent and active efforts to get an apartment. This assistance is to be rendered through the planned system of loan and relief funds offering cheap loans, and a system of tax exemptions and reduction for families who actively try to solve their own housing problem.

This new conception of social policy encounters considerable obstacles in the people's consciousness. Some prove even more difficult to overcome than the financial difficulties (so the Under-secretary of State in the Ministry of Labour and Social Matters told the author when interviewed) due to the people's claims on consciousness. Activity to improve one's own and one's family's situation is limited; people seem unable to plan their family expenses rationally taking into account their living conditions and financial resources.

Changing the people's mentality is a difficult and time-consuming task; it can thus be expected that state social policy will continue to meet with criticism from both opinion-makers and a considerable part of society. As follows from sociological studies (Kurczewski, 1992), most members of society expect the state first and foremost to provide social security, to ensure jobs corresponding to qualifications, to provide free health services, and so on. In the present conditions, the state cannot possibly meet such expectations.

REFERENCES

Kąkol, K. (1950), *Akcja Socjalna w Polsce* (Social Action in Poland) (Lodz).

Kurczewski, J. (1992), *Na Przełomie ustrojów. Prawa i obowiązki obywateli w opinii publicznej* (At the Turning-Point of Systems: The Rights and Duties of Citizens in Public Perception) (Warsaw).

National Census (1991), Rodzina w świetle wyników naradowego spisu powszechnego (Warsaw).

Panek, T. (1992), *Poverty and the Determinants of Income in Households in 1992* (Warsaw).

Pernal, A. (1991), 'As a Family We're Strong', mimeo.

Program Rządowy (1991), 'Government Program: Social Security of Citizens', mimeo.

Statistical Yearbook (1992), *Rocznik Statystyczny* (GUS, Warsaw).

Tymowski, A. (1991), 'Social Policy in the Polish Market Economy', mimeo.

DECREES AND ORDINANCES

Decree of 8 January 1946 on amending and supplementing the Act of 28 March 1933 on social insurance (Journal of Laws 1946, No. 4).

Decree of 28 October, 1947 on family insurance (Journal of Laws 1947, No. 66).

Ordinance of the Council of Ministers of 17 November 1959 on amending the conditions of acquisition of the rights to family allowance (Journal of Laws 1959, No. 64).

Act of 6 July 1972 on extension of maternity leaves (Journal of Laws 1972, No. 27).

Ordinance of the Minister of Labour, Wages, and Social Matters of 31 May 1971 on family allowances (Journal of Laws 1974, No. 21).

Ordinance of the Council of Ministers of 29 November 1975 on unpaid leaves for working mothers who take care of small children (Journal of Laws, 1975, No. 24).

Ordinance of the Minister of Labour, Wages, and Social Matters of 4 November 1980 amending the ordinance on family allowances (Journal of Laws 1980, No. 25).

Ordinance of the Council of Ministers of 17 July 1981 on educational leaves (Journal of Laws 1981, No. 19).

Ordinance of the Minister of Labour, Wages, and Social Matters of 15 March 1983 on the amount of family and nursing allowance due to some groups of the insured (Journal of Laws 1983, No. 15).

Ordinance of the Council of Ministers of 9 May 1986 on family allowances for children of individual farmers (Journal of Laws 1906, No. 21).

16. Marriage, Motherhood, and Old-Age Security in the UK

Heather Joshi

Legal marriage gives public recognition of a couple's commitment to each other. The institution serves many functions, among them: bearing and rearing children, a division of labour between husband and wife, a pooling of resources, regulation of property, regulation of sexuality, and the provision of emotional and economic stability. This chapter draws attention to a particular aspect of the last feature: marriage as a source of financial security for women in old age. Wives, especially mothers, are almost invariably the financially dependent partner, usually outlive their husbands, and are normally 'provided for' as widows. Marriage is the major mechanism by which those whose work is unpaid gain access to income. This chapter argues that this function may need protection and strengthening alongside the development of adequate alternatives through the market and the state.

Legal marriage contrasts with *de facto* partnerships in that it confers rights to a share in property and to the inheritance of survivors' benefits in insurance and pension schemes. The existence of these rights is sometimes the only reason cohabiting couples gives for getting formally married. It produced a rash of weddings in Sweden, for example, when widow's benefits in the state earnings related scheme were about to be discontinued. Pension coverage is also one of the reasons given by those homosexual couples who regret the absence of legal recognition of their partnerships (Coxon, 1992).

Marriage is by no means a guarantee of old-age security. Couples who stay together are pooling risks, but this does not eliminate the risk that they may not jointly accumulate enough assets or pension rights to provide for a comfortable old age, particularly if both have chequered employment careers, or if pension funds run into difficulty. The risks are, however, compounded if the partners fail to share, or the marriage fails altogether. In the case of divorce, the risk pooling ceases, eligibility to widow's benefits is cut off, and cumulated pension rates to date are not always divided. Some countries have the legal apparatus to do this (e.g. Germany, the USA and Canada), but not, as yet, the UK (Joshi and Davies, 1991, 1992*b*).

The issue of marriage as a source of old-age security has to be set in the context of the other institutions which provide resources for the elderly, and of trends which are tending to obscure the continuing importance of social protection to those whose work is largely unpaid, outside the paid labour market. The institutions, discussed in Section 1, through which the elderly acquire financial resources (as well as services) are the family, the market, and the state. Three relevant trends, described in Section 2, are ageing, privatization, and increased employment of women on the labour market. Sections 3 to 7 explore the pension consequences for women of marriage, motherhood, and divorce, based on the illustrative example of a British couple. Section 8 explores, briefly, measures which would strengthen the social protection of those with unpaid work. This chapter concludes by drawing out the links between motherhood, old-age insecurity, and the reproduction of generations, and questions the need for state regulation of the consequences of private decisions.

1. Institutions

1.1 Family

Family transfers of cash are primarily between spouses, in the pooling of their incomes while both living, and in the inheritance of benefits by the surviving spouse. If a couple's income and assets are viewed as jointly received or owned, the question of the direction of transfer does not arise. If individuals are seen as earning separate resources, all of which go into a common pool, then one would think of transfers generally occurring from higher-earning husbands to their wives. (Davies and Joshi, 1992*b*) To the extent that couples do not actually pool all their income, the transfers between spouses are moderated. Countries with community of property written into family law formalize the assumption usually made, for example in statistics on income distribution and income-maintenance programmes, that married couples pool their resources. In practice the pooling of resources by couples is far from universal or complete (Brannen and Wilson 1987; Vogler 1989; Lister 1992).

The family also provides a channel for transfer of resources between generations—parents to children and vice versa—as well as the transfers within a generation, between spouses. In most industrial societies offspring are no longer treated as primarily responsible for keeping elderly parents in terms of cash, though the position on personal care for the frail has been taken over less completely by the market and the state. The displacement of parenthood as a source of old-age security as societies modernize may help reinforce falling fertility (Cigno, 1991*b*), but it certainly justifies the focus here on the interdependence of spouses as the most important source of old-age security within the family.

1.2 The market

The market economy provides resources to the elderly through their ownership of assets—financial and property—and through the labour market. Relatively few, in Britain, own substantial wealth, and in these days of falling retirement ages throughout Europe, relatively few elderly people have much in the way of current earnings. The item of market income that is of growing importance is the occupational pension, a hybrid of labour and capital markets. It is related to past employment and earnings, and is regarded by some as deferred pay. Others see it as a form of asset, even if the description of deferred pay is also applicable (Davies and Joshi, 1992*a*). Funded pension schemes do indeed represent a collection of assets, collectively owned, in trust, on behalf of their members (and, arguably, their spouses). Although this form of provision has been spreading, in Britain the coverage is disproportionately in favour of men. Low coverage of part-time jobs and intermittent employment records means that the gap between men's and women's earnings in the labour market tends to be magnified in their private pension rights.

1.3 The state

The state affords access to cash resources through state-run pension schemes, preferential tax treatment, and means-tested payments. In Britain, contributory state pensions are two-tier, basic flat rate and an earnings related component (SERPS) for those not contracted out into an approved occupational or personal pension scheme. Preferential tax treatment operates through an additional tax allowance to elderly people, and, more importantly, through the exemptions offered to pension schemes whose own funds are allowed to accumulate free of taxation (subject to some limits on the generosity of the benefits). This effective subsidy of 'private' pensions means that there is no clear distinction between market and state provision.

Means-tested payments, the safety net of last resort, consist of housing benefits and Income Support. As these are assessed on the combined resources of couples, state and family support are also intertwined. It is elderly women living alone who are, at the moment, most dependent on means-tested supplements.

Another way in which state and family interact in the UK, rather more to women's advantage, is that credit for state pension is given for periods of unpaid caring work. Home responsibility protection was introduced from 1978, under Barbara Castle's Social Security Pensions Act 1975. Complete years after this date when contributions were not paid because of responsibility for children or the care of a severely disabled invalid could be credited towards basic pension (up to a maximum of twenty). In 1988 home responsibility protection was extended to the earnings-related tier, in partial compensation for the abandonment of Barbara Castle's plan to base SERPS entitlement on the best twenty years. Generations coming up for retirement in the next few decades will not be able to draw fully on these provisions, as they do not operate retrospectively. Even for those generations who only entered the labour force after 1978, the benefit of credits to state pension rights will only be as valuable as the state pension itself. The prospects on this count are not too good, in view of the trends discussed next.

2. Trends

2.1 Ageing

The increased proportion of elderly people to the young, is partly the result of greater longevity but largely of falling birth rates. It means that the number of earners who can be called upon to contribute to each elderly person's income has been falling and is expected to continue to fall, both within any individual family and on the national scale of contributors and beneficiaries of a state pension scheme. Projections of the rising financial burden of state pay-as-you-go have led to reductions in planned benefits in various countries. In Britain, for example, the 1986 Social Security Act cut the value of the state earnings related pension. The issue of pension provision to an ageing population has been presented as one of intergenerational conflict (Johnson, *et al.*, 1989). While interest is often fixed on intergenerational issues such as curbing the claims of a 'selfish generation', the question of the distribution of benefits within generations still needs attention.

2.2 *Privatization*

The second trend, privatization, is occurring in Western as well as Eastern Europe. It involves the rolling back of state provisions in favour of arrangements made through the market for labour and capital. In the context of British pensions, this means more provision is arranged by employers (occupational pensions) or by individuals (personal pensions) rather than the state (National Insurance and supplementary pensions). Market-based arrangements cannot be designed to redistribute benefits. Benefits tend to be entirely earnings related, although variations in the rate of return on different funds mean that the values of benefits may not be predictable, particularly in money purchase schemes which typify the personal pension sector. Provisions for contracting out of state earnings-related pensions and the sheltering of pension funds from income tax mean that the private nature of the market pension sector should not be overstated. It is heavily subsidized by the Exchequer and linked in a number of ways to provisions in the state pension scheme. Another limit to privatization is that it affects far more men than women. This is mainly because, as noted above, women tend to be left outside private pension coverage.

2.3 *Women into Paid Work*

This brings us to the third trend, increased participation by women in the labour market. Between 1950 and 1990 the participation of adult women in the British labour force nearly doubled, which largely involved married women. This implies that wives can no longer be presumed, as Beveridge did, normally to devote most of their time to unpaid duties (Beveridge, 1942). Marriages no longer represent a total division of labour between paid and unpaid work, but they still normally represent some division of labour between partners. It would seldom be correct to infer from a wife's labour market participation that she is economically independent, as seems to be implied by the clean-break provisions of the 1971 Divorce Reform Act. Wives normally earn a lot less than their husbands although they now normally earn for much of their marriages. This reflects unequal division of paid and unpaid work between spouses, wives taking the major responsibility for child-rearing and other caring work, along with unequal treatment of males and females by the labour market. Thus marriage still involves a degree of financial dependency between spouses, which provides the partner with lower earnings with a source of financial security. It gives the primary carer an interest in the earnings, assets, and pensions of the primary earner, which are legally recognized by derived rights to benefits such as widow's pension.

3. Women's Rights and the Family

The cause of women's rights appears to accord with a move, suggested by the EC Draft Directive on Social Security of 1987, towards individualization of benefits, pensions to each person on the basis of their labour-market record, and no derived right for spouses (see Lister, 1992). A contrary argument is put here. Such a move is not in the interests of many women, or indeed in the interests of the reproductive functions of the family. There is a case to strengthen the claims of partners in each others' pension rights, particularly in the case of divorce.

Between generations the implicit contract is weakening, and conflict threatens. The same could be said of gender relations within each generation, but here conflict is not only counter-productive, but counter-reproductive. Some form of co-operation between men and women (preferably not female subordination) is surely needed to sustain social and biological renewal. Marriage as an institution, and among its other functions, safeguards the interests of unpaid workers, as specialization in domestic work reduces earning power in paid work (Cigno, 1991*a*), and indeed subsequent pension entitlement. As divorce increases, the institution becomes less reliable, and this contract too weakens, the implicit contract that underpins the division of labour between spouses, and establishes the unpaid worker's entitlement to share in income, property, and pensions.

4. Pensions, Gender, and Marital Status: A British example

4.1. Lifetime earnings

Poverty in old age is, and promises to remain, a higher risk for women living on their own than men, at least in Britain (Joshi and Davies, 1991). Men's and women's own incomes diverge in old age in reflection of a divergence in their earnings at younger ages, particularly when a major part of old-age income is a pension related to past earnings. Men's and women's earnings diverge over a working lifetime for a number of reasons which tend to compound one another. Men tend to encounter higher wage opportunities than similarly qualified females; they also tend to acquire more training and qualifications and to work for longer hours and more years. The extra years are due partly to women taking breaks from paid work for domestic reasons, but even those who do not, tend to retire earlier because of the difference in pensionable ages still applying in British state pensions, 60 for women and 65 for men.

Apart from the curiosity of unequal pension ages (which can be viewed as both an advantage or a disadvantage for women) the sources of divergence probably apply to some extent in most European countries. They represent the interaction between the division of labour in the home and unequal treatment in the labour market, persisting, at least in Britain, despite equal-pay legislation. My estimates of the effects on the rate of pay of employed women relative to that of men are that unequal treatment accounts for at least as much of the gap as the adaptations British mothers make as a result of motherhood (Joshi, 1991).

These effects are illustrated for a couple of following patterns observed in 1980 over a hypothetical lifetime in a simulation (Joshi and Davies, 1991). Both the man and the woman are assumed to have the same (modest) qualifications, but the woman's lifetime earnings are 59 per cent of his if she never marries, 53 per cent if she marries but has no children, and only 27 per cent if she has two children. The difference between the last two steps represents the cash opportunity cost of bearing two children, around half the lifetime potential for a married woman.

Before proceeding to look at the pension entitlements implied by these earning streams, it should be noted that such an example is not universal. Our experiments for Britain suggested that these relativities are more likely to extend to couples who are less well-qualified than to graduates, where all the gaps were much closer, the earnings of the mother of two falling only to 69 per cent of the man's. The relativities also widen out where men are better qualified than women. We have also attempted to make comparable estimates of mothers' forgone earnings for other countries in relation to the central British case (Davies and Joshi, forthcoming, Joshi and Davies, 1992*a*). In West Germany they appear to be of similar magnitude to Britain, but markedly less in Sweden where there is more public daycare and part-time employment is more remunerative. In France, mothers' work histories appear to polarize into those who forego little employment and those who forgo a lot.

4.2 Pensions Earned

Returning to the 'central case' we can see the relative sizes of the earnings-linked pension that would be earned. In addition to these, men and women would both earn a basic pension of similar value, given the credits available for home responsibility, (years without paid contributions but in which benefit was paid for child or invalid care). Since this basic pension is currently below the level at which single pensioners qualify for means-tested assistance, it is of particular interest to look at the earnings-related pension which, in effect, determines whether and how far old-age income exceeds the poverty line. The earnings related pension may be private if the occupational scheme provided by the employer is acceptable for contracting out of the state scheme. If not, there is the state earnings related pension scheme known as SERPS. Contracted-out schemes can be very much more generous than SERPS, by a factor of five on our assumptions (no job changing, no inflation), and, as we have seen, men are more likely than women to be contracted-out. We must, therefore, look at the pension outcomes of the earnings differences set out above, allowing for some different combinations of pension coverage.

First let us assume both the man and the woman spend their entire careers covered only by the state scheme. The unmarried woman in the central case would be eligible for a weekly pension worth 58 per cent of the man's, the married woman with no child, 50 per cent, and the married mother of two, 29 per cent. The relativities are slightly narrowed as compared with earnings due to the operation of a ceiling on banded earnings and home-responsibility protection. The pension cost of rearing two children is 42 per cent of the pension of the wife with no child. The weekly pension to which the man in the central case would be eligible under SERPS nearly matches the basic pension, but those of the women hardly come up to the level needed to bring them out of the means testing.

If everyone in the central case were covered by a good final-salary scheme our calculations are that the three women would have pensions relative to the man's of 68, 56 and 21 per cent respectively. The differentials widen out as a result of differing pension ages and the lack of cover assumed for years of part-time employment. The pension losses due to motherhood are 62 per cent (of the childless wife's pension). All these final-salary pensions, even the mother's, are well above the adequacy threshold. There is nearly a fivefold gap between the two types of scheme. Men are more likely to have the better cover and women to rely on SERPS. The mother of two covered by SERPS only would have a pension of only 7 per cent of the man's occupational benefit.

5. Pensions Shared

The calculations in the previous section illustrate the pecuniary attractions for women of joining forces with a husband for the purpose of income security in old age. If we may assume that couples pool their pensions, married women are likely to be better provided for by sharing a husband's pension than are unmarried women. In this illustration, being in a couple sharing 107 per cent of a man's private pension looks better than being a spinster on SERPS getting 14 per cent to herself. From the cash point of view, position of wives is strengthened on widowhood. They would normally inherit half their former spouse's pension, and they would no longer have to share their own with him. If access to a man's good pension puts married women in a more secure position than women who have never married, despite the latter's greater earnings, divorce can make financing their old age particularly precarious. Our report illustrates the poor pension prospects of women who divorce after having incurred earnings losses on behalf of their partnership. Provisions (as in Germany) to split the pension rights of divorcing parties, would be of substantial help in some, but not all, cases (Joshi and Davies, 1991). Pension splitting cannot be a solution where there is not much pension to split, and will not divert very much to a woman after a short marriage.

The pension calculations presented in Section 4 illustrate the fact that, though few wives are totally dependent on their husbands for income in old age, many are partially so. Where it operates, the pooling of income and pensions within and after marriage provides a channel for compensating those whose work has been unpaid, and redressing other sources of inequality between men and women in paid work.

6. Home Responsibility Protection and the Pension Cost of Motherhood

The pension consequences of motherhood can be summarized for this example. The married mother of two 'loses' almost half the earnings she would have received married but childless. If she is in the state earnings related scheme her forgone pension is proportionately less (42%), home-responsibility protection mitigating but not obliterating the pension cost of motherhood. In the less likely case of her being in the final-salary scheme, the proportional pension losses are more (62%), though the absolute value of this pension is still better than SERPS (on our assumptions), bearing out the point that the market cannot be expected to provide compensation or reward for non-market work. In the SERPS, years of non-contribution due to home responsibility (up to a maximum of twenty) are dropped from the denominator when calculating average lifetime earnings. The formula does not compensate for reduced hours or reduced pay consequent upon motherhood and can actually penalize part-time workers. Sweden, Germany, and France all have some feature of their pension scheme to credit mothers with contributions. In Germany, for example, earnings are credited, at 75 per cent of the average, for up to three years per child. British home-responsibility provisions seem at least as generous, so it seems unlikely that the pension costs of motherhood would be any more than mitigated even in the European schemes.

7. Pensions per Contribution

These sort of inequalities in pension benefits, to the female disadvantage, coexist with inequalities in benefit-to-contribution ratios in which women appear to receive better treatment, or value for money, than men (Owen and Joshi, 1990; Stahlberg, 1990). Such calculations bring in the duration of pension receipt, longer for women because of their greater longevity, as well as, in Britain, their earlier pension age. These are the main reasons for the higher benefit to contribution ratio in SERPS, though home-responsibility protection adds a minor part to the female advantage. In Stahlberg's calculations for the Swedish state earnings related pension (which simulate average rather than illustrative lifetimes), the female advantage on the (larger) benefit to contribution measure is much smaller, and arises out of preferential treatment in ATP (Alternatives to Transfer Payment) to part-time workers and its formula, basing pension level on the best fifteen years' earnings. Such measures show that the system already distributes resources from men to women and leads some commentators to conclude that it is women who are particularly generously served by 'over-generous' state pension schemes (Hemming and Kay, 1982).

The fallacy of this line of argument is the acceptance of paid contributions as a valid point of reference where low earnings may be evidence of unpaid contributions to the reproduction and maintenance of future, current, and past members of the paid labour force. This is another way of questioning the politically hallowed 'contributory principle' to collective pension schemes, or at least whether it need involve the rigid linking of benefits to earnings that would obtain if benefit to contribution ratios were indeed equal. The undoubted fact that it is difficult to quantify and monitor unpaid work should not mean that it gets completely overlooked.

8. Policy for the protection of unpaid work

It tends to be thought that trends in women's work are bringing wives 'independence', at least financially, from their husbands so that the benefit system need no longer recognize marital status in such features as additions for dependent wives, pensions for surviving widows (or indeed in splitting pension rights after divorce). These should be no longer necessary as women 'earn their own pensions'. The attractions of this view are strengthened by the fact that formal marriage is itself becoming less popular, in parts of Europe at least. But the qualification is needed that women's own pensions must be big enough on their own for separate treatment to be considered. Unless 'big enough' means 'equal to their husbands', eliminating wives' pensions would achieve independence at a price. Independence without equality has been a familiar experience in the Women's Movement (whose highest achievement in the USA is jokingly said to be the Dutch treat). The price to be paid for independence through individual benefits is lower pensions, in widowhood at least, than would be enjoyed in the current (British) regime.

Sweden is now phasing out widows' pensions, and other European countries are likely to be harmonizing on a pattern of individualized earnings-related pensions. The point made here is that this has the curious feature that people who give their time, energy, and future earning power to rearing the next generation of contributors will end up with lower pension entitlements as a result.

Resolutions of this paradox could come from a number of directions, which should not be seen as mutually exclusive, and indeed probably need to be pursued in combination:

   (i) measures to improve women's access to the paid economy—a long-term objective, but of limited value to transitional generations at least;

  (ii) measures to facilitate both men and women combining paid work with nurturing and caring—such as more flexible hours for employment, schools, and other facilities;

 (iii) enhancement of the credits available for caring-responsibilities in earnings related pension provision—e.g. in the British context, reducing the pension penalty of part-time employment, or extending credits retrospectively to those rearing children before 1978;

 (iv) facilitation of the splitting of pension rights when *de jure* or *de facto* partnerships end;

  (v) reducing the pension–earnings link by enhancing the basic, universal component of collective schemes, following Danish lines of a pension based on residence, not paid contributions. Such development could be financed out of general taxation, but there is a case for doing so by scaling down the higher earnings related benefits.

In an experiment with examples similar to that quoted in Section 4, Joshi and Davies (1992*c*) found that there were limits to what could be achieved with any one option on its own, for example, allowing home-responsibility credits to mothers in low paid part-time jobs (option iii). We also found that the resources released from abolishing SERPS would make surprisingly little difference to a flat-rate pension if the contracted-out person gained but did not contribute. These approaches should not be seen as alternatives because different solutions would suit different people, and social policy should presumably not favour one type of behaviour over another. Although some may adjust the legal status of their partnerships because of the rules of pension schemes, it seems unlikely that many people will adjust their behaviour in partnering, reproduction, and employment very much because of pension prospects. It would be unfair to penalize those who followed non-standard strategies.

However much collective interventions and support may change the balance of labour within some households, specialization between spouses has a long history, and probably a long future. Therefore, though this may be controversial, it seems to me that the features of the pension system which recognize partners' interests in each other's pensions should not be set aside. The rules may need to be adapted to treat the partners symmetrically, whichever of them undertakes more unpaid work, and to allow for more forms of partnership than legal marriage, but the rules still play a part. Rather than abolish widow's pensions, for example, survivors of either sex from *de facto* as well as legal unions should be covered, at least in the basic pension, and to 'top up' their own entitlement. Further, as suggested above, interests in partners' pension rights should be recognized more effectively in the dissolution of marriages or other partnerships. The retention of unequal pension ages does not however seem so important for solving the problem of inferior pensions for unpaid contributions.

Conclusions

Earnings-related pension schemes tend to penalize people whose work is not all paid, even the mothers who produce the next generation of contributors. Whether or not it is desirable to increase the birth-rate and whether or not improving mothers' old-age security, on its own, would have such an effect, it seems desirable to improve their pension prospects. There is a case on grounds of equity alone, and it might at least help deter further falls in current levels of fertility. Independent pensions, equivalent to men's, seem a long way off for some, particularly when pension systems are under pressure to reduce their generosity. Until such time as all citizens have comfortable pensions as of right, it will be important to monitor the distribution of benefits and contribution of unpaid work to society. A number of ways of improving the pensions of those whose work is outside the market have been indicated, along with arguments for preserving, though modernizing, familial structures which redistribute purchasing power.

The editor has expressed a worry that overhauls of family law in eastern Europe might 'throw out the baby with the bathwater'. A further concern here is that the modernization of the work-place and of social protection should not add to the difficulties of sustaining the reproductive phase of the life-cycle—throwing out the mother along with the baby! As the family evolves, the state seems better fitted than the market to help sustain its multiple functions. Mothers need support from both the family and the state to protect them from the market penalties of raising the next generation.

Acknowledgements

The research on which this paper draws has been supported financially by the Joseph Rowntree Foundation and the ESRC. It has also relied heavily on the collaboration of Hugh Davies. The views expressed are the author's alone. An earlier version of sections 4 onwards was presented to the European Population Conference 1991 in Paris, and appears in Volume 2 of its Proceedings (éditions INED, Paris). The material is reproduced here with the editor's permission. Thanks are also due to my husband for taking the children off to the seaside while this chapter was being finalized.

REFERENCES

Beveridge, W. (1942), *Social Insurance and Allied Services* Cmd. 6404 (HMSO, London).

Brannen, J. and Wilson, G. (eds.) (1987), *Give and Take in Families* (Allen and Unwin, London).

Cigno, A. (1991*a*), *Economics of the Family* (Oxford University Press, Oxford).

—— (1991*b*), 'Children and Pensions', Presidential Address to the European Society for Population Economics, Pisa.

Coxon, A. (1992), Contribution to BBC Radio 4, *Analysis,* 'The Matrimonial State', 9 July.

Davies, H. and Joshi, H. (1992*a*), 'Pensions in Divorce: Illiquid Assets in Dissolving Unions', *Family Law*, 22 (Jan.) 21–4.

—— —— (1992*b*), 'Sex, Sharing and the Distribution of Income', paper presented to the 6th Annual Conference of the European Society for Population Economics, Gmunden, Austria. Typescript, Department of Economics, Birkbeck College.

—— —— (forthcoming), 'The Forgone Earnings of Europe's Mothers', in O. Ekert (ed.), *The Cost of Children*, Proceedings of EAPS Symposium, Barcelona, Oct. 1990 (INED, Paris).

Hemming, R. and Kay, J. (1982), 'The Cost of the State Earnings-Related Pension Scheme', *Economic Journal*, 92/366: 300–19.

Johnson, P., Conrad, C., and Thomson, D. (eds.) (1989), *Workers versus Pensioners: Intergenerational Justice in an Ageing World* (Manchester University Press, Manchester and New York, in association with the Centre for Economic Policy Research).

Joshi, H. E. (1991), 'Sex and Motherhood as Sources of Women's Economic Disadvantage', in D. Groves and M. Maclean (eds.), *Women's Issues in Social Policy* (Routledge, London), 179–93.

—— and Davies, H. (1991), 'The Pension Consequences of Divorce', Discussion Paper 550 (CEPR, London).

—— —— (1992a), Child Care and Mothers' Lifetime Earnings: Some European Contrasts, CEPR Discussion Paper 600.

—— —— (1992b), 'Pensions, Divorce, and Wives' Double Burden', *International Journal of Law and the Family* (in press).

—— —— (1992c), 'The Paid and Unpaid Roles of Women: How should Social Security Adapt?', paper prepared for Social Security: Fifty Years After Beveridge, University of York. Typescript, Department of Economics, Birkbeck College.

Lister, R. (1992), *Women's Economic Dependency and Social Security* (Equal Opportunities Commission, Manchester).

Owen, S. and Joshi, H. (1990), 'Sex, Equality and the State Pension', *Fiscal Studies*, 11/1: 53–74.

Stahlberg, A.-C. (1990), 'Life-Cycle Redistribution of the Public Sector: Inter- and Intragenerational Effects', in I. Persson (ed.), *Generating Equality in the Welfare State: The Swedish Experience* (Norwegian University Press, Oslo), 98–121.

Vogler, C. (1989), 'Labour Market Change and Patterns of Financial Allocation within Households', ESRC Social Change and Economic Life Initiative, Working Paper 12, Nuffield College, Oxford.

17. Divorcing Children: Roles for Parents and the State

Martin Richards

Introduction

The basic argument of this chapter is simple: that parental divorce often damages the life chances of children and the state could, and should, act more firmly to head off some of this damage. In Britain, as in most industrialized countries, the state does intervene at divorce, adopting the rhetoric of preserving or enhancing the best interests of the child. However, such good intentions usually fail because there is little understanding or agreement about what the best interests might be. Where there are clear policies they are usually more concerned at reducing government spending, whether on the judicial system or on direct or indirect support for post-divorce households with children. The chapter will begin by outlining the evidence about the effects of parental divorce for children, before turning to the issue of state intervention in the arrangements that may be made for children.

Consequences of parental divorce for children

Children of divorcing parents tend to show a period of disturbed behaviour—either acting-out disruptive behaviour or depressive and anxious patterns. This may last through the whole process of divorce beginning months or years before a separation and continuing some time after this. School work often shows some falling-off around the time of separation and, as effects for educational attainment may be cumulative, children are likely to leave school with fewer qualifications and have a reduced chance of going on to a university (see Maclean and Wadsworth, 1988; Hetherington and Arasteh, 1988; Chase-Landsdale and Hetherington, 1990; Elliott and Richards, 1991; Wallerstein, 1992; Kiernan, 1992).

Some effects may persist into adulthood and studies in Britain and the United States have found lower occupational status and earnings, earlier marriage and divorce, and increased frequency of psychological and psychiatric problems (Amato and Keith, 1991). In short, parental divorce may be associated with downward social mobility for the children.

Of course, effects of divorce are very variable depending on many aspects of the particular circumstances and such things as the age of the children, the social position of the family, and the living arrangements after the separation. Not all children show significant persistent effects. However, these are sufficiently common and of such importance—we are talking of effects which, in some cases, influence the life-long chances for adults—that it seems reasonable that we should regard these as the prime concern which we need to consider when discussing interventions at divorce (Richards, 1991).

Why should parental divorce have these long term effects? Clearly, this is a very complex question and there are no simple answers. But we may point to a number of key interrelated factors which play a crucial role in a young person's journey from their childhood home into their independent life as a young adult. My approach is to consider the ways in which parental divorce may influence these. These factors are educational attainment and vocational training, leaving home and setting up an independent life elsewhere, forming a cohabitation or a marriage, and the beginning of reproduction. Parental divorce has been shown to influence all these factors. It is through varying combinations of these factors that divorce is likely to have its effect on social mobility (Richards, 1991). But the significance of the divorce effect is variable depending on both individual and social factors. The analysis of the follow-up study of the cohort of children born in 1958, for example, suggest that girls from middle-class homes show the strongest effects in early adulthood while boys from working-class backgrounds are least affected (Richards and Elliott, 1992). Moreover, the links are certainly complex. Nevertheless, we can point to a number of crucial effects of parental divorce. So, for instance, a child that does badly at school is more likely to leave at the minimum age with few or no qualifications and is less likely to proceed to further education or training and so has reduced job prospects. Children who have left education are more likely to leave home and live independently. Marriage and cohabitation are more probable for those living independently and, associated with these, are earlier reproduction, which in turn may further reduce employment possibilities, especially for women (Tasker and Richards, 1992). The association between leaving home, marriage, and cohabitation is probably the end result of two different processes; leaving home because a decision has been taken to get married, and because those living independently may be more likely to form relationships that develop more rapidly into cohabitation or marriages. Where relationships are difficult or strained at home a young person may choose to leave earlier than otherwise. A poor relationship with a step-parent is a significant factor for some. Social-class differences are very important here, not least because of the need for financial resources to find independent accommodation. We should also note that matters which are controlled by government action such as rules for job-training allowances, welfare benefits and poll tax may have a direct bearing on the financial consequences for parents and young people of the latter staying or leaving home (see Roll, 1990). Availability of jobs and housing are also of obvious significance.

Divorce is associated with a sharp drop in income for homes with children. In Britain, a majority of households containing divorced women and their children become dependent on state benefits for at least a period of time (see Maclean, 1991) and some remain caught in the poverty trap. Inadequate income reduces children's educational attainment and in many other ways has adverse effects on their life chances. While parental remarriage, and probably cohabitation, may improve incomes, the levels are seldom restored to those preceding the divorce. Even if these events have beneficial effects for household income, they may lead to further psychological and social disruptions for children. Follow up studies (e.g. Kiernan, 1992) tend to show small but consistently negative effects for children from remarriage homes as compared with those where a mother remained on her own after the divorce.

After divorce most children live with their mothers, and fathers become, at best, occasional visitors in their lives. Research in Britain and the USA suggests that within a short time of separation many children cease to have a relationship with their father (see Seltzer, 1991). The breaking of established relationships with fathers and other family members may have significant effects on a child's social development and their capacity to form and sustain relationships with others. When a father disappears from a child's life that child often feels a persistent sense of abandonment and loss which damages their self esteem and sense of worth. Lack of self esteem, in turn, has many psychological and social consequences. The loss of a parent and kin could also have economic and social effects for children which may continue into adult life. Fathers who are in contact with their children are more likely to be contributing towards their support and, though there seems to be no direct evidence to make the point, other transfers of money and practical support are likely to be reduced or cease where divorce ends effective contact (see Finch, 1990).

Conflict between parents before and after divorce is associated with poorer outcome for children. Where parents are living together, if the conflict is conducted in such a way that children are not directly involved, they seem to be protected from some of its consequences (see Rutter, 1988). An important point here is that the effects of inter-parent conflict for children may be relatively benign if the children are able to see their parents settle their differences and restore good relationships. Conflict in the closing stages of a marriage or after separation may be more serious because it is less likely that this happens and because children, and the arrangements for their care, are more likely to be the subject of disputes. Conflict between parents will often erode parent–child relationships or end them.

Separating and divorced adults tend to have higher rates of psychological and physical illness (Elliott, 1991). Parents who are ill, depressed, preoccupied, and generally under stress are less effective as parents and their children may lack sustained support and emotional engagement. Such parental difficulties may further exacerbate the psychological problems of the children of divorce.

These problems may also be increased by moves which may mean a change of school and loss of friends and familiar peers. Changes of school tend to be associated with poorer educational attainment. Divorce may not simply lead to a single move but, for some, is the beginning of continued changes as a lone parent moves in and out of further relationships (and households).

The analysis I have sketched out provides a set of clear issues which could become goals for policies related to divorce and children. Such policies should aim to encourage the maintenance of a child's existing relationships with parents and the wider family and kin, ensure an adequate income to post-divorce households with children, reduce as far as possible conflict between divorcing parents or, at least, encourage its expression in areas that do not involve children, encourage the provision of emotional and practical support for divorcing parents who have the care of children and, finally, avoid as far as possible moves of house or school. On this latter point we should note that the availability of reasonably priced housing, whether to rent or buy, is of particular importance to divorcing couples and their children. I have necessarily stated the policy objectives in broad terms. It will not always be desirable to strive to maintain relationships with both parents. The evidence suggests that it is the breaking of already existing relationships which has ill effects for children. In rare cases, existing relationships may be detrimental to children if they continue. However, I suspect that such cases are much less common than many professionals working in the field choose to believe. It is also important to realize that the loss of a parent usually means the permanent loss of half of a child's kin relationships which may have profound emotional, social, and financial consequences.

Parental and kin relationships and maintaining children

Earlier in this chapter I argued that children are likely to do better in the long term if they maintain relationships with both their parents and the kin network on both sides of their family after a parental divorce. We know that in practice, in Britain, the United States, and elsewhere, the usual pattern is for children to live with their mother after divorce and for around half of fathers (at best) to remain in regular contact. As far as mothers are concerned, we should expect the post-divorce pattern we see, as it is simply the same situation as is found within marriage. The bulk of child care is provided by women in marriage, as it is afterwards. In only very few cases is the mother's position of the primary care-taker challenged at divorce. What had been the mother's role as principal care-taker in the joint household becomes that of residential parent in a single-parent household. While she may be faced with all sorts of increased difficulties in this new situation—juggling child care and employment, housing, and financial difficulties, etc.—the basic role remains the same. The complications arise in trying to see how a father can fit into the post-divorce pattern when the mother's primary role within one household is translated into that of a single parent (or one with a new partner). Within a typical marriage the father is out at work each day while the mother is either at home as a full-time carer of children, or combines work, and, importantly, the organization of substitute child care while she is working, with child care and domestic work. A father fits what care-taking he does, and his other time with the children, into the basic pattern set up and maintained by the mother. In most households fathers engage with their children when the mother is present too. This is unlike the typical pattern for a mother who will spend a lot of time on her own with her children. Or to put it in other terms, if a father is to maintain a relationship with his children his role *vis à vis* children is likely to change at separation much more radically than that of a mother. He has to become a sole care-taker for the times he is with his children, unless he simply passes on the care to a new partner or a relative.

A change for a mother is that there may be times when she is *not* with her children, if they are visiting their father. For some women this can pose a significant psychological threat to their role as a mother and it is frequently experienced as a loss. So, at many separations, a mother may not wish her children to go to see their father, and a father may be unable or unwilling to change his life to become a part-time sole carer. Control over visiting, and more generally over contact with a father, may be one of the few areas in which a mother may feel she has some power so it is not surprising that so many disputes become focused on these issues. Where a divorce has been initiated by a mother and the father feels he is losing his marriage, wife, and home, he may push for as much time with his children as possible as a way of retaining some element of his past life. Again, this may help to add emotional fuel to conflicts over children which stand, in practical and symbolic ways, as the bones for contention.

New partners may further complicate the picture. Father involvement tends to fall off if either he or his ex-spouse acquires a new partner. This is likely to be for somewhat different reasons on each side. The residential mother may have fantasies about creating a new family for which ties with the 'old' father may seem a threat best met by keeping the children around and denying them visits to the other parent. For the non-residential parent, a relationship with a new partner may feel threatened by the occasional presence of children who are reminders of the old marriage and intimacy with another woman. Running through these situations is a very persistent prejudice that children should never have more than two parents and when a new one arrives, an old one has to go. I suggest that children have a much greater tolerance for non-standard family forms than adults (see Funder, 1991). Indeed discomfort about such arrangements seem particularly strong among professionals who deal with children who often seem to regard such arrangements as 'confusing' for children (see Kelly, 1991*a*). I suspect this is a matter of projection and the potential confusion lies more with the adults than with the children. A parallel argument could be mounted here about the concept of adoption and the great adult fantasy that it is possible to create and end kinship relationships at the stroke of a court order.

It is usual to regard children as conservatives in their views of family life. Certainly they may resent change and can be very sensitive about the ways others may regard their living arrangements. However, children may have few presuppositions about the roles various adults in their lives should play. One can cite cases of children who see nothing but gain in the addition of further adult figures who can come to occupy quasi-parental roles in their lives. But we know too little about how children experience arrangements in non-traditional family structures and we should be very wary about assuming on their behalf the existence of strong views in favour of idealized family forms.

There is also the issue that conflict between parents may lead to a reduction in contact between parents and this can erode the parent–child relationship. I shall have more to say about this below.

Changing the world

Given the pervasiveness of a pattern which places little emphasis on the need for continuing relationships between children and non-residential parents, and the strength of the beliefs and institutions that support this, change is not going to be easy. The evidence suggests that very little has occurred over recent decades in the United States (Seltzer, 1991; Folberg, 1991) and the situation seems similar in the UK. A first step which we have begun to take in The Children Act 1989 is to make the legal change so that at least we do not take parental responsibility from most fathers at divorce.

But can we do more? Certainly if there were better ways of settling disputes between parents, conflict were reduced, and some of the emotional tensions that so often continue between past spouses were addressed more directly, we might expect more fathers to stay in the picture. I will discuss this further below. Apart from this, it seems a matter of creating a culture of expectation so that we accept, as the slogan goes, 'Divorce is for adults, not children'. We need small changes on many fronts. Schools, for instance, should be encouraged (required?) to send information to both parents if they do not share the same address. Divorcing parents should receive written information about the post-divorce needs of children and the range of workable residence and visiting patterns.

In many jurisdictions, including our own, there have been recent changes in the law designed to increase child support from fathers after divorce. As yet, it is too early to say whether these schemes are likely to improve the economic standing of households with children after divorce. First indications are that they have little financial impact (see Pearson, *et al.*, 1992) which may well be because they are more concerned with controlling government expenditure than with the welfare of children and those who care for them. However, it is possible that these schemes may serve a symbolic function in indicating to non-resident parents that their responsibilities towards their children—financial and otherwise—do not end simply because they cease to share the same address.

Other effects that might follow more effective attempts to collect maintenance from fathers concern second families. At present, a father can effectively wipe the slate clean and start again with a second family. Ensuring transfers to existing children, and giving them preference over subsequent ones, might depress fertility in second families. Would that be an undesirable result?

A difficulty we should not duck here is the difference between his and her divorce. He is likely either to have been left, or to be leaving for someone else. If the former, he may feel a strong sense of injustice at losing his marriage, children, and house while continuing to pay support—or at least that is a way that a vocal minority will put it. If he is moving into a new relationship, guilt can provide some motive to pay, but a new partner may increasingly resent supporting another woman's children. Of course, not everyone is driven by such motives. However, the coming of legal 'no fault' divorce has perhaps allowed us to believe that couples separate with a similar detached view of divorce. They don't. Blame, accusation, and strong feelings of injustice are the norm at divorce and they get in the way of couples making reasonable arrangements about children and money. Neither legal fiction of the lack of fault or imposed orders do anything to relieve the situation, rather the reverse.

Indeed, neither the public ordering of the court, nor most private ordering provides an adequate arena for expression of the feelings that accompany marital separation. Studies of the legal process of divorce (see Davis and Murch, 1988) show that many of the participants feel that the legal procedures do not engage what they see as the 'real' issues. Affidavits take instances from a private reality and present them in a context where they lose most of their meaning. There is always a deep sense of betrayal when events from a private and once shared reality are forced into public in the provocative legal prose of an affidavit. People are not allowed their say in a manner that fits their own sense of justice. They are told to look forward at a time when their prime concern is history and its rewriting. The wounds go very deep but they often feel that the doctor is not even interested in seeing them.

Most mediation takes the same stance. Agendas are strictly controlled and anyone who tries to talk about how the present situation came about is wrapped over the knuckles and told—directly or indirectly—to attend to the business at hand and look to the future (Dingwall and Greatbatch, 1990).

Marriage, as Berger and Kellner (1964) argued in a perceptive paper that has deservedly become a classic, involves the joint construction of a private shared and exclusive reality. Identities are anchored in the shared meaning of the relationship (Askham, 1984). Maybe, legally, we do not become one any more, but we aspire to a social and psychological fusion (Reibstein and Richards, 1992). It follows, therefore, that the process of uncoupling is very painful and provokes powerful irrational feelings (Vaughan, 1987; Weiss, 1975). Yet we try to get people to divide their lives, children, and property without even acknowledging the deep sense of anger, love, betrayal, and hate that most are feeling.

At separation, many people are literally out of their minds. They will do things and treat people in ways they never have before and never will again. Any family lawyer can provide numerous examples of what has to be regarded as typical behaviour: he broke into her house and tipped the contents of the dustbin into the double bed where she and her new partner sleep; she went through the family photograph album cutting him out of each photo; he slashed the tyres of her, once their, car; she burnt the postcard he sent to the children while he way away on a business trip. We expect them both to be calm and rational, yet we present them with a system that allows them to take their irrational behaviour into the public arena of the court where it may be validated by the professionals who have become drawn into their warring world. Court contests seem to be designed to allow the trivia of everyday life to become elevated to a point where it becomes the basis of long-term decision-making. The result is adults and children who may feel damaged and bruised by their experience, who are a great deal poorer, and who do not necessarily have any sensible solutions to their problems. I suggest that until we begin to address the feelings of the participants at divorce we cannot expect people to make sensible decisions about the long-term interests of their children.

My noting of the restrictiveness of some styles of mediation may have seemed rather dismissive. A major problem is that under this term is gathered together a very wide range of activities. It is not simply that there are many variants in practice, but there is dispute about some basic approaches and techniques. A common model is of a kind of public-school debating contest with each team represented by one of the spouses and the neutral chair seeing that everyone keeps to the point and to time. There tends to be a polarization between those who come from the pragmatic dispute-resolution tradition, often with a background of labour-disputes work, and those who draw on more therapeutic frameworks. There is little thought about how the two might be combined in the very special circumstances of a dispute between two parties who were once intimate and emotionally interdependent and whose union may have represented a bridge between two kinship networks. Some of the influence from family therapy has been less than helpful as it puts little stress on the ambivalence of loss and love that may dominate the feelings of each warring spouse. Not surprisingly, mediation has had a somewhat mixed press in evaluation studies (see Bruch, 1988). But not all evaluation has been negative (Kelly, 1991*b*). There have been concerns expressed by some feminists that women are disadvantages by the 'privatization' of the law (e.g. Bottomley, 1985), but such fears, at least judged by practice in the USA, seem unfounded (Kelly and Duryee, 1992).

My guess, and it can be no more on present evidence, is that mediation can be effective if (a) it is comprehensive and we get rid of the silly British fiction that we can sort out issues to do with children without discussing where they will live or how they are to be financially supported; (b) it allows clients to express something of their feelings and so engage the private reality that was their marriage (drawing here on appropriate psychodynamic traditions); (c) it provides some help and encouragement to couples to see that their quarrels can be conducted in ways that are more or less damaging for them and/or their children; (d) it is offered in context where other services such as counselling and direct support for children are also available; and finally (e) it deals in realistic and practical solutions for individual cases rather than idealized and generalized arrangements (see Richards, 1990).

I think mediation is the best hope we have, but it needs more money, more experimental schemes, and more hard thinking about its dynamics and how they may relate to the psychology of uncoupling. When it is done in the spirit I am proposing it does have some interesting effects. Children receive higher levels of financial support, agreements are more likely to be kept, and there is more contact between non-residential parents and their children (Kelly, 1991*b*). But we need to be careful to judge post-divorce arrangements by appropriate criteria. Increased contact between children and non-residential parents may mean that there is more scope for continuing conflict between parents. Some continuing conflict may be a reasonable price that has to be paid for the better contact (Masheter, 1991) but good mediation can help to ensure that it does not stand in the way of necessary discussions about children (Kelly, 1991*b*).

One other very important point needs to be made about the ways in which couples end their marriages. Most go on to further marriages or cohabitations after divorce and recoupling often stimulates fertility. Sadly, however, second and subsequent relationships are more prone to divorce than first-time marriages. It seems reasonable to assume the unfinished business of the first marriage—emotional as well as financial—is an important determinant of the stability of the second. Addressing the psychological issues of divorce and providing couples with a forum in which to do this might have significant benefits for any subsequent relationship and children that might be born in these.

I am sure it is right for the Law Commission (1990) to recommend that divorce is available on demand with a suitable delay in which to sort out arrangements about children and money and without the need to provide the usually fictional historical account of the marriage in a legal format. Courts are not the place in which to argue about the private world of intimate relationships. The present system seems to have the worst combination of offering opportunities through affidavits to rehearse all sorts of marital quarrels which break faith with an erstwhile partner but then to ignore these issues and give the divorce on the nod (see Burgoyne *et al.*, 1987).

It is much more difficult to see how the courts might be used to settle those cases of disputes about children that mediation cannot shift. Perhaps we should try to follow the same kind of system as the proposed formula for determining levels of child support and we should define the areas of acceptable dispute in litigation over children. Perhaps the easier cases are the few where there is a straight dispute about residence (custody); about where the children should live. The vast majority of such disputes concern parents who are as fit and able to care for children as any other; i.e. they are what Winnicott might have called 'good enough' parents, who have both played some part in the care of the children before the separation. Relying on evidence of who did most during the marriage is not always very relevant as the divorce changes most things. Also the needs of children change through development and with the roles that the two partners may take. Perhaps all that is required is for each parent to establish that they have practical plans for how they would look after children under whatever scheme they are proposing for their future care. In these disputes parents often try to suggest, directly or indirectly, that their partner is unfit to have the care of children. I suggest that such evidence should be inadmissible. If there are such concerns, these should be dealt with by the appropriate child-protection procedures and only when any such issues have been resolved should a custody hearing take place. The principle of the primacy of the welfare of the children should still obtain in such situations but I suggest it should be given a single simple definition, that the children should reside with whichever parent is able to convince the court that they are the parent most likely to foster and maintain the children's links with the other parent and the wider family. Such a criterion has a long history (1 Kings 3: 16–28) and should ensure that attention is focused on the welfare of the children rather than the supposed moral worth of each parent. One of the benefits of any clear guide like the Solomon principle is that it reduces the scope for disagreement. While few are likely to object to the concept of the best interests of the child, it is a concept which allows for the maximum range of disagreement. As the most cursory glance at what (married) parents do with their children (or indeed the changing whims of probation and social-work practice on judicial decision-making) makes clear, there is the widest divergence of views of what constitutes the best interests of children. That diversity of view means that bargaining in the shadow of the law provides maximum scope for disagreement. Leaving decisions to a court remains an uncertain gamble, but this allows at least a ray of hope for the most unlikely cases and so encourages litigation.

The seeking of clearer guidelines or principles for resolution of custody disputes seems to be becoming an increasing preoccupation in the more progressive jurisdictions. The most favoured principle at present seems to show a preference for the primary care-taker. Essentially this means confirming the *status quo*—making the parent who provided the bulk of the care-taking within marriage, the residential parent after divorce. In most cases such a principle is simply a return to the maternal presumption which dominated in the days before the best-interests concept became established. Not surprisingly, those feminists who see child custody as an issue of gender politics have argued strongly for the primary care-taker principle (Smart and Sevenhuijsen, 1989). In some jurisdictions in the USA, where the principle has been adopted, there have been problems and not all the supposed benefits have been found (Crippen, 1990).

The most detailed proposal for an approach of this kind has come from New Zealand (Hassall and Maxwell, 1992). Here we might expect the results to be rather different from the USA because these would operate in the context of a family court system which places strong emphasis on the needs of children. The plan is a detailed one which is a development from the present mediation-based system. It places a family care conference—involving the parents, children, perhaps members of the wider family, an advocate for the children, and a mediator, but no lawyers—at the centre of the system. The proposal not only gives a list of tasks that can be used to define who is the primary care-taker but lays down norms for a 'standard' interim arrangement for children to be with their parents. Clearly, there is plenty of scope for argument about what principles decisions should be based on but two points about the New Zealand proposal are particularly attractive: the emphasis on providing a context for decision making before the legal system is engaged, and the attempt to reduce uncertainty and set standards for appropriate arrangements. Of course, some cases will proceed to court and not all parents will behave in ways that remotely approach the standards set. But the proposals do seem to stand a good chance of reducing court cases (and so legal costs) and may help to protect the interests of children.

Disputes around access, and matters such as the removal of children from the jurisdiction, are perhaps the hardest to resolve, not least because they are so often an arena in which the conflicting emotions of the once intimate are played out. It seems unlikely that there are any simple principles to guide solutions here. What about the father who consistently fails to turn up on agreed access days or the mother who refuses to let a father see his children despite access orders? In the latter case do we put the mother in prison as the occasional exasperated judge has tried to do or transfer the children to the father? Nothing is gained by the former and in the latter situation perhaps the father is unable or unwilling to take them. Similarly, heavy-handed treatment is unlikely to encourage a father to take his responsibilities more seriously. I think the best we can suggest is mediation, compulsory if necessary, and a court hearing at the very last resort where appropriate. The problem is, of course, that in the end, we cannot impose arrangements on parents who are determined to thwart an order. Such cases are rare but if everything has been exhausted—mediation with due attention to the psychodynamic agenda, a determined attempt to discover the reasons for the refusal, an informal meeting with a judge, and court hearing—there is nothing for it but occasional supervised access visits until such time as children are old enough to make their own choices.

Acknowledgements

Some of my research on the consequences of divorce has been supported by a grant from the Health Promotion Research Trust. Jill Brown and Sally Roberts, as always, have provided excellent administrative and secretarial services.

REFERENCES

Amato, P. R. and Keith, B. (1991), 'Parental Divorce and Adult Well-Being: A Meta-analysis', *J. Marriage and the Family*, 53: 43–58.
Askham, J. (1984), *Identity and Stability in Marriage* (Cambridge University Press, Cambridge).
Berger, P. and Kellner, H. (1964), 'Marriage and the Construction of Reality', *Diogenes*, 46: 1–25.
Bottomley, A. (1985), 'What is Happening to Family Law? A Feminist Critique of Conciliation', in J. Brophy and C. Smart (eds.), *Women-in-Law: Explorations in Law, Family and Sexuality* (Routledge & Kegan Paul, London).

Bruch, C. S. (1988), 'And How are the Children? The Effects of Ideology and Mediation on Child Custody Law and Children's Well-Being in the United States', *Int. J. of Law and the Family*, 2: 106–26.

Burgoyne, J., Ormrod, R., and Richards, M. P. M. (1987), *Divorce Matters* (Penguin Books, London).

Chase-Lansdale, L. and Hetherington, E. M. (1990), 'The Impact of Divorce on Life Span Development: Short and Long-Term Effects', in D. L. Featherman and R. M. Lerner (eds.), *Life-Span: Development and Behaviour* (Erlbaum, Hillsdale, NJ).

Crippen, G. (1990), 'Stumbling Beyond the Best Interests of the Child: Reexamining Child Custody Standard-Setting in the Wake of Minnesota's Four Year Experiment with the Primary Caretaker Preference', *Minnesota Law Review*, 75: 427–503.

Davis, G. and Murch, M. (1988), *Grounds for Divorce* (Clarendon Press, Oxford).

Dingwall, R. and Greenbatch, D. (1990), *Divorce Conciliation: A Report to the Wates Foundation* (Centre for Socio-Legal Studies, Oxford).

Elliott, B. J. (1991), *Divorce and Adult Health: The Mediating Effects of Gender*, unpublished paper: Child Care and Development Group, University of Cambridge.

—— and Richards, M. P. M. (1991), 'Children and Divorce: Educational Performance and Behaviour, Before and After Parental Separation', *Int. J. of Law and the Family*, 5: 258–76.

Finch, J. (1990), *Family Obligation and Social Change* (Polity Press, Cambridge).

Folberg, J. (ed.) (1991), *Joint Custody and Shared Parenting*, 2nd edn (Guilford Press, New York).

Funder, K. (1991), 'Children's Construction of their Post-Divorce Families: A Family Sculpture Approach', in K. Funder (ed.), *Images of Australian Families* (Longman Cheshire, Melbourne).

Hassell, I. and Maxwell, G. (1992), *A Children's Rights Approach to Custody and Access* (Office of the Commissioner for Children, Wellington, NJ).

Hetherington, E. M. and Arasteh, J. D. (eds.) (1988), *Impact of Divorce, Single Parenting, and Stepparenting on Children* (Lawrence Erlbaum, Hillsdale, NJ).

Kiernan, K. E. (1992), 'The Impact of Family Disruption in Childhood and Transitions made in Young Adult Life', *Demography*.

Kelly, J. B. (1991*a*), 'Examining Resistance to Joint Custody', in J. Folberg (ed.), *Joint Custody and Shared Parenting*, 2nd edn (Guilford Press, New York).

—— (1991*b*), 'Mediated and Adversarial Divorce Resolution Processes: A Comparison of Post-Divorce Outcomes, *Family Law*.

—— and Duryee, M. A. (1992), 'Women's and Men's Views of Mediation in Voluntary and Mandatory Mediation Settings', *Family and Conciliation Courts Review*, 30, 34–49.

Law Commission (1990), *The Grounds for Divorce*, Law Commission, No. 192 (HMSO, London).

Maclean, M. (1991), *Surviving Divorce: Women's Resources after Separation* (Macmillan, London).

—— and Wadsworth, M. E. J. (1988), 'The Interests of Children after Parental Divorce: A Long Term Perspective', *Int. J. of Law and the Family*, 2: 155–66.

Masheter, L. (1991), Post Divorce Relationships between Ex-Spouses: The Role of Attachment and Interpersonal Conflict. *J. Marriage and the Family*, 53: 103–10.

Pearson, J., Thoennes, N., and Anhalt, J. (1992), 'Child Support in the United States: The Experience in Colorado', *Int. J. of Law and the Family*, 6: 321–37.

Reibstein, J. and Richards, M. P. M. (1992), *Sexual Arrangements* (Heinemann, London).

Richards, M. P. M. (1990), 'Divorce Cambridge Style: New Developments in Conciliation', *Family Law*, 436–8.

—— (1991), 'Children and Parents after Divorce', paper presented at the Seventh World Conference of the International Society on Family Law, Opatija, Yugoslavia, 1991, and to be published in the proceedings of the meeting.

Richards, M. P. M. and Elliott, B. J., 'The Economic Status of Families Before and After Divorce' (in preparation).

Roll, J. (1990), 'Young People: Growing up in the Welfare State', Family Policy Studies Centre Occasional Paper No. 10, London.

Rutter, M. (1988), 'Functions and Consequences of Relationships: Some Psychopathological Considerations', in R. A. Hinde and J. Stevenson-Hinde (eds.), *Relationships within Families* (Clarendon Press, Oxford).

Seltzer, J. A. (1991), 'Relationship between Fathers and Children who Live Apart: The Father's Role after Separation', *J. Marriage and the Family*, 53: 79–102.

Smart, C. and Sevenhuijsen, S. (eds.) (1989), *Child Custody and the Politics of Gender* (Routledge, London).

Tasker, F. and Richards, M. P. M., 'The Attitudes to Marriage and the Marital Prospects of the Children of Divorce: A Review' (submitted for publication).

Vaughan, D. (1987), *Uncoupling: Turning Points in Intimate Relationships* (Methuen, London).

Wallerstein, J. S., 'The Long-Term Effects of Divorce on Children: A Review', *J. Amer. Acad. Child and Adolescent Psychiatry* (in press).

Weiss, R. (1975), *Marital Separation* (Basic Books, New York).

Index